Vertical Integration
in
Cable Television

Vertical Integration in Cable Television

David Waterman
Andrew A. Weiss

The MIT Press
Cambridge, Massachusetts
London, England
and
The AEI Press
Washington, D.C.
1997

Published by

The MIT Press
Cambridge, Massachusetts
London, England

and

The AEI Press
Washington, D.C.

Library of Congress Cataloging-in-Publication Data

Waterman, David
    Vertical integration in cable television / David Waterman, Andrew A. Weiss
        p. cm. — (AEI studies in telecommunications deregulation)
    Includes bibliographical references and indexes.
    ISBN 0-262-23190-5 (cloth: alk. paper)
    1. Cable television—Vertical integration—United States.
2. Competition—United States. I. Weiss, Andrew. II. Title.
III. Series.
HE8700.72.U6W38   1997
384.55'51—dc21   96-51422
                                                                       CIP

Printed in the United States of America

To Sharon, Chloe, and Jason,
and to Christina, Alan, and Fiona

Contents

Foreword

DRAMATIC ADVANCES IN COMMUNICATIONS and information technologies have been imposing severe strains on a government regulatory apparatus devised in the pioneer days of radio and are raising policy questions with large implications for American economic performance and social welfare. Before the passage of the Telecommunications Act of 1996, one was compelled to ask, Is federal and state telecommunications regulation impeding competition and innovation, and has that indeed become its principal if unstated function? Is regulation inhibiting the dissemination of ideas and information through electronic media? Does the licensing regime for the electromagnetic spectrum allocate that resource to less than its most productive uses? Now that the 1996 act is in place, is it likely to correct any of those ill effects?

David Waterman and Andrew A. Weiss assess the effects of vertical integration in the cable television industry. The study is one of a series of research volumes addressing those questions commissioned by the American Enterprise Institute's Telecommunications Deregulation Project. The AEI project is intended to produce new empirical research on the entire range of telecommunications policy issues, with particular emphasis on identifying reforms to federal and state regulatory policies that will advance rather than inhibit innovation and consumer welfare. We hope this research will be useful to legislators and public officials at all levels of government and to the business executives and, most of all, the consumers who must live with their policies. The volumes have been written and edited to be accessible to readers with no specialized knowledge of communication technologies or economics; we hope they will find a place in courses on regulated industries and communications policy in economics and communications departments and in business, law, and public policy schools.

Each volume in the Telecommunications Deregulation Project has been discussed and criticized in draft form at an AEI seminar involving federal and state regulators, jurists, business executives, professionals, and academic experts with a wide range of interests and viewpoints and has been reviewed and favorably reported by anonymous academic referees selected by the MIT Press. I wish to thank all of them for their contributions, noting, however, that the final exposition and conclusions are entirely the responsibility of the authors of each volume.

I am particularly grateful to Paul W. MacAvoy, Williams Brothers Professor of Management Studies at the Yale School of Management, and J. Gregory Sidak, F. K. Weyerhaeuser Chair in Law and Economics at AEI, for conceiving and overseeing the project's research and seminars, and to Frank Urbanowski, Terry Vaughn, and Victoria Richardson of the MIT Press for their support and steady counsel in seeing the research to publication.

CHRISTOPHER C. DeMUTH
President, American Enterprise Institute
for Public Policy Research

Acknowledgments

THIS VOLUME HAS BENEFITED in its conception and progress from the contributions and comments of many. We especially thank Timothy J. Brennan, Charles L. Jackson, Leland L. Johnson, Paul W. MacAvoy, David J. Salant, Martin L. Stern, Lawrence J. White, anonymous referees, and participants at an American Enterprise Institute symposium, where we presented a preliminary draft of this study. We also thank Leigh Tripoli and Julie Bassett of AEI and Victoria Richardson and Ann Sochi of MIT Press for their professional contributions to the editorial and production process. We are especially indebted to J. Gregory Sidak for his support and his very detailed comments and editorial contributions. Any errors and shortcomings nevertheless remain with us.

Completion of the research we report in this book required efforts extending far beyond our own. Erik Deutsch, Joseph M. Hinshaw, Krishna P. Jayakar, Guy Katz, and Zhaoxu Yan provided able research assistance. Cable industry executives generously granted interviews to help us understand the industry's inner workings. Staff members of the Federal Communications Commission went out of their way to assist us in finding and interpreting documents. And we shall always be grateful for the extraordinary librarianship of Carolyn M. Spicer of the University of Southern California and Francis G. Wilhoit of Indiana University.

Finally, we acknowledge A. C. Nielsen Co. for their generosity in providing the data used in our econometric analysis, and we thank Indiana University and the University of Southern California for financial and administrative support.

Access to a number of government agency studies and comments to regulatory proceedings has contributed importantly to our work. An economic study prepared in 1979 for the Federal Communications Commission by Yale Braunstein documented horizontal and vertical ownership ties in the cable industry and identified a number of policy issues foreshadowing those we face today. Within a wide-ranging report on the cable industry published in 1988, the National Telecommunications and Information

Agency presented updated cable industry ownership data and discussed related policy issues then coming to the forefront.

In 1990 the FCC released a comprehensive study of the cable industry. Based on the descriptive data and voluminous comments filed in the commission's inquiry, the report identified and discussed possible procompetitive and anticompetitive effects of vertical integration in cable and discussed policy implications. In 1994, 1995, and 1997 the FCC released its first, second, and third annual reports on the status of competition in the cable television industry, as required by the 1992 Cable Television Consumer Protection and Competition Act. Those reports updated industry ownership data and drew policy inferences.

Comments of interested parties to the FCC in the proceedings and testimony in congressional hearings leading up to the 1992 Cable Act contain data and theories of cable firm behavior, and they have advanced public interest justifications for alternative policies toward vertical integration in cable. Notable among supporting documents in those proceedings are several economic studies to which we had access. Janusz Ordover and Yale Braunstein discussed motives and effects of horizontal and vertical integration in cable in a 1988 study. In 1989 Benjamin Klein analyzed the motives and effects of vertical integration in cable and presented extensive data about vertical ownership ties in the industry. Of two 1993 studies by Stanley M. Besen, Steven R. Brenner, and John R. Woodbury, one analyzed proposed FCC restrictions on horizontal and vertical ownership ties in cable, and the other analyzed proposed regulations of exclusive contracting and the pricing of programming services to cable's competitors. A 1994 study by Economists, Inc., presented more recent data on horizontal and vertical ownership ties in the industry.

DAVID WATERMAN
ANDREW A. WEISS

About the Authors

DAVID WATERMAN is associate professor of telecommunications at Indiana University, Bloomington. He was previously a faculty member of the Annenberg School for Communication at the University of Southern California. Before joining USC, Professor Waterman was the principal of Waterman & Associates, a Los Angeles consulting firm. He has also served as research economist at the National Endowment for the Arts in Washington.

Professor Waterman has written widely on the economics of the motion picture, cable television, and other information industries in scholarly journals and edited books. His recent research has focused on market structure and public policy issues in cable television, the economics of motion picture and video production and distribution, and international trade in media products.

Professor Waterman received a Ph.D. in economics from Stanford University in 1979.

ANDREW A. WEISS is professor of economics at the University of Southern California. He has been at USC since 1984, where he has taught courses in statistics and econometrics. His research interests include theoretical and applied econometrics, forecasting, and time-series analysis. In addition to the cable television industry, his recent research has focused on simultaneity in count data models, forecasting with asymmetric cost functions, and specification testing in ordered logit and probit models.

Professor Weiss received a Ph.D. in economics from the University of Sydney in 1984.

Vertical Integration
in
Cable Television

1

Introduction

IN 1974, along with its recommendation that cable television systems of the future be common carriers, President Nixon's Cabinet Committee on Cable Communications proposed a complete vertical divestiture of cable systems from program suppliers.[1] At that time, approximately 12 percent of all U.S. households with television subscribed to cable, and only a handful of locally or regionally distributed cable programming networks was available.[2]

Although several of those programming networks were owned and operated by cable systems or chains of systems called multiple cable system operators (MSOs), the committee's recommendations were apparently based on expectations, rather than on any perceived misbehavior by those integrated cable firms. The local monopoly status of cable systems meant that they were likely to become the sole gatekeepers of which programs would be available to local subscribers. Thus, the committee wanted to eliminate any incentives that cable systems might have to exclude or otherwise disadvantage program suppliers with which they had no vertical affiliation. Such behavior, the committee contended, would be anticompe-

---

1. CABINET COMMITTEE ON CABLE COMMUNICATIONS, REPORT TO THE PRESIDENT (1974) [hereinafter CABINET COMMITTEE REPORT]. The report is commonly called the Whitehead Report, after its principal investigator, Clay T. Whitehead. It recommended a transition period before vertical separations were implemented.

2. Throughout this book, the term *network* refers to program suppliers, as distinct from a network of hardware serving communications needs at the facilities level, such as local exchange carriers, satellite master antenna systems, or even cable systems. In accordance with the Federal Communications Commission's terminology, we refer to firms that offer or might offer multichannel video services at the retail level as multichannel video programming distributors.

titive, inconsistent with the First Amendment objective of preserving free and open access to consumers by program creators, and would limit a cable consumer's freedom to "pick and choose from among a diverse range of entertainment, information, and services."[3]

Of course, the committee's recommendations were never implemented. But, as it expected, the supply of cable programming has indeed flourished. More than 100 nationally distributed networks, as well as many regional networks, are now available to cable operators. Vertical integration between those programming suppliers and cable systems has also become widespread.[4] As recent Federal Communications Commission reports[5] and our own compilation in chapter 3 document, many of the largest "basic" networks (such as TBS, CNN, and The Discovery Channel) and "premium" cable networks (such as HBO and Cinemax) have become vertically affiliated with MSOs. Equity sharing—the holding of equity in a single cable network by two or more MSOs—has become prevalent. We also document a growing degree of horizontal concentration of cable system ownership by MSOs in terms of their national shares of cable subscribers and a tendency for the largest MSOs to be disproportionately responsible for vertical relationships with cable networks.

Those structural developments captured legislative attention in a series of congressional hearings beginning in 1988.[6] The hearings culminated in

---

3. CABINET COMMITTEE REPORT, *supra* note 1, at 25.

4. Consistent with its common usage in FCC and most other government documents, we often use the term *vertical integration* interchangeably with *vertical ownership* or *vertical affiliation*. As shown in chapter 3, many vertical ties between program suppliers and cable systems involve minority ownership, but that is not integration in the strict economic sense, because vertical control of assets is not ostensibly involved.

5. Competition, Rate Deregulation and the Commission's Policies Relating to the Provision of Cable Television Service, Report, MM Dkt. No. 89-600, FCC 90-276, 67 Rad. Reg. 2d (P&F) 1771 (1990); Implementation of Section 19 of the Cable Television Consumer Protection and Competition Act of 1992: Annual Assessment of the Status of Competition in the Market for Delivery of Video Programming, First Report, CS Dkt. No. 94-48, FCC 94-235 (1994) [hereinafter 1994 FCC Cable Report]; Implementation of the Cable Consumer Protection and Competition Act of 1992: Annual Assessment of the Status of Competition in the Market for the Delivery of Video Programming, CS Dkt. No. 95-61, FCC 95-491 (Dec. 11, 1995); In the Matter of Annual Assessment of the Status of Competition in the Market for the Delivery of Video Programming, Third Annual Report, CS Dkt. No. 96-133, FCC 96-496 (Jan. 2, 1997) [hereinafter 1997 FCC Cable Report].

6. *Competitive Issues in the Cable Television Industry: Hearings Before the Subcomm. on Antitrust, Business Rights, and Competition of the Sen. Comm. on the Judiciary*, 100th Cong., 2d Sess. (1988); *Media Ownership: Diversity and Concentration: Hearings Before the Subcomm. on Communications of the Sen. Comm. on Commerce, Science, and*

1992 with the passage of the Cable Television Consumer Protection and Competition Act.[7] Certain sections of the act directed the FCC to establish regulations governing the behavior of integrated cable systems. Accordingly, the FCC promulgated a variety of such regulations, including channel-occupancy limits—restrictions on the number of channels that an integrated cable system can fill with programming in which it has an attributable interest—and a limit on the number of homes passed in which a single MSO can have an interest. In addition, the commission imposed regulations intended to ensure nondiscriminatory access to programming by multichannel, multipoint distribution service (MMDS) systems, direct broadcast satellites (DBS), satellite master antenna television (SMATV) systems, home satellite dish (HSD) owners and program distributors,[8] "overbuilt" cable systems (those competitive cable systems constructed within the same franchise), and other existing or potential competitors to established cable systems. At this writing, some of those regulations are being contested in the courts or are under reconsideration at the FCC.

The Telecommunications Act of 1996,[9] signed into law in February 1996, does not directly affect vertical ownership ties between cable operators and cable networks. The act does, however, remove the 1970 telephone company–cable cross-ownership ban;[10] local telephone exchange carriers (LECs) are now permitted to offer both cable service and telephone service within their telephone service areas. LECs that do so become cable operators in the eyes

---

Transportation, 102d Cong., 1st Sess. (1989); *Cable TV Consumer Protection Act of 1989: Hearings Before the Subcomm. on Communications of the Sen. Comm. on Commerce, Science, and Transportation*, 101st Cong., 2d Sess. (1990); *Cable Television Regulation (pt.2): Hearings Before the Subcomm. on Telecommunications and Finance of the Sen. Comm. on Energy and Commerce*, 101st Cong., 2d Sess. (1990); *Cable TV Consumer Protection Act of 1991: Hearing Before the Subcomm. on Communications of the Sen. Comm. on Commerce, Science, and Transportation*, 102d Cong., 1st Sess. (1991).

7. Pub. L. No. 102-385, 106 Stat. 1460 (1992) (codified at 47 U.S.C. §§ 521–55).

8. HSD is distinct from direct broadcasting satellites. The HSD industry, often known as the television receive only (TVRO) industry, utilizes larger, three- to five-meter dishes designed to receive television signals from the same low-power, C-band satellites that transmit to cable system headends. The DBS industry primarily includes companies such as DirecTV and United States Satellite Broadcasting, which utilize relatively small, approximately one-half-meter rooftop dishes at a subscriber's premises to receive signals from high-power satellites in the Ku-band. Those companies, most notably Primestar, that transmit directly to intermediate-size home dishes via medium-power satellites in the lower portion of the Ku-band are also usually considered part of the DBS industry.

9. Pub. L. No. 104-104, 110 Stat. 56 (1996); S. 652, 104th Cong., 2d Sess. (1996).

10. The FCC's 1970 cross-ownership ban was codified by the Cable Communications Policy Act of 1984, Pub. L. No. 98-549, 98 Stat. 2780 (1984).

of the law and are subject to the vertical restraints and other provisions of the Cable Act of 1992. The 1996 act also permits LECs to offer video services by other means, with more limited vertical restraints affecting programming supply functions in which a LEC may have ownership interests.

TOPICS TO BE EXAMINED

The main questions we consider in this book mirror the recent policy debate in cable television and echo the concerns of Nixon's cabinet committee. Does vertical integration in cable foster anticompetitive behavior and raise barriers to entry into the system, to the detriment of economic efficiency, program diversity, or the First Amendment freedoms of program creators? Or does integration lead to more efficient cable industry operation and benefit consumers as well as program suppliers, who might not otherwise have market opportunities? What policies toward vertical integration in the cable industry should we have? What policies should apply to vertical integration between programming suppliers and the multichannel video programming distributors (MVPDs) that either now or soon will compete with cable?

One objective of this book is to evaluate relevant policy outcomes of the 1992 Cable Act and the 1996 Telecommunications Act. Recent legislative and regulatory activity, however, is only one part of the debate about the benefits and costs of ownership ties between the upstream creators or packagers of information and the downstream distributors of that information to consumers. That debate has involved not only cable, but other mass media, and, as legal barriers to content-creation by the LECs have fallen, the telephone industry as well.[11] The vertical ownership issue will persist: in cable, as policy formulation continues, as well as in telephony and other media, as those technologies press their entry into multichannel video distribution. We intend our analysis to serve as a resource to policy makers confronting new questions about vertical ownership and control in the media.

In addressing the issues, we must take into account the extraordinary pace of technological change in video programming distribution. Cable system operators have accelerated the installation of high bandwidth capacity and fiber optic–based transmission systems, and, along with some of their

---

11. BRUCE M. OWEN, ECONOMICS AND FREEDOM OF EXPRESSION (Ballinger Publishing Co. 1975) contains an economic analysis of vertical ownership in media industries. *See also* United States *v.* Western Electric Co., Op. No. 82-0192 (D.D.C. July 25, 1991); Roger G. Noll, *The Role of Antitrust in Telecommunications*, 5 ANTITRUST BULL. 40 (Fall 1995); BRUCE M. OWEN & STEVEN S. WILDMAN, VIDEO ECONOMICS (Harvard University Press 1992).

rivals, they are beginning to deploy digital video compression equipment that can multiply channel capacities of their transmission systems by a factor of four or more. Down the road, now experimental video-on-demand (VOD) systems may allow a subscriber to select electronically programs from large libraries to view programs at times of his own choosing. How might those and other technological developments affect our conclusions about vertical integration's economic effects or the need for regulations governing integration?

Cable's dominance of the multichannel video program distribution industry is also eroding—a prospect that would diminish many of the economic and First Amendment–related social concerns about vertical integration in cable that we set forth below. In 1994 DirecTV and United States Satellite Broadcasting (USSB) began nationwide high Ku-band DBS service. As a result of the FCC's 1992 and 1994 Video Dialtone rulings, subsequent court decisions,[12] and, most recently, the 1996 Telecommunications Act, the LECs have begun entering the video marketplace. Still, DBS, MMDS, SMATV, and HSD distributors have together garnered less than 12 percent of today's MVPD market, with many of those subscribers outside cable franchise areas.[13] In only a few markets do established cable systems face competition from overbuilt cable systems.[14] One economic study suggests that although established cable systems will face increasingly effective competition within the next decade, cable overbuilders and the technological alternatives to cable system video delivery face a long, if not uphill, battle.[15] A premise of

12. Telephone Company–Cable Television Cross-Ownership Rules, §§ 63.54–63.58, Mem. Op. & Order on Recons., CC Dkt. No. 87-266, 7 F.C.C. Rcd. 5069 (1992); Telephone Company–Cable Television Cross-Ownership Rules, §§ 63.54–63.58, and Amendments of Parts 32, 36, 61, 64, and 69 of the Commission's Rules to Establish and Implement Regulatory Procedures for Video Dialtone Service, RM-8221, CC Dkt. No. 87-266 (Nov. 7, 1994).

13. According to the FCC, basic cable subscribers accounted for approximately 88.7 percent of a total of 71.6 million multichannel video households as of September 1996. MMDS accounted for 1.7 percent; SMATV for 1.5 percent; HSD for 3.2 percent; and DBS for 4.9 percent. 1997 FCC Cable Report, *supra* note 5, app. F. Fifty-two percent of DirecTV and USSB subscribers and a large proportion of HSD subscribers were reported in 1995 to be outside areas wired for cable. Mark Landler, *The Dishes Are Coming: Satellites Go Suburban*, N.Y. TIMES, May 29, 1995, at 19.

14. 1994 FCC Cable Report, *supra* note 5. The report states that in 1990 there were forty-one to forty-nine "overbuilt" systems (¶ 55) of a national total of approximately 10,000 and that as of September 1994 the extent of overbuilding "seems to have remained quite limited" (¶ 60).

15. LELAND L. JOHNSON, TOWARD COMPETITION IN CABLE TELEVISION (MIT Press and AEI Press 1994).

this book is that public policy toward vertical integration in cable and other multichannel video technologies should try to anticipate, but not presume, effective competition to established cable television systems operators.

We address those issues principally through economic analysis. To make our work more accessible, however, we use a nontechnical approach whenever possible.

ORGANIZATION, KEY FINDINGS, AND RECOMMENDATIONS

In chapter 2 we detail the current economic controversies about vertical integration in cable television and define the corresponding policy issues. We then assess the costs and benefits of integration in cable systems to economic efficiency, as well as to two First Amendment–related criteria: the access that program suppliers have to cable subscribers and program diversity. In chapter 3 we document the current horizontal and vertical market structure of the cable television industry and briefly describe its historical development. Ownership ties between MSOs and cable program suppliers have become extensive, though by no means ubiquitous. The horizontal concentration of MSOs in national shares of cable subscribers has risen steadily in recent years. The largest individual MSOs now account for the largest numbers of vertical ownership affiliations with cable networks.

In chapters 4 and 5 we consider the competitive advantages of vertical integration to cable firms and the likely effects of integration on consumers. Chapter 4 is concerned with efficiency advantages of integration; a variety of anecdotal evidence suggests that cable subscribers benefit from transactions efficiencies and from the creative and financial resources of cable system operators that are made available by integration. In particular, reduced risks of opportunistic behavior and resolution of other contracting problems are likely to reduce programming input costs, thus increasing efficiency. More important, the extensive history of MSOs' involvement in cable programming suggests reduced risks of entry, improved access of programming suppliers to subscribers, and greater program diversity.

Chapter 5 turns to strategic advantages of vertical integration, with emphasis on potentially anticompetitive effects of vertical integration on the supply of cable programming. While integration is likely to facilitate anticompetitive behavior in the cable programming supply that may occur, integration's role is fundamentally ancillary to that of the buying, or monopsony, power of MSOs in the programming market. The historical experience also shows that vertical integration is only one among a number of strategic devices that cable programming suppliers might employ to establish and maintain their market positions. In the presence of MSO monopsony power, vertical integration may also have a procompetitive effect by increasing the flow of cable system revenues back to the production industry.

Chapter 6 reports the results of an econometric analysis of the effects of vertical integration on the carriage, pricing, and promotion of cable networks. While differences are often insignificant or minor, a consistent general pattern emerges: Integrated cable systems tend to "favor" the programming with which they have ownership ties, either by carrying those networks more frequently than would otherwise be expected or by pricing them lower or marketing them more vigorously. Our analysis also shows that integrated systems tend to disadvantage unaffiliated networks in those same respects, at least if the latter are good substitutes for affiliated programming. Integrated systems also tend to offer fewer cable networks in total, although the differences are very small. The dominant effect appears to be that integrated cable systems replace unaffiliated networks with similar, affiliated networks. A separate analysis of the effects of vertical integration on larger channel capacity systems suggests that those effects of integration will persist, though they will diminish, as channel capacities expand or VOD systems are developed. In general, the statistical results are consistent with either the realization of transactions efficiencies or vertical foreclosure models.

In chapter 7 we consider strategic, potentially anticompetitive uses of vertical integration by established cable operators to retard or prevent the entry of competing MVPDs. Vertical integration, especially via majority ownership ties, is likely to facilitate such strategies. Again, however, there is no evidence that vertical integration is a decisive element in any anticompetitive behavior that may have occurred. While exclusive contracting and input price differentials have procompetitive explanations, the record shows that both integrated and nonintegrated firms have engaged in the same range of potentially anticompetitive behavior. Evidence that program suppliers tend to charge higher prices to MMDS, SMATV, and other entrants can be explained, if not by cost differences, by variations in the bargaining power that MVPDs are likely to have in setting input prices. Those variations have relatively little to do with vertical integration.

Those findings lead to five principal policy conclusions discussed in chapter 8. First, regulatory attempts to limit discriminatory behavior by vertically integrated cable systems against unaffiliated program suppliers are impractical or counterproductive and should be abandoned. In particular, the 1992 Cable Act's channel-occupancy limits can do little to reduce such discrimination, except to the extent that they may induce vertical divestiture. Channel limits could make it more difficult for new networks to enter, because of reduced incentives for cable operators to offer their financial support.

Second, the FCC's program-access regulations should not, as they currently do, apply only to vertically integrated program suppliers. While an economic argument can be made in favor of nondiscriminatory access provisions in general, the lack of evidence that vertical integration is decisive in any discrimination that may take place indicates that any such regulations should apply equally to integrated and nonintegrated program suppliers. To the extent that the current program-access regulations affect the sales behavior of integrated programming suppliers, they may also encourage vertical divestiture.

Third, the evidence does not support an economic case for vertical divestiture. Because vertical ownership ties are only one strategic resource that cable firms might employ to establish and defend their competitive positions, there is no assurance that a policy of vertical divestiture would appreciably reduce either entry barriers to new cable networks or facilities-level barriers to alternative multichannel providers. Evident sacrifice to efficient operation, especially of the creative and financial resources that cable operators can bring to the supply of cable programming, would result. Vertical divestiture would also have far-reaching effects on media-firm organization, since the great majority of large media corporations produce or distribute programming that appears on cable systems at one time or another. Antitrust authorities should, however, actively monitor the extent of vertical ownership ties to programming suppliers, especially those that the largest MSOs develop.

Fourth, if the FCC's right to impose a limit on the proportion of homes that any single MSO can reach is upheld by the courts, then the FCC should reduce its limit from 30 percent to no more than 20 percent. While systematic evidence to document the extent to which individual MSOs might now exert monopsony power were not available, it is reasonable that an MSO with substantially less than 30 percent of the national market could anticompetitively affect competition in cable-programming supply because of economies of scale in cable network distribution. Conversely, it appears unlikely that a 20 percent or even lower limit would result in major sacrifices to economies of scale in cable system operations or to the creative and financial resources necessary to develop new programming and new technology. Antitrust authorities should, in any case, monitor merger activity among the largest MSOs with consideration of the unusual cost conditions of cable networking.

Fifth, we find no reason to apply structural or behavioral restrictions involving vertical integration by alternative MVPDs, including LECs, that may compete with cable. Specific program-access constraints on suppliers that are vertically affiliated with alternative MVPDs would be counterproductive to the objective of encouraging their entry. Any favoritism that new entrants—or established cable operators—might show to vertically affiliated program suppliers would be of limited social interest because consumers would be able to choose among alternative video distributors.

We conclude that to the extent there are economic or other social problems with the cable television industry's performance, policy solutions lie not with regulatory or other restraints on vertical ownership, but with reducing or containing the horizontal market power of cable system operators at both the local and the national market levels.

2

Social Concerns and Policy Issues

We NOW SET OUT the economic and policy controversies about vertical integration in cable television and other video media that led us to write this book.

CONTROVERSIES ABOUT VERTICAL INTEGRATION

Many contributors to the legal proceedings leading up to the 1992 Cable Act identified potentially procompetitive, efficiency-promoting advantages of vertical integration in cable. As we discuss in later chapters, such advantages are implied by an extensive general economic literature on industrial organization. In summary, integration between cable systems and networks might increase industry efficiency by reducing risk and otherwise facilitating the process of contracting between cable firms. Integration between cable systems and networks might also promote innovation in programming and increase the availability of financial resources for program development and distribution.

Few dispute the efficiency advantages of vertical integration, but claims that integration in cable has socially harmful effects have been intensely debated. We therefore devote disproportionate attention in this work to the allegations of harm. The concerns about detrimental effects of integration that have motivated the recent policy process fall into two main categories: concern that integrated cable systems might favor their vertically affiliated networks to the disadvantage of unaffiliated program suppliers; and concern that integrated cable systems might use their vertical ties to restrict potential or existing competitive multichannel video programming distributors from access to programming.

Favoring Vertically Affiliated Networks

Reflecting the Nixon cabinet committee's original apprehensions, many observers in recent legal proceedings have assumed or feared that unaffiliated networks tend to be excluded from the program menus of vertically integrated cable systems. Further, those observers claim, integrated networks are priced or promoted preferentially.

A consequence of such behavior could be an undesirable reduction in the amount or variety of programming available to local cable subscribers. Or, if enough cable systems favor their vertically affiliated suppliers, unaffiliated networks might be forced out of business altogether. Vertical integration could also prevent the entry of new networks that promise to compete with existing integrated networks, especially if vertically affiliated cable systems account for a large share of the national market.

Attracting attention, for example, has been the ownership by Tele-Communications, Inc. (TCI) and Time Warner since 1987 of approximately 23 percent and 19 percent, respectively, of Turner Broadcasting System (TBS), the operator of CNN. In October 1996 Time Warner acquired 100 percent of TBS from TCI and other shareholders, although TCI received in exchange approximately a 9 percent equity stake in Time Warner.[1] As documented in chapter 3, those two MSOs (including their minority holdings) together accounted for approximately 47.4 percent of U.S. basic cable subscribers (28.3 percent by TCI and 19.1 percent by Time Warner) in September 1996. Do MSO ties to CNN dim prospects for a competing general news channel, such as MSNBC or the Fox News Channel?[2] Numerous claims of anticompetitive behavior involving TCI, Time Warner, and other MSOs have also been presented in legal proceedings and in the popular press. Those accounts often pertain to relatively extensive vertical ownership ties. Our data show that by late 1995, TCI was vertically affiliated with at least twenty-five nationally distributed cable networks, and Time Warner with at least sixteen.

Restricting Access of Alternative Multichannel
Video Programming Distributors to Programming

In an extensive report on the cable industry released in 1990, the FCC cited many complaints by multichannel, multipoint distribution service systems

---

1. See the postscript to this book for a discussion of the Time Warner–TBS merger.

2. MSNBC—a joint venture of Microsoft Corp. and NBC—and Fox News Channel, 100 percent owned by News Corp., entered the market in the summer and fall of 1996, respectively.

(wireless cable), satellite master antenna television operators, and other existing or potential competitors to cable systems that cable networks with vertical ownership ties to established cable systems refused to do business with them or offered them programming only on discriminatory terms.[3] Parallel testimony and evidence were submitted in several congressional hearings from 1988 to 1991 and reiterated in the FCC's implementation proceedings following the 1992 act.[4]

Of understandably little concern at the time of the Nixon cabinet committee report, wireless and other technological alternatives to local monopoly cable television systems add a new dimension to the vertical integration issue. While the economic prospects of those alternatives may be uncertain, effective competition to local monopoly cable systems seems to offer a natural solution to nagging problems that many observers attribute to the cable industry: excessively high prices, poor service, and notably, for purposes of this study, any undesirable variations in the available diversity and prices of programming resulting from vertical integration. It is likely that effective competition would make discrimination by an integrated cable system against unaffiliated networks unprofitable. In any case, such distortions would be of little social interest if alternative delivery systems were widely available to consumers.

POLICIES TOWARD VERTICAL INTEGRATION IN CABLE

Numerous proposals for constraining vertical integration and the behavior of integrated firms have emerged from the recent policy process; some of them are now incorporated into FCC regulations as a result of the 1992 act. This study focuses in particular on three issues: restrictions against disadvantaging of unaffiliated program suppliers; nondiscriminatory access to programming; and partial or complete vertical disintegration.

*Restrictions against Disadvantaging
of Unaffiliated Program Suppliers*

There is a long history to the idea that monopoly cable systems should be required to offer some kind of nondiscriminatory access to suppliers of

---

3. Competition, Rate Deregulation, and the Commission's Policies Relating to the Provision of Cable Television Service, Report, MM Dkt. No. 89-600, FCC 90-276, 67 Rad. Reg. 2d (P&F) 1771 (1990) ¶ 117 [hereinafter 1990 FCC Cable Report].

4. Implementation of Sections 12 and 19 of the Cable Television Consumer and Competition Protection Act of 1992: Development of Competition and Diversity in Video Programming Distribution and Carriage, First Rep. & Order, MM Dkt. No. 92-265, 8 F.C.C. Rcd. 3359 (1993) [hereinafter First Rep. & Order on Competition and Diversity].

programming that they might otherwise choose not to carry. Depending on their channel capacities, many systems have been required since the 1960s to set aside a block of channels for commercial lease. Those leased access requirements have failed. Program suppliers have not taken meaningful advantage of those channels on either integrated or nonintegrated cable systems, although some have attributed that to weakness of the provisions as now written.[5]

To address the perceived discrimination by integrated systems against unaffiliated networks, Congress took a new tack in the 1992 act. The act directed the FCC to set a limit on the proportion of a cable system's channel capacity that it could occupy with programming in which the system's operator has an attributable interest.[6] In 1993 the FCC set that channel-occupancy limit at 40 percent (for systems with fewer than seventy-five channels) and defined *attributable interest* to be 5 percent or more of total equity.[7] The main objective of those limits was to reduce the incentive of vertically integrated cable operators to favor their affiliated services to the disadvantage of unaffiliated services.[8]

Nondiscriminatory Access to Programming

Should overbuilt cable systems and alternative multichannel video programming distributors be given nondiscriminatory access to programming distributed by suppliers that are vertically integrated with established cable operators? As mandated by the 1992 act, the FCC established regulations in 1993 that require cable program suppliers in which cable systems have an attributable interest to make programming available on the same terms and conditions to all competing delivery systems.[9] As the commission notes, the

---

5. *See, e.g.*, Donna A. Lampert, *Cable Television: Does Leased Access Mean Least Access?*, 44 FED. COMM. L.J. 245 (1992); *see also* STANLEY M. BESEN & LELAND L. JOHNSON, AN ECONOMIC ANALYSIS OF MANDATORY LEASED CHANNEL ACCESS FOR CABLE TELEVISION (RAND Corporation 1982).

6. Pub. L. No. 102-385, § 11(c), 106 Stat. 1487.

7. First Rep. & Order on Competition and Diversity, *supra* note 4. The FCC declined to change that ruling on reconsideration in April 1995; Implementation of Sections 11 and 13 of the Cable Television Consumer Protection and Competition Act of 1992: Horizontal and Vertical Ownership Limits, Cross-Ownership Limitations and Anti-Trafficking Provisions, Rep. No. DC 95-52, MM Dkt. No. 92-264 (Apr. 5, 1995).

8. In the Matter of Implementation of Sections 12 and 19 of the Cable Television Consumer Protection and Competition Act of 1992: Development of Competition and Diversity in Video Programming Distribution and Carriage, Second Rep. & Order, MM Dkt. No. 92-265 (1993) ¶ 41.

9. First Rep. & Order on Competition and Diversity, *supra* note 4.

act generally prohibits "unfair methods of competition" and "unfair or deceptive acts or practices" by all cable operators and programmers. But the act singles out the vertically integrated program suppliers (along with all satellite broadcast program vendor superstations such as WTBS) for specific FCC regulation. Among other restraints, those regulations prohibit integrated programmers and superstations from any price discrimination in the distribution of cable programming in any market, except for differences a programmer can justify on the basis of cost, volume difference, creditworthiness, or similar factors. Those programmers and superstations are also prohibited from entering into exclusive dealing contracts—or, implicitly, from refusing to deal—with any multichannel video distributor unless they can demonstrate that those contracts are in the public interest.

Partial or Complete Vertical Disintegration

Should cable systems be vertically disintegrated from cable program suppliers, or should the extent of their interests in those suppliers be limited? The 1992 Cable Act instructed the FCC to study the possibility of "imposing limitations on the degree to which multi-channel video programming distributors . . . may engage in the creation or production of video programming."[10] No such limits were imposed.

The question of partial or complete vertical separations in cable is nevertheless an important and longstanding policy issue. Divestiture would certainly be a way to resolve the problems that have been attributed to vertical integration in cable. Beginning with the cabinet committee report, the general idea of vertical separation in information industries has also received legislative, judicial, and academic attention on First Amendment grounds.[11]

RELATED ISSUES IN CABLE TELEVISION

The debates about vertical integration cannot be separated from two other policy issues in cable: horizontal concentration of MSOs; and the general question of whether any nondiscriminatory program-access requirements should be imposed on all cable programming suppliers, not just those vertically integrated with cable systems.

---

10. Pub. L. No. 102-385, § 11, 106 Stat. 1487.

11. *See also* BRUCE M. OWEN, ECONOMICS AND FREEDOM OF EXPRESSION (Ballinger 1975) and BRUCE M. OWEN & STEVEN S. WILDMAN, VIDEO ECONOMICS (Harvard University Press 1992).

With respect to MSO concentration, the FCC had considered but rejected limits on the national market shares of MSOs, as defined by the total number of basic subscribers or homes passed that they reach.[12] The 1992 act did, however, direct the FCC to establish such limits to "[prevent] larger vertically integrated cable systems from creating barriers to entry of new video programmers and from causing a reduction in the number of media voices available to consumers."[13] Accordingly, in 1993 the FCC directed that no more than 30 percent of all cable homes passed could be served by any one system owner.[14] At this writing, the FCC's right to set a limit has been struck down by a lower court, but the ruling is currently under appeal; the rules are also under reconsideration by the commission.[15] Horizontal mergers and acquisitions of cable systems by MSOs are also an antitrust issue.

The issue of MSO size is inseparable from a study of vertical ownership because the plausibility of most economic theories of vertical foreclosure depends on the presence of horizontal market power. For example, it is unlikely that an integrated MSO could have much anticompetitive impact on the entry or market survival of unaffiliated national networks unless that MSO controlled a substantial share of the national market.

The second implicit issue—access to programming by competing multichannel delivery systems, independent of vertical integration's influence—is a complex one. As we discuss in chapter 7, program-access complaints have involved both vertically affiliated and unaffiliated programming suppliers. Our main concern in this study is the extent to which vertical integration may *facilitate* anticompetitive attempts to restrict program access. Vertical integration does not in itself motivate such anticompetitive behavior; cable systems must have an incentive to restrict program access to alternative video distributors, even in the absence of vertical integration. The economic justifications for program-access regulations in general, however, inevitably underlie our study of access restrictions with respect to vertical integration.

---

12. 1990 FCC Cable Report, *supra* note 3, ¶ 76.

13. First Rep. & Order on Competition and Diversity, *supra* note 4, ¶ 37.

14. Pub. L. No. 102-385, § 11, 106 Stat. 1487 (codified at 47 U.S.C. § 533(f)(1)(A)); Implementation of Sections 11 and 13 of the Cable Television Consumer Protection and Competition Act of 1992; Horizontal and Vertical Ownership Limits, Cross-Ownership Limitations and Anti-Trafficking Provisions, Second Rep. & Order, MM Dkt. No. 92-264, 8 F.C.C. Rcd. 8576 (Oct. 23, 1993).

15. In the Matter of Annual Assessment of the Status of Competition in the Market for the Delivery of Video Programming, Third Annual Report, CS Dkt. No. 96-133, FCC 96-496 (Jan. 2, 1997) ¶ 130.

POLICIES TOWARD VERTICAL INTEGRATION
BY COMPETITORS TO CABLE TELEVISION

We noted that the FCC's 1993 program-access regulations apply only to programming suppliers in which an attributable interest is held by a cable system operator. Should those or other vertical restraints also be applied to ownership ties between programming suppliers and alternative multichannel video programming distributors?

Local exchange carriers are perhaps of special interest. The FCC's 1992 and 1994 Video Dialtone rulings first permitted LECs to offer video services within their local market areas, but only as common carriers. The Telecommunications Act of 1996 generally permits a LEC to choose among video services in the following ways: as a wireless multichannel video programming distributor; as a "cable operator" (and thus subject to local franchise requirements and other existing legislation affecting cable operators); or as a common carrier through an "open video system" (OVS), certified by the FCC to be offering nondiscriminatory capacity for unaffiliated programmers.[16] Open video systems do not require a franchise and are subject only to certain provisions of the 1992 Cable Act, notably the program-access regulations.

Contrary to popular assumption, the LECs were never prohibited from owning programming suppliers such as cable networks. The Video Dialtone rulings did, however, prohibit the LECs from owning more than a 5 percent interest in any *programmer*—the intermediary that actually packages and provides the programming to consumers over LEC facilities.[17] The 1996 act formally removes that last vertical ownership restriction and leaves the LECs free to integrate into program supply functions, whichever of the three video service options they select.[18]

The 1996 legislation thus raises new policy questions with respect to appropriate regulatory treatment of LEC-provided video services.

---

16. Telecommunications Act of 1996, Pub. L. 104-104, 110 Stat. 56 (Feb. 8, 1996) § 302 (a).

17. Amendments of Parts 32, 36, 61, 64, and 69 of the Commision's Rules to Establish and Implement Regulatory Procedures for Video Dialtone Service, RM-8221, CC Dkt. No. 87-266 (Nov. 7, 1994).

18. Court decisions had ruled the cross-ownership ban on joint operation of cable and telephone systems in the same market to be unconstitutional and thus permitted several of the regional Bell operating companies to ignore those ownership restrictions before the 1996 act.

CRITERIA FOR EVALUATING SOCIAL COSTS
AND BENEFITS OF VERTICAL INTEGRATION

Before proceeding, we need to be explicit about what we hope the cable and other multichannel video industries can achieve in pricing, program variety, and other dimensions of social benefit. As we shall see, appropriate criteria on economic and other social grounds are often consistent, but they do conflict in important respects. We distinguish two criteria to evaluate the performance of multichannel video media: economic efficiency and objectives related to the First Amendment.

The goal of economic efficiency underlies the methodology of this study and is a central focus of it. In simplest terms, efficiency means that resources are allocated in a way that reflects the demands of consumers and the opportunity cost of using those resources for other purposes. Efficiency in the cable industry would imply that the programming and other attributes of cable service reflect the preferences of potential subscribers and that the prices of those services do not exceed a firm's actual costs of providing them. A subscription price for a premium cable network in excess of its cost, for example, would be inefficient because some potential subscribers willing to pay more than the true cost would remain unserved. That circumstance in turn implies that additional hardware, administrative measures, or other resources needed to provide additional subscriptions to that network—perhaps coming from other cable networks or from different industries altogether—would increase consumer welfare and thus be socially desirable.[19]

In general, economic efficiency can be improved either by lowering costs or by reducing the market power of firms that are sustaining prices above costs. The evaluation of efficiency in media industries such as cable television is complicated, however, by the presence of economies of scale and product differentiation. As detailed in chapter 5, media products tend to have large economies of scale in distribution: There is a high "first copy" cost of creating a television program, but the marginal costs of distributing it to additional viewers through broadcast, cable, or other media are very low. Those cost conditions imply a trade-off between the number of media products that can be created and distributed and their average cost per viewer or reader. That leads to a hard question: Are consumers better off with two cable news programs with different slants at a cost of $10 per viewer or with a single, homogenized news program at a cost of $7.50 per viewer? In

---

19. *See* WILLIAM J. BAUMOL & J. GREGORY SIDAK, TOWARD COMPETITION IN LOCAL TELEPHONY (MIT Press and AEI Press 1994), ch. 3, for a more thorough discussion of economic efficiency.

economic terms the answer depends on the full array of prices that each individual consumer would be willing to pay for those alternatives. Unfortunately, such information is rarely revealed by the marketplace.[20]

That uncertainty about consumer preferences means that we usually cannot tell whether a change in the number of different products available or a change in their retail prices really improves efficiency. Theoretically, lower costs could even lead to reduced efficiency, or anticompetitive behavior could increase efficiency. Such perverse effects could occur if product variety (or prices) happened to move toward the optimum level in the process. In this book we simply assume that any reduction in a firm's costs will lead to greater efficiency. We assume that the ability of firms to maintain output prices above competitive levels,[21] to maintain input prices below competitive levels, or to engage in anticompetitive behavior against other firms reduces efficiency. Despite those simplifying assumptions, efficiency effects can still be difficult to assess in the cable industry.

Our second criterion for evaluating social welfare, First Amendment–related objectives, has two main elements: ease of access to the public by program creators and program diversity. Policy debates about access by program suppliers through cable have centered on whether cable operators are obligated to provide channel space to all comers on nondiscriminatory terms because of their local monopoly status.[22] As the cabinet committee

---

20. Technically speaking, the difficulty here arises from an inability to measure the amount of consumer surplus that would result from either alternative. The dilemma would be resolved by the market if the program distributors could perfectly price discriminate and thus extract the full value of consumer surplus. For classic analyses of the product variety–economic welfare problem, *see* Avinash K. Dixit & Joseph E. Stiglitz, *Monopolistic Competition and Optimal Product Diversity*, 67 AM. ECON. REV. 297 (1977), and A. Michael Spence, *Product Selection, Fixed Costs, and Monopolistic Competition*, 43 REV. ECON. STUDIES 217 (1976). A more specific model is set out in A. Michael Spence & Bruce M. Owen, *Television Programming, Monopolistic Competition, and Welfare*, 91 Q.J. ECON. (1977).

21. The typical measure of market power in economics is the ability of a firm to raise its price above marginal cost. Owing to economies of scale, however, the best outcome that can be achieved is a programming industry with a variety of differentiated products priced at average cost. In such a market, prices are bid to competitive levels by the threat of entry, although individual firms must have some market power to maintain price above marginal cost. Those conditions describe the Chamberlain monopolistic competitive equilibrium. Our definition of market power as the ability to price above competitive levels follows that of William M. Landes & Richard A. Posner, *Market Power in Antitrust Cases*, 94 HARVARD L. REV. 937, 977 (1981).

22. *See, e.g.*, Timothy J. Brennan, *Vertical Integration, Monopoly, and the First Amendment*, 3 J. MEDIA ECON. 57 (1990); Daniel L. Brenner, *Cable Television and Freedom of Expression*, DUKE L.J. 329 (1988).

recognized, the access issue is implicitly related to vertical integration because integration might reduce the incentives of operators to offer the programs of unaffiliated suppliers. By another interpretation, however, integration might facilitate access by providing financial support to under-capitalized program creators. In either case, ease of access generally implies low barriers to entry by program suppliers and thus promotes competition and efficiency. Therefore, ease of access and economic efficiency are generally consistent, reinforcing objectives.

Program diversity is a more controversial, sometimes perplexing, criterion for evaluating media performance. Diversity can be defined in different ways. It may mean the degree to which available programs appeal to the interests or needs of distinct audience segments or the degree to which programs reflect a variety of different *sources* of origination or points of view.

The perceived social objective of achieving the "widest possible" pro-gram diversity permeates legislative and judicial debates about cable televi-sion and other media policy and has been interpreted by the Supreme Court in several landmark cases as a legitimate goal of the First Amendment.[23] Those court decisions, as well as the legitimacy of program diversity as a social objective, have been criticized by some economists and legal scholars as paternalistic and irrelevant. They argue that the First Amendment's legitimate purpose is to protect the right to speak—to have access to cable subscribers—not the right to hear.[24]

We nevertheless consider program diversity in our evaluation of video media performance, at least because of its widespread acceptance by the judicial and legislative bodies that set media policy in the United States. A substantive argument in favor of maximizing the diversity of programming also seems to be implicit in its governmental acceptance: A wide range of

---

23. Section 601 of the Cable Communications Policy Act of 1984, for example, states that one of its purposes is to "assure that cable communications provide and are encouraged to provide the widest possible diversity of information sources and services to the public." Pub. L. No. 98-549, § 601, 98 Stat. 2780 (1984) (codified at 47 U.S.C. § 521). In Associated Press *v.* United States, 326 U.S. 1, 20 (1945), the Supreme Court asserted that a goal of the First Amendment is to foster "the widest possible dissemination of information from diverse and antagonistic sources." More recently, in Metro Broad-casting *v.* FCC, 497 U.S. 547, 567 (1990), the Supreme Court stated, "Safeguarding the public's right to receive a diversity of views and information . . . is . . . an integral component of the FCC's mission."

24. *See* BRUCE M. OWEN, ECONOMICS AND FREEDOM OF EXPRESSION (Ballinger 1975) and J. Gregory Sidak, *Telecommunications in Jericho*, 81 CAL. L. REV. 1209 (1994). THOMAS G. KRATTENMAKER & LUCAS A. POWE, JR., REGULATING BROADCAST PRO-GRAMMING (MIT Press and AEI Press 1994), offer an extensive, critical discussion of FCC policies that have attempted to promote program diversity in broadcasting.

available opinion and entertainment products may promote social and political awareness or other democratic values.

Although one measurable dimension of diversity is simply the number of available programs, program diversity is impossible to measure fully. One can count the number of separate ownership or creative sources from which a given menu of programs originates. The degree of content differences among available programs, however, or the extent to which they really serve diverse audience groups, is subjective and prone to wide interpretation.

As our foregoing discussion of economic efficiency implies, there is no necessary relationship between diversity and efficiency. Diversity is generally expensive to achieve, however, owing to the inverse relationship between the number of programs that can be produced and the average cost per program. From an economic perspective, pursuing the "widest possible" diversity is therefore bound to become inefficient and undesirable at some point. Thus, there is an inherent conflict between the diversity and efficiency objectives.

In summary, economic efficiency and First Amendment–related objectives are often difficult to measure and sometimes conflict. Where ambiguities or conflicts arise, we offer our own best judgments or defer to the reader.

3

Market Structure of the Cable Television Industry

W<small>HAT IS THE</small> E<small>XTENT</small> of vertical and horizontal integration in the cable television industry, and how did that market structure develop? Answers to those questions serve two purposes. First, they indicate the dimensions of any existing policy problems. Second, they provide a basis for understanding the economic motives and effects of vertical integration considered in subsequent chapters.

We begin with a brief description of the kinds of programming available on cable systems. We then detail the extent of vertical and horizontal ownership ties between MSOs and program suppliers. Finally, we trace major trends and developments leading up to that ownership structure.

T<small>YPES OF</small> C<small>ABLE</small> P<small>ROGRAMMING</small>

Essentially, a cable system is a local retailer of an array of differentiated products, usually in the form of programming networks. Although the particular menus of more than 10,000 individual local systems in the United States are very diverse, their main elements are: basic cable networks, local and nearby broadcast stations, dedicated channels, premium networks, and pay-per-view (PPV) networks.

Basic cable networks are cable-originated networks, such as MTV, CNN, and Home Shopping Network, and superstations, such as WTBS and WGN.[1] Most basic networks sell advertising and are offered to subscribers

---

1. Superstations are actually local broadcast stations nationally distributed by common carriers via satellite to cable systems.

in bundles, either as part of a basic service package or as part of an expanded basic package available for an extra charge.

Local and nearby broadcast stations also sell advertising and are usually included in basic service packages.

Dedicated channels are public access, educational, local government, and leased-access channels. They are typically mandated by local franchise agreements or, in the case of leased access, by the Federal Communications Commission and are usually included in a basic service package.

Premium networks include nationally distributed services, such as HBO, Showtime, and The Disney Channel, and some regional sports networks. They usually sell no advertising and charge substantial additional fees to basic subscribers on an à la carte basis.

Pay-per-view networks include Viewer's Choice and Request Television. Offering mostly movies and sports events, they charge a consumer by the program.

Many cable systems also offer electronic program guides, other character-generated programming, and audio services. Some cable systems, as well as LECs or consortia of LECs and cable companies, are experimenting with two-way interactive services in which subscribers use a set-top box or other device to communicate with the cable headend or telephone office, or with other subscribers on the system.[2] Those services include "distance education," video games, banking, telephone service, Internet access, and video on demand (VOD). Another service being offered experimentally by some cable systems is near video on demand, essentially a large-capacity PPV system occupying perhaps 200 cable channels, a large proportion of which shows identical programs, usually movies, at staggered intervals.

OWNERSHIP STRUCTURE

Market structure and ownership ties in the cable industry change constantly. The picture of ownership we report here, however, demonstrates the prominent role of vertical ownership in cable since the programming supply industry's beginnings.

Table 3-1 provides information on sixty-five full-time nationally distributed cable networks operating as of November 1995. We rank basic, premium, and PPV networks separately according to their audience reach or

---

2. *See* PETER KRASILOVSKY, INTERACTIVE TELEVISION TESTBEDS (Benton Foundation Communications Policy Working Paper No. 7, 1994), for descriptions of seventeen of those experiments. Other more recent experiments have been announced in the trade press.

subscribership. We include all basic and PPV networks that reached at least 10 percent, as well as premium networks that reached at least 1 percent, of U.S. households with cable TV or another multichannel video service as of the end of 1994. Thus, the table accounts for all networks of current economic significance. Owners listed in the table held at least a 5 percent share of their network's equity as of November 1995.

Table 3-1 shows vertical integration to be extensive, although not ubiquitous. Forty-one of the sixty-five networks shown in table 3-1 had vertical ties to MSOs. Among the fifty-one basic networks listed, thirty were integrated with MSOs. Of the twenty-one nonintegrated basic networks, C-SPAN and C-SPAN II were supported with cable-operator funds. Seven of the eight premium networks and four of the six PPV networks were vertically integrated.

Because networks with vertical ties tended to be larger and more commercially viable, the above counts understate the economic significance of vertical ownership. Seven of the ten most widely distributed basic networks had MSO ties, and those ten accounted for approximately three-fourths of the $6.5 billion gross revenues of the basic networking industry in 1995.[3] All four of the national home shopping networks, whose gross revenues of approximately $3.3 billion in 1995[4] are divided between operators and networks based on realized sales volume, also had vertical ties. Among national premium networks, the four full premium networks having vertical ties accounted for 74 percent of national full premium subscriptions.[5] National premium networks earned approximately $2.2 billion in 1995.[6] The four integrated PPV networks accounted for approximately two-thirds of PPV movie revenues, although cable PPV is not yet of major economic significance. All PPV networks grossed roughly $.3 billion in revenues in 1995.[7]

---

3. That total is for forty-eight commercially supported basic networks tracked by PAUL KAGAN ASSOCIATES, CABLE TV PROGRAMMING, Sept. 30, 1996, at 1.

4. PAUL KAGAN ASSOCIATES, KAGAN MEDIA INDEX, Feb. 29, 1996, at 15.

5. Time Warner networks, HBO, and Cinemax had 51 percent; the Viacom networks, Showtime, and The Movie Channel had 23 percent. PAUL KAGAN ASSOCIATES, PAY TV NEWSLETTER, June 29, 1995, at 2; Dec. 31, 1994, at 2. Full premium networks exclude Encore and Flix, the two minipay networks listed in table 3-1. Encore and Flix are typically sold at a far lower price and contribute a very small amount to total premium network revenues.

6. PAUL KAGAN ASSOCIATES, PAY TV NEWSLETTER, June 30, 1996, at 2.

7. The calculation is based on PAUL KAGAN ASSOCIATES, KAGAN MEDIA INDEX, Feb. 29, 1996, at 15. Approximately 50 percent of the total $587 million cable system revenues from PPV in 1995 is assumed to accrue to the networks.

Table 3-1
Characteristics and Ownership of Full-Time Nationally Distributed Cable TV Networks
November 1995

Network	Content	Subscribership Reach (%)[a]	Launch Date	Current Ownership (5% equity or more)	First Cable System Affiliation (5% equity or more)
Basic Networks					
Cable News Network (CNN)[b]	general news	97.0	1980	Turner Broadcasting [*TCI* (23%); *Time Warner* (19%)]	1987 (*TCI, Warner Cable*)
ESPN	sports	96.9	1979	Walt Disney/ABC (80%); Hearst Corp. (20%)	none
TBS[b]	movies, series, specials, sports (superstation)	96.2	1976	Turner Broadcasting [(*TCI* (23%); *Time Warner* (19%)]	1987 (*TCI, Warner Cable*)
USA Network[c,d]	movies, series, specials, sports	95.7	1980	*Viacom* (50%); MCA (50%)	launch (*UA-Columbia*)
The Discovery Channel	science, nature, travel	95.1	1985	*TCI* (48%); *Cox Cable* (24%); *Newhouse* (24%)	1986 (*TCI, Cox Cable, Newhouse*)

Network	Programming	Rating	Year	Ownership	Distribution
C-SPAN I[e]	public affairs	94.2	1979	Cable Satellite Public Affairs Network	none
TNT[b]	movies, series, specials, sports	93.8	1988	Turner Broadcasting [(TCI (23%); Time Warner 19%)]	launch (TCI, Warner Cable)
Nickelodeon/Nick at Nite[c,f]	children's, family entertainment	93.0	1979	Viacom (100%)	launch (Warner Cable)
The Nashville Network (TNN)[g]	music videos and specials	91.0	1983	Gaylord Entertainment Co. (100%)	launch (Group W Cable)
The Family Channel	movie, series, specials	90.8	1977	International Family Entertainment [TCI (18%)]	1990 launch (TCI, Time Warner)
Lifetime Television[h]	women's, family, informational	90.2	1984	Hearst Corp. (50%); Walt Disney/ABC (50%)	launch (Viacom, Hearst)
Arts & Entertainment Network (A&E)[i]	cultural, foreign movies, series	89.8	1984	Walt Disney/ABC (38%); Hearst Corp. (38%); NBC (25%)	launch (RCA Cable, Hearst Corp.)
MTV: Music Television[c]	music videos and specials	87.7	1981	Viacom (100%)	launch (Warner Cable)
The Weather Channel[j]	weather	84.7	1982	Landmark Communications (100%)	launch (Telecable)
Headline News[b]	general news	83.8	1982	Turner Broadcasting [(TCI (23%); Time Warner (19%)]	1987 (TCI, Warner Cable)
CNBC	consumer-oriented, business news	78.9	1989	NBC (100%)	launch (Cablevision Systems)

(Table continues)

Table 3-1 (continued)

Network	Content	Subscribership Reach (%)[a]	Launch Date	Current Ownership (5% equity or more)	First Cable System Affiliation (5% equity or more)
QVC Network	home shopping	77.0	1986	*Comcast* (57%); *TCI* (43%)	1987 (*TCI*)
Video Hits One (VH-1)[c]	music videos and specials	76.1	1985	*Viacom* (100%)	launch (*Warner Cable*)
American Movie Classics (AMC)	classic movies	73.3	1984	*Cablevision Systems* (75%); NBC (25%)	launch (*Cablevision Systems*)
Black Entertainment Television (BET)	black-oriented entertainment and informational	61.5	1980	BET Networks [*Time Warner* (15%); Robert Johnson (55%); *TCI* (18%)]	launch (*TCI*)
WGN/UVI	movies, series, specials, sports (superstation)	59.4	1978	Tribune Broadcasting (100%)	none
Prevue Guide[k]	program guide, previews	58.4	1988	United Video [*TCI* (36%)]	1988 (*TCI*; Scripps Howard)
C-SPAN II[e]	public affairs	53.9	1986	Cable Satellite Public Affairs Network	none
EWTN: The Catholic Cable network	religious	53.3	1981	Eternal World Television Network (100%)	none
The Learning Channel (TLC)	educational	49.2	1980	*TCI* (48%); *Cox Cable* (24%); *Newhouse* (24%)	1991 (*TCI*, *Cox Cable*, *Newhouse*)

Network	Programming		Year	Ownership	Notes
Comedy Central[l]	comedy entertainment	47.5	1991	Time Warner (50%); Viacom (50%)	launch (Time Warner, Viacom)
Home Shopping Network I	home shopping	43.5	1985	TCI (80%)	1992 (TCI)
E! TV[m]	entertainment industry informational	42.7	1990	Time Warner (50%); Cox Cable (10%); Continental (10%); Comcast (10%); TCI (10%); Newhouse (10%)	launch (ATC, Cox Cable, Continental, Comcast, Newhouse)
Home Shopping Network II	home shopping	40.0	1986	TCI (80%)	1992 (TCI)
Sneak Prevue[k]	previews (PPV guide)	39.8	1991	United Video Corp. [TCI (36%)]	launch (Scripps Howard)
Mind Extension University	educational	38.9	1987	Jones International (100%)	launch (Jones International)
Country Music Television (CMT)[g]	music videos and specials	38.8	1983	Group W Satellite Communications (33%); Gaylord Entertainment Co. (67%)	1991 (Crown Media)
TBN Cable Network	religious	37.7	1978	Trinity Broadcasting Network (100%)	none
Faith & Values[n]	religious	33.6	1988	National Interfaith Cable Coalition (51%); TCI (49%)	1995 (TCI)

27

(Table continues)

Table 3-1 (continued)

Network	Content	Subscribership Reach (%)[a]	Launch Date	Current Ownership (5% equity or more)	First Cable System Affiliation (5% equity or more)
The Box	interactive music videos	32.8	1985	VJN Partners [*TCI* (6%)]	1988 (*Newhouse*)
The Travel Channel	travel informational	30.5	1987	Landmark Communications (100%)	none
fX	movies, series	27.5	1994	News Corp. (100%)	none
ESPN2	sports	26.4	1993	Walt Disney/ABC (80%); Hearst Corp. (20%)	none
Telemundo	Spanish-language entertainment and informational	23.8	1987	Telemundo Group (100%)	none
Bravo	cultural, foreign movies, series	23.6	1980	*Cablevision Systems* (50%); NBC (50%)	launch (*Cablevision Systems; Cox Cable; Daniels Associates*)
WWOR	movies, series, special, sports (superstation)	19.8	1979	Chriscraft, Inc. (100%)	none
Cartoon Network[b]	children's	19.1	1992	Turner Broadcasting [*TCI* (23%); *Time Warner* (19%)]	launch (*TCI, Time Warner*)
WPIX	movies, series, special, sports (superstation)	18.1	1984	Tribune Broadcasting (100%)	none

Q2	home shopping	1994	*Comcast* (57%); *TCI* (43%)	launch (*Comcast, TCI*)
Sci-Fi Channel	science fiction movies, series	1992	*Viacom* (50%); *MCA* (50%)	1994 (*Viacom*)
America's Talking	all talk	1994	NBC (100%)	none
Court TV	courtroom trials	1992	*Time Warner* (33%); *Cablevision Systems* (33%); *TCI* (33%)	launch (*Time Warner, Cablevision Systems, TCI*)
TV Food°	food, fitness	1993	Providence Journal Co. (n.a.); *Continental* (n.a.), Landmark Communications (n.a.), *Scripps Howard* (n.a.), Tribune Broadcasting (n.a.)	launch (*Colony, Continental, Scripps Howard, Adelphia, Times Mirror*)
Nostalgia Television	classic movies, series	1985	Concept Communications (22%); Richard K. Diamond (15%)	none
The New Inspirational Network	religious	1978	The Inspirational Network Inc. (100%)	none
International Channel	foreign language	1990	ICN Entertainment (50%); *TCI* (50%)	1994 (*TCI*)

(Table continues)

Table 3-1 (continued)

Network	Content	Subscribership Reach (%)[a]	Launch Date	Current Ownership (5% equity or more)	First Cable System Affiliation (5% equity or more)
		Premium Networks			
Home Box Office (HBO)	movies, series, specials, sports	27.3	1972	Time Warner (100%)	launch (Manhattan Cable)
The Disney Channel	family-oriented movies, series and specials	18.3	1983	Walt Disney Co./ABC (100%)	none
Showtime	movies, series, specials, sports	12.3	1976	Viacom (100%)	launch (Viacom)
Cinemax	movies, series, specials, sports	10.2	1980	Time Warner (100%)	launch (ATC)
Encore (minipay)[p]	movies	8.2	1991	TCI (90%); John Sie (10%)	launch (TCI)
The Movie Channel (TMC)	movies	4.7	1979	Viacom (100%)	launch (Warner Cable)
Starz[q]	movies	2.1	1994	TCI (90%); John Sie (10%)	launch (TCI)
Flix (minipay)[p]	movies	1.2	1992	Viacom (100%)	launch (Viacom)

PPV Networks

Network	Content		Year	Owner	Status
Viewer's Choice 1	movies, specials, sports	18.2	1985	Viewer's Choice Networks [*TCI* (10%); *Time Warner* (20%); *Continental* (10%); *Cox Cable* (20%); *Comcast* (10%); *Newhouse* (10%); *Viacom* (10%);Walt Disney/ABC (10%)]	launch (*Viacom*)
Spice	adult	17.3	1988	Graff Pay-per-View (100%)	none
Request Television I	movies, specials, sports	17.1	1985	Reiss Media [TCI (40%); News Corp.]	1992 (*TCI*)
Playboy At Night	adult	14.5	1989	Playboy Enterprises (100%)	none
Hot Choice	movies, specials	13.4	1986	Viewer's Choice Networks [*TCI* (10%); *Time Warner* (20%); *Continental* (10%); *Cox Cable* (20%); *Comcast* (10%); *Newhouse* (10%); *Viacom* (19%): Walt Disney/ABC (10%)]	launch (*Viacom*)
Action Pay-per-View	movies	10.7	1990	BET Networks [*TCI* (18%); *Time Warner* (15%); Robert Johnson (55%)]	1994 (*TCI, Time Warner*)

(Table continues)

31

. Table 3-1 (continued)

Notes: Italics indicate a vertical ownership relationship with a cable operator. Base equals 65.0 million multichannel video system subscribers.

a. The percentage of subscribers to cable and other multichannel video systems that have the network available. For pay-per-view, we include only addressable cable homes. For basic networks, data are for year-end 1994.

b. As of November 1995, the proposal by Time Warner to acquire 100% equity of Turner Broadcasting Networks was under review by the Federal Trade Commission.

c. Viacom settled terms for the sale of its cable systems to TCI in 1995.

d. Continuous equity ownership by MSOs until Time Inc. (ATC) sold its one-third interest in 1987 to Paramount and MCA, which at that time also owned one-third each. Reacquired in 1994 as a result of the Viacom–Paramount Communications merger.

e. Cable operators have provided 95% of funding since launch but have no ownership interest.

f. Nick at Nite was launched by Viacom (33%) and Warner Cable (67%) in July 1985.

g. Gaylord Broadcasting sold its cable system interests in 1995.

h. Created by a merger of Daytime (launched by Viacom) and Cable Health Network (launched by Hearst). Viacom sold its remaining 33% interest in Lifetime in 1994.

i. Arts & Entertainment combined assets of The Arts Channel (launched in 1980 by a joint venture of Hearst Corp. and ABC) and The Entertainment Channel (launched by RCA Cable and Rockefeller Center in 1980). MSOs were continuously involved until Hearst Corp. sold its cable system interests in 1989.

j. Landmark Communications sold Telecable in 1984.

k. TCI acquired 36% equity and majority voting interest in United Video in 1995. United Video had been divested by Scripps Howard in 1992.

l. Created by a 1991 merger of HA! TV (launched by Viacom in 1990) and The Comedy Channel (launched by Time Warner in 1989).

m. Originally launched as Movietime in July 1987.

n. Created by a merger in October 1992 of VISN (launched in 1988) and ACTS (launched in 1984). The name was later changed to Faith & Values. TCI reportedly supported the network financially without actual ownership until mid-1995.

o. Ownership shares are undisclosed but presumed to be 5% or greater.

p. Minipay networks offer primarily classic movies that are generally offered at a low additional price, such as $1, so their revenues are substantially lower than full premium networks. The Encore service actually consists of seven thematic channels, of which the great majority of subscribership is for the main channel.

q. Starz is marketed as Encore 8.

Source: See the appendix to this chapter.

Notably unaffiliated, by contrast, were some of the largest networks of each type: ESPN, the second largest basic network in subscribership; The Disney Channel, the second largest national premium network; and Spice, the second most widely available PPV network. Although not shown in the table, pervasive vertical ownership prevails for regional sports networks. All the twenty most widely subscribed basic and premium regional sports networks had ownership ties to MSOs in November 1995.[8] The table also shows a growing number of regional cable news networks. Some of those were integrated (Long Island 12, owned by Cablevision Systems) and some not (Orange County News Channel, owned by Freedom Newspapers), but generally those are of very minor economic significance.

A substantial change to the statistical picture of vertical integration in table 3-1 occurred in 1996 with Viacom's sale of all its cable systems to TCI. As a result, five basic networks, including two of the largest ten, and three premium networks, including the third largest, became unaffiliated with any MSO.[9] Although Viacom was a relatively small MSO, serving less than 2 percent of U.S. households, that divestiture has reduced the proportion of the table 3-1 networks that are vertically integrated to just over one-half.

Note also that a number of MSOs have become integrated into program production. Many of the networks in which MSOs have equity interests produce a portion of their own cable programming. Time Warner also owns Warner Brothers Pictures, a movie and television studio whose products are eventually exhibited on a variety of PPV, premium, and basic cable networks. Time Warner and TCI have recently been vertically affiliated with both New Line Cinema, a small movie production and distribution company, and Castle Rock Productions, a producer of movies and television programs, via Turner Broadcasting's sole ownership of those companies.[10]

Table 3-1 also shows that minority ownership in networks by MSOs and the sharing of network equity among two or more MSOs are both common. At least among basic and PPV networks, individual MSOs tend to own 50 percent or fewer shares of network equity. A single MSO held a majority of network equity in only nine cases among the thirty integrated basic networks in table 3-1 and in no cases among the six integrated PPV networks. Majority

---

8. Our tabulation is based on "total potential subs" reported by PAUL KAGAN ASSOCIATES, MEDIA SPORTS BUSINESS, Aug. 31, 1994, at 3.

9. The ownership status of PPV, home shopping, and regional networks would be unaffected.

10. The 1996 Time Warner–TBS merger shifts all direct vertical ownership of those studios to Time Warner.

ownership by a single MSO was the case, however, for all seven integrated premium networks.

On the other hand, the table shows a prevalence of network equity sharing by MSOs. The equity of at least sixteen of the thirty integrated basic networks and that of three of the four integrated PPV networks was shared among two or more MSOs. In total, MSO ownership cumulated to more than a 50 percent share of equity in more than half the integrated network cases, including at least thirteen of the thirty integrated basic network cases. In some instances, such as TCI's 36 percent equity ownership of United Video Corporation (parent company of the Prevue Guide and Sneak Prevue), a minority of equity ownership reportedly accompanied a majority of voting stock.[11] Nevertheless, the frequency of minority holdings by individual MSOs, as well as the presence of equity sharing by MSOs, leaves ambiguous the degree of vertical control that MSOs or their corporate parents actually exercised.[12]

Table 3-2 reorganizes the same network ownership data as of late 1995 by MSO for the twelve largest MSOs in the United States. Rankings are according to the total number of basic cable subscribers served. Table 3-2 demonstrates that larger MSOs accounted for the great majority of vertical affiliations with nationally distributed program suppliers. Three MSOs, including the two largest, were prominent among them. By September 1995 the twelve largest MSOs accounted for 70 percent of U.S. basic cable subscribers. With very minor exceptions, those MSOs directly accounted for all of the 5 percent or greater network equity ownerships indicated in table 3-1.[13]

---

11. John M. Higgins, *TCI Buying Control of United Video*, MULTICHANNEL NEWS, June 26, 1995, at 1. Other MSOs apparently have equity shares of less than 5 percent in some networks, including some of the "unaffiliated" networks in table 3-1. Beginning in 1986, for example, several publicly traded basic networks, including Home Shopping Network, The Travel Channel, The Nostalgia Network, and QVC, offered MSOs shares of stock in exchange for agreements to carry their services. PAUL KAGAN ASSOCIATES, CABLE TV PROGRAMMING, Dec. 27, 1987, at 7.

12. The Time Warner–TBS merger significantly reduces the extent of both direct MSO minority ownership and equity sharing in cable programming supply owing to TCI's transfer of its 23 percent equity in TBS to Time Warner, whose 19 percent share in those networks now increases to 100 percent. That transaction affects five TBS networks in table 3-1 (CNN, Headline News, TBS, TNT, and the Cartoon Network). TCI retains an indirect minority ownership in the Turner and other Time Warner networks via its 9 percent equity in Time Warner.

13. Colony Communications and E. W. Scripps, respectively the fourteenth and sixteenth largest MSOs in November 1995, owned undisclosed minority shares in the TV Food Network.

Table 3-2
Network Ownership Affiliations of the Twelve Largest MSOs
November 1995

MSO	Percentage Share of Total Cable Households[a]	Number of Vertically Affiliated Full-time National Networks (5% equity or more, minimum carriage criteria)	Affiliated Networks (minimum carriage criteria)
TCI[b]	20.1 (25.5)	25	AMC (50%); Action Pay-per-View (18%); Black Entertainment Television (18%); The Box (6%); Court TV (33%); The Discovery Channel (48%); The Learning Channel (48%); E! TV (10%); Encore (90%); The Family Channel (18%); Home Shopping Network I (80%); Home Shopping Network II (80%); QVC Network (43%); Q2 (43%); Request 1 (40%); Starz (90%); Cartoon Network (23%); CNN (23%); Headline News (23%); TNT (23%); TBS (23%); Prevue Guide (36%); Sneak Prevue (36%); Viewer's Choice 1 (10%); Hot Choice (10%)
Time Warner[c]	16.5	16 [18]	Action Pay-per-View (15%); Black Entertainment Television (15%); Cinemax (100%); Comedy Central (50%); Court TV (33%); E! TV (50%); HBO (100%); QVC (10%); Q2 (10%); Cartoon Network (18%); CNN (18%); TBS (18%); TNT (18%); Headline News (18%); Viewer's Choice 1 (20%); Hot Choice (20%)

[Advance Publications/Newhouse Broadcasting programming affiliations: The Discovery Channel (24%); The Learning Channel (24%); E! TV (10%); Viewer's Choice 1 (10%); Hot Choice (10%)] |

(Table continues)

Table 3-2 (continued)

MSO	Percentage Share of Total Cable Households[a]	Number of Vertically Affiliated Full-time National Networks (5% equity or more, minimum carriage criteria)	Affiliated Networks (minimum carriage criteria)
Comcast[d]	5.5 (5.9)	5	E! TV (10%); QVC Networks [QVC Network, Q2] (10%); Viewer's Choice 1 (10%); Hot Choice (10%)
Cox Cable	5.3	5	The Discovery Channel (24%); The Learning Channel (24%); E! TV (10%); Viewer's Choice 1 (20%); Hot Choice (20%)
Continental Cablevision[e]	5.1 (5.3)	4	E! TV (10%); TV Food Network (n.a.); Viewer's Choice 1 (10%); Hot Choice (10%)
Cablevision Systems	4.6	3	AMC (75%); Bravo (50%); Court TV (33%)
Adelphia Communication	2.7	—	—
Cablevision Industries[f]	2.2	—	—
Jones International	2.2	1	Mind Extension University (100%)
Viacom[g]	1.9	11	Comedy Central (50%); Flix (100%); Nickelodeon/Nick at Nite (100%); MTV (100%); VH-1 (100%); Sci-Fi Network (50%); USA Network (50%); Showtime (100%); The Movie Channel (100%); Viewer's Choice 1 (10%); Hot Choice (10%)

Falcon Cable	1.8	—	—
Sammons Communications[h]	1.8	—	—
Total	69.7		

Note: Base is 60.9 million basic subscribers as of July 31, 1995.

a. Numbers in parentheses include all attributable interests.

b. Based on subscriber counts as of September 30, 1995, as reported in Paul Kagan Associates, *Cable TV Investor*, November 22, 1995, p. 16. TCI majority ownership affiliations totaled 13,415,000 subscribers as of July 31, 1995. Unconsolidated holdings included 3,000,500 "joint venture and other off-balance-sheet subscribers," plus 198,000 Garden State Cable subscribers (40% owned by Lenfest) and 109,000 Sonic Communications subscribers (37% owned by Intermedia Partners). TCI owns 50% of Lenfest and 54% (unconsolidated) of Intermedia. Not included are TCI's pending acquisitions of 100% of Viacom cable systems (1,158,000 subscribers) and Western Communications (328,000 subscribers).

c. Includes approximately 1,500,000 cable system subscribers served by Advance Publications/Newhouse Broadcasting. In 1995 Time Warner and Newhouse entered a joint venture agreement, 67% owned by Time Warner, the terms of which call for management of all Newhouse systems by Time Warner. Cable network holdings of Newhouse are indicated in brackets under Time Warner, since ownership control is not direct. Not included is Time Warner's pending acquisition of Cablevision Industries (2,300,000 subscribers).

d. Total holdings include Garden State Cable (40% owned, 198,000 subscribers). Not included are 751,000 subscribers from pending acquisition of E. W. Scripps cable systems.

e. Total holdings include Insight Communications (34% owned, 159,000 subscribers). Not included are 814,000 subscribers from pending acquisition of Colony Communications.

f. Acquisition by Time Warner pending.

g. Acquisition by TCI pending.

h. Breakup pending; subscribers to be allocated to TCI, Lenfest, and other smaller MSOs.

Sources: Paul Kagan Associates, *Cable TV Investor*, September 18, 1995, and other issues.

Among the MSOs in table 3-2, programming ownership ties are obviously skewed toward the largest operators. TCI accounted for the greatest number of U.S. basic cable subscribers in late 1995 and had the largest number of full-time national network affiliations, although most were of minority ownership. The second largest MSO, Time Warner, had the second largest number of national network affiliations.[14] Most of the other top twelve MSOs had interests in at least a few networks. Prominent among those were the primarily majority-owned interests of Viacom, owner of the tenth largest MSO. The 1996 sale of Viacom's cable systems to TCI leaves vertical ties to cable programming overwhelmingly in the hands of the two largest MSOs.

Also notable, but not included in table 3-2, were regional and national sports network holdings of TCI and of Cablevision Systems Development Corporation, the sixth largest MSO. TCI declared equity interests as of December 31, 1994, in fifteen regional sports networks, and shared with Cablevision Systems the equity in two national sports networks (Prime Network and SportsChannel America) that feed sports programming to regional networks.[15] Cablevision Systems also had interests in eight regional sports networks at the end of 1994.[16] The twenty largest regional sports networks were integrated with TCI or Cablevision's systems or both.[17] Holdings of other MSOs were very minor.

Historical Developments in Market Structure

Cable Networking. As the wide variety of network launch dates in table 3-1 shows, there has been a steady flow of entry into cable networking since satellite delivery made national distribution of cable networks practical in the mid-1970s.[18]

---

14. Note that the larger, bracketed number of Time Warner–affiliated networks in column 3 reflects Time Warner's indirect corporate relationship with five cable networks in which Advance Publications/Newhouse Broadcasting has a minority ownership interest. As indicated in notes to table 3-2, in 1995 Time Warner and Newhouse entered into a joint venture, majority-owned by Time Warner, under which Time Warner operates Newhouse's cable systems.

15. TELE-COMMUNICATIONS, INC., 1995 FORM 10-K (1996), at 118.

16. CABLEVISION SYSTEMS DEVELOPMENT CORP., 1994 FORM 10-K (1995), at 27.

17. In 1996 News Corp. entered into a 50–50 joint venture with TCI to operate Prime Sports, relaunched as Fox Sports, a group of nine regional sports networks in which TCI has an equity interest. In the Matter of Annual Assessment of the Status of Competition in the Market for the Delivery of Video Programming, Third Annual Report, CS Dkt. No. 96-133, FCC 96-496 (Jan. 2, 1997) ¶147 [hereinafter 1997 FCC Cable Report].

18. For histories of cable networking and its regulation, *see* Yale Braunstein, Recent Trends in Cable Television Related to the Prospects for New Television Networks

Table 3-3
Trends in Channel Capacity and Addressability

Number of Channels	% of U.S. Cable Households Served			
	1983	1989	1992	1995
54 or more	4	21	33	41
30–53	45	66	60	55
20–29	23	9	4	2
0–19	26	2	1	—
N/A	2	2	2	2
Total	100	100	100	100
Addressable systems	11	32	36	40

Sources: Channel capacity: *Jerrold Television and Cable Factbook,* March/April of individual years; addressability: Paul Kagan Associates, *Kagan Media Index,* March 30, 1993, p. 10; July 31, 1994, p. 8; *Pay TV Newsletter,* April 29, 1996, p. 2.

Much of that entry flow has been stimulated by a steady growth of cable system channel capacities, which, as table 3-3 shows, continues. More than two-fifths of all subscribers are now served by systems of fifty-four channels or more, and rebuilt systems in that category are regularly coming on line.

Another technology factor creating entry opportunities for cable networks in the past decade or so is addressability—the ability of a system operator to deliver a particular program efficiently to a particular subscriber. That ability makes unbundled sales more efficient and is particularly important for PPV networks, and in the future, near video on demand systems. As table 3-3 also shows, addressable technology is diffusing rapidly. It reached more than 40 percent of subscribers by the end of 1995. That diffusion is generally coincident with the entry of several national PPV networks beginning in 1985. Cable system rebuilds or upgrades that incorporate addressability will probably continue.

Vertical ties between MSOs and program suppliers have developed in different ways, but especially from backward integration by MSOs or their parent companies. Table 3-1 reports the date, if any, that each of the sixty-five networks became vertically affiliated with cable systems and the cable operators involved. In thirty-one of the sixty-five cases, a cable

---

(submitted to FCC Network Inquiry Special Staff Aug. 1979); Stanley M. Besen & Robert W. Crandall, *The Deregulation of Cable Television*, 44 LAW & CONTEMP. PROBS. 77 (1981); R. A. Gershon, *Pay Cable Television: A Regulatory History*, COMMUNICATIONS & L. 3 (June 1990); R. A. Gershon, *Home Box Office: A 20-Year Perspective*, in CABLE TELEVISION HANDBOOK (R. Picard ed., Carpelan Press 1993).

operator was involved in the network's launch. In a few other instances (for example, The Discovery Channel and QVC), one or more MSOs acquired an independently launched network within a year or two of its launch. Other suppliers, such as the Turner Broadcasting networks, were well established before an MSO or its parent company acquired equity in them. In a few cases integration has occurred via merger. Viacom's 1994 integration with USA Network and the Sci-Fi Channel, for example, resulted from Viacom's acquisition of Paramount Pictures, which at that time held a 50 percent interest in those two basic cable networks.

The table documents numerous ownership changes over the years, including some notable divestitures of formerly integrated networks that are now unaffiliated, such as CNBC and Lifetime. Overall, forty-six of the sixty-five networks, including nearly all the largest, have been vertically affiliated with an MSO at one time or another during their histories.

The data in table 3-1 suggest that from the mid-1980s until late 1995, the extent of vertical integration in cable increased. Thirty-nine of the sixty-five total networks had been launched by the end of 1985. Of those, sixteen (41 percent) were vertically integrated at that time. The integration of forty-one of the sixty-five (63 percent) networks suggests an upward trend over that period.

Despite that apparent growth in the significance of integration, unaffiliated networks have managed to enter and prosper without the benefit of affiliation with system operators. Among independently launched early entrants later reaching top industry ranks were WTBS (now TBS) in 1976, Christian Broadcast Network (now the Family Channel) in 1977, and CNN in 1980. Following those were the Disney Channel in 1984, and Home Shopping Network (now HSN I) and Request Television (now Request 1) in 1985. Among the twenty-six networks in table 3-1 launching in 1986 or later, thirteen entered independently, and seven of them remained unaffiliated with any MSO as of November 1995. Among those unaffiliated networks were ESPN2, fX, and America's Talking, which launched in 1992 or later but managed to reach our minimum carriage criteria by late 1995.[19]

MSOs. Since the mid-1980s, MSOs have had steadily rising horizontal concentration of their national shares of subscribers. The FCC reported that

---

19. Entry of those three networks was apparently aided by retransmission consent agreements reached as a result of the 1992 Cable Act. See chapter 4 for further details. America's Talking was relaunched in 1996 as MSNBC, a joint venture of Microsoft Corp. and NBC.

in 1985, the largest four MSOs accounted for 24.9 percent of U.S. basic subscribers.[20] Table 3-2 shows that by November 1995, the national shares of the top four MSOs had increased to 47.4 percent, or to 53.2 percent when all their attributable interests were included.[21]

Those changes have been overwhelmingly due to growth of the two largest MSOs. TCI's total national subscriber share increased from 9 percent in 1985 to 25.5 percent (including all attributable interests) in November 1995. The 1989 merger of Time Inc. and Warner Communications added together their respective 8.7 percent and 3.3 percent shares,[22] and further acquisitions increased Time Warner's total share to the 16.5 percent indicated in table 3-2.

The accumulation of network holdings by TCI and Time Warner has been largely coincident with their horizontal growth. Indeed, network launches and acquisitions involving those two MSOs are mainly responsible for the general growth in cable industry vertical ties between 1985 and 1995. Twenty-three of TCI's twenty-five vertically affiliated national networks and fourteen of Time Warner's sixteen directly affiliated national networks were launched or acquired by those MSOs between the ends of 1985 and 1995.

Since 1993, there has been a renewed wave of horizontal mergers and acquisitions involving larger MSOs.[23] Among those, table 3-2 reflects TCI's 1993 acquisition of Telecable, the seventeenth largest MSO, Time Warner's 1994 entry into a majority-owned joint venture with Newhouse, then the seventh largest MSO, and Cox Communications' acquisition of Times Mirror's cable systems, then the tenth largest MSO.

Not shown in table 3-2 are several 1996 mergers that have increased national shares of all four of the largest MSOs.[24] TCI's acquisition of Viacom and other properties increased its attributable national share of basic

20. Competition, Rate Deregulation and the Commission's Policies Relating to the Provision of Cable Television Service, Report, MM Dkt. No. 89-600, FCC 90-276, 67 Rad. Reg. 2d (P&F) 1771 (1990), at app. G.

21. The FCC's definition of an attributable interest is a 5 percent or greater ownership share.

22. We derived those figures from *Cable Impact: Changes Likely in Systems, Management*, BROADCASTING, Mar. 13, 1989, at 31.

23. The transactions reported in this paragraph are summarized from Implementation of Section 19 of the Cable Television Consumer Protection and Competition Act of 1992: Annual Assessment of the Status of Competition in the Market for Delivery of Video Programming, First Rep., CS Dkt. No. 94-48, FCC 94-235 (1994), at 141–47; Mark Robichaux, *Cable TV Consolidates Rapidly in the Hands of a Few*, WALL ST. J., Feb. 8, 1995, at B4; and PAUL KAGAN ASSOCIATES, CABLE TV INVESTOR, various issues.

24. 1997 FCC Cable Report, *supra* note 17, ¶¶ 132–133. Market share data in this

subscribers to 28.3 percent as of September 1996. Time Warner's national subscriber share (all majority-owned) increased to 19.1 percent by that date with its acquisition of Cablevision Industries, the eighth largest MSO. Mergers with other MSOs made Continental Cablevision the third largest cable operator with a 7.7 percent share and Comcast the fourth largest with a 6.9 percent share. Both of those shares include majority and minority holdings.[25] Nine of the twenty largest MSOs as of December 31, 1992, have now disappeared, mostly because of mergers with larger MSOs.

Accompanying the brisk pace of MSO mergers and acquisitions has been a rapid movement toward clustering—a process by which MSOs are attempting to consolidate system ownership within separate geographical regions. Many cable system trades among MSOs have reportedly been made for that purpose, especially in the past two or three years.

CONCLUSION

The historical prevalence of vertical ownership ties suggests that there must be important economic advantages to vertical integration between cable systems and programming suppliers, especially for the larger MSOs. In chapters 4 and 5, respectively, we classify those economic advantages into efficiency advantages involving the pursuit of more efficient use of resources and presumably increasing economic welfare, and strategic advantages involving the exercise of horizontal market power at system or network levels and that may or may not be anticompetitive in effect.

APPENDIX: DATA COLLECTION METHODOLOGY FOR CABLE PROGRAMMING NETWORK OWNERSHIP

Characteristics and Ownership of Full-Time Nationally Distributed Cable Networks

We assembled data for our categories as delineated below.

---

paragraph are based on PAUL KAGAN ASSOCIATES, CABLE TV INVESTOR, Jan. 7, 1997, at 8, and on 1997 FCC Cable Report, app. F.

25. In 1996 U S West's 100 percent acquisition of Continental Cablevision created an indirect ownership link between MSOs. Mark Landler, *U S West Continental Ambitions,* N. Y. TIMES, Feb. 28, 1996, at C1. U S West also holds a 25 percent equity stake in Time Warner Entertainment, Time Warner's cable system and programming division. Note also TCI's 9 percent equity stake in Time Warner, owing to the 1996 Time Warner–TBS merger.

Networks. We included all national basic, premium, and PPV networks transmitting programs via satellite for at least sixteen hours per day that met our minimum subscribership criteria. We did not include multiplexed networks, which are time-shifted versions of another network. Our primary sources for identification were the *Jerrold TV and Cable Factbook*, no. 63 (1995); National Cable Television Association, *Cable TV Developments* (Spring 1995); and Paul Kagan Associates, *Cable TV Programming* and *Pay TV Newsletter* (various issues).

Content. We based those categories on *Cable TV Developments* (Spring 1995), program guides, and network media kits.

Share of Total Subscribership. Data for individual networks are from *Cable TV Programming* (Feb. 27, 1995); *Cable TV Developments* (Spring 1995); *Pay TV Newsletter* (May 31, 1995); and network media kits. All subscribership data are for December 31, 1994, or the nearest available date. In cases where data were unavailable, we contacted the networks in question. We obtained the base for all share calculations from *Cable TV Programming* (Feb. 27, 1995, 5).

Launch Dates. We used *Cable TV Developments* (Spring 1995), *Cable TV Programming*, *Pay TV Newsletter*, and network media kits to compile those data. Note that data from different sources occasionally conflict.

Current Ownership and First Cable System Affiliation. Our primary sources for current ownership data were: *Cable TV Programming* (October 25, 1995, 4–5); *Cable World* (November 27, 1995, 65–66); various recent issues of *Cable TV Programming* and *Pay TV Newsletter*; *MultiChannel News*, *Broadcasting & Cable*; and Implementation of Section 19 of the Cable Television Consumer Protection and Competition Act of 1992: Annual Assessment of the Status of Competition in the Market for Delivery of Video Programming, First Report, CS Dkt. No. 94-98, FCC 94-235 (1994), app. G.

Historical Ownership. Historical ownership data are collected from the above sources and also from Yale Braunstein, "Recent Trends in Cable Television Related to the Prospects for New Television Networks," submitted to the Federal Communications Commission in August 1979; Competition, Rate Deregulation and the Commission's Policies Relating to the Provision of Cable Television Service, Report, MM Dkt. No. 89-600, FCC 90-276, 67 Rad. Reg. 2d (P&F) 1771 (1990); annual financial reports; and earlier issues of the trade publications cited.

Reported percentages of equity ownerships vary from source to source for a number of networks and were not always available as of November 1995. Where conflicts among different sources arose, we generally relied on annual reports and FCC data in favor of trade literature reports, but we did use the latter if they were the only sources reporting all owners with equity percentages adding up to 100 percent. Trade literature and other sources seem to conflict in some cases because of confusion between the total percentage of equity owned and the percentages of particular types of stock (for example, voting stock) held. We could not always resolve those conflicts.

For purposes of comparison with ownership data reported by the FCC in 1994 and 1995, we used more restrictive criteria for inclusion in terms of minimum subscribership, minimum equity owned, hours of broadcast, and the like. Those data also are reported for different dates in several cases.

Network Ownership Affiliations of the Twelve Largest MSOs

We calculated percent share of total cable households data as of July 31, 1995, based on Paul Kagan Associates, *Cable TV Investor* (September 18, 1995, 9–10). Table 3-2's market-share data differ slightly from those reported by Kagan, because, as detailed in footnotes to its table, Kagan calculated market share in several cases by prorating subscribership of minority holdings (and in a few cases of majority holdings) among MSOs according to their shares of equity. In all cases in which total attributable holdings (5 percent or greater ownership) are shown, we included all subscribers of systems in which an MSO has an attributable ownership interest.

Network ownership data are as of November 1995 and are directly compiled from table 3-1. Note that the percentages in many cases indicate the percentages of ownership in another company that owns all of a network's equity.

The base of 60.9 million basic cable subscribers and 92.2 million cable homes passed as of July 31, 1995, is reported in Paul Kagan Associates, *Kagan Media Index* (August 31, 1995, 8).

4

Efficiency Advantages of Vertical Ownership in Cable

To UNDERSTAND WHETHER vertical integration in cable is beneficial or detrimental to the public, we first investigate how such organization might promote economic efficiency. We focus on three advantages of particular interest to cable: transactions efficiencies; the enhanced availability of capital and creative resources; and risk reduction by means of signaling commitment. We offer theory and evidence suggesting that those factors contribute to economic welfare and that although integration impedes program diversity and ease of access by program creators in some respects, it may improve them in others.

TRANSACTIONS EFFICIENCIES

An important motive for vertical integration in many industries is more efficient contracting between the buyer and seller.[1] The reality of doing

---

1. An extensive theoretical and empirical literature on this subject has followed from seminal work of Ronald H. Coase. *See* Ronald H. Coase, *The Nature of the Firm*, 4 ECONOMICA (n.s.) 386 (1937). Other significant contributors include Oliver E. Williamson, *The Vertical Integration of Production: Market Failure Considerations*, 61 AM. ECON. REV. 112 (1971); Benjamin Klein, R. A. Crawford & Armen A. Alchian, *Vertical Integration, Appropriable Rents, and the Competitive Contracting Process*, 21 J. LAW & ECON. 297 (1978); Oliver E. Williamson, *Transaction Cost Economics: The Governance of Contractual Relations*, 22 J. LAW & ECON. 233 (1979); Steven Shavell, *Risk Sharing and Incentives in the Principal and Agent Relationship*, 10 BELL J. ECON. 55 (1979). For surveys of this literature, *see* ROGER D. BLAIR & DAVID L. KASERMAN, LAW

business in the cable industry provides plentiful examples of contracting problems that can occur in the absence of mutual ownership ties.

Affiliation agreements between cable systems and cable networks are negotiated at the MSO level and usually contain terms and conditions governing all the systems within the MSO offering a network. The main components of the agreements are the term of agreement (usually two to five years), an input price schedule, cooperative arrangements for sharing expenses and efforts to promote the network in question, and reporting and payment procedures. Often other provisions specify a network's program content, channel positioning, or the package of other networks with which it may be offered to subscribers.

An ownership relation between transacting parties will likely aid the enforcement of cable affiliation agreements and otherwise facilitate the contracting process. Thus, the parties can reduce the risks of opportunistic behavior and of changing conditions and can eliminate or reduce what economists call double marginalization.

Reducing Risk of Opportunistic Behavior

An affiliation agreement cannot effectively constrain all behavior, either during or after a contract period. After an agreement is signed, for example, an MSO might decide not to promote a network to its subscribers. As one trade article put it, basic cable networks "deluge" cable operators with videos, literature, and other promotional materials intended to enhance viewing—and thus advertising revenues—of their networks.[2] Premium and PPV networks are especially dependent on sales efforts at the system level to increase their subscribership or buy rates. Often, affiliation agreements require an MSO to apply its best efforts to promoting networks. Such provisions, however, are difficult to monitor.

Promotion can apparently have major effects on subscriber demand, especially for premium services. Before 1992, the two leading premium cable network distributors, Time Inc. and Viacom, vigorously competed to induce cable operators to promote their services. Employing so-called

---

AND ECONOMICS OF VERTICAL INTEGRATION AND CONTROL (Academic Press 1983); Michael L. Katz, *Vertical Contractual Relations*, in 1 HANDBOOK OF INDUSTRIAL ORGANIZATION 655 (Richard L. Schmalensee ed., Elsevier Science Publishers 1989); Martin K. Perry, *Vertical Integration: Determinants and Effects*, in 1 HANDBOOK OF INDUSTRIAL ORGANIZATION 655 (Richard L. Schmalensee ed., Elsevier Science Publishers 1989).

2. Richard Katz, *Attention Shoppers*, CABLEVISION, Nov. 4, 1991, at 25.

time-lock campaigns, those suppliers induced operators to offer subscribers special prices for their networks during specified periods of the year. Typically, those periods were several months long, alternating between both networks. As part of a private antitrust suit settled in August 1992, Time and Viacom agreed to refrain from such marketing practices and to engage in cooperative marketing of all four of their respective premium networks.[3] The trade press reported that a primary motive for that settlement was to reduce the churn that arose from customers' jumping from one premium channel subscription to another.[4] Such switching, however, was evidently not a particular problem for the cable systems vertically affiliated with premium networks, at least not for those owned by Time.[5]

Conversely, cable operators face risks of opportunistic behavior by networks. After a contract expires, for example, a network can raise its input price to extract the value of accrued subscriber loyalty to a network. As we discuss in chapter 5, a month after Satellite News Channel folded, CNN's owner, Ted Turner, announced that CNN would more than triple its monthly fees to cable systems.[6] At that time, CNN had no ownership affiliations with cable systems, and there seems to be no evidence of similar pricing behavior by CNN after its vertical affiliations in 1987.

Reducing Risk of Changing Conditions

A change in the quality of a network's programming, rapid technological changes that affect network or system costs, or a changing legal environment can work to the disadvantage of either contracting party during an affiliation period.

Extraordinary advances in video technology and regulatory uncertainties would seem to make cable especially vulnerable to such problems. Certain FCC rules following from the 1992 Cable Act, for example, encouraged cable operators to move some basic networks to higher-priced, ex-

---

3. Viacom Inc. and Showtime Networks, Inc. *v.* Time Inc., Home Box Office, Inc., American Television & Communications Corporation, and Manhattan Cable Television, Inc., Complaint, No. 89-3119 (S.D.N.Y., 1989, unsealed Feb. 7, 1992) [hereinafter *Viacom*]. The *Viacom* complaint alleged that Time used those campaigns and other marketing practices to induce operators not to promote Viacom networks. The settlement is discussed in Richard Katz, *High Time for Showtime,* CABLEVISION, Nov. 2, 1992, at 23, and W. Walley, *Time Warner, Viacom Settle,* ELECTRONIC MEDIA, Aug. 24, 1992, at 2.

4. Katz, *supra* note 3.

5. *Viacom, supra* note 3, ¶¶ 37–56.

6. PAUL KAGAN ASSOCIATES, CABLE TV PROGRAMMING, Dec. 16, 1983, at 1.

panded basic tiers to evade rate regulation. Most basic networks, however, prefer to be on the most widely distributed tiers to maximize advertising revenues. Some affiliation agreements specify higher per subscriber fees if a network is carried on an expanded tier.[7] Recent lawsuits and heated debates in the industry suggest that such conditional input pricing has failed to stem regulation-induced operator incentives to retier networks. For example, A&E and USA recently sued unaffiliated cable operators for moving their programming to higher tiers.[8] In any case, it is clear that passage of the 1992 Cable Act unexpectedly changed the optimal contract between systems and basic networks, a problem that ownership ties would likely alleviate.

Double Marginalization

A classic prescription of economic theory is that an efficient vertical contract between a manufacturer and a retailer requires that the marginal input price the manufacturer charges the retailer be equal to the manufacturer's true marginal cost of producing and distributing that input.[9] If not, the retailer will underutilize the input, and the combined profits of the manufacturer and retailer will be lower than they could otherwise be.

Suppose, for example, that a certain vertically unaffiliated cable network charges an MSO ten cents per subscriber, but its true marginal cost of distribution to another subscriber is only five cents, the remainder contributing to the upfront fixed cost of programming the network. The cable system will, of course, perceive its marginal cost to be ten cents. If those firms were vertically integrated, however, the cable system branch would perceive the true marginal cost of five cents and would be induced to set the subscription price lower or to promote the network to subscribers more aggressively—to the mutual benefit of network and system.

In theory, at least, double marginalization can be resolved without vertical integration simply by a contractual agreement. For example, most premium and at least some basic network contracts specify quantity dis-

---

7. For example, one basic network contract specifies a 7.5 cent per subscriber charge if more than 80 percent of the system's subscribers receive the network and 18 cents per subscriber if less than 80 percent receive it.

8. Kim Mitchell & R. Granger, *Operators Call New Contracts "Obscene,"* MULTICHANNEL NEWS, Mar. 29, 1993, at 1; Kim Mitchell, *USA and A&E Sue Two Ops over à la Carte Tiers,* MULTICHANNEL NEWS, Mar. 27, 1993, at 1.

9. For seminal work on that classic economic dilemma, *see* Joseph J. Spengler, *Vertical Integration and Antitrust Policy,* 58 J. POL. ECON. 347 (1950); Fritz Machlup & M. Taber, *Bilateral Monopoly, Successive Monopoly, and Vertical Integration,* 27 ECONOMICA 101 (1960).

counts with respect to the total number of subscribers that a network attracts. In effect, such discount schemes lower the marginal per subscriber fees that a network charges to a cable system without sacrificing the total revenues that flat-rate pricing could return to the network.

In practice, however, a network can set a marginal input price equal to its true marginal cost only by sacrificing other contractual objectives—again because of conflicting incentives and uncertainty. Unless both parties to a contract stand to profit from a marginal increase in subscribership, for example, mutual incentives to promote a network to subscribers cannot be preserved. In affiliation agreements, larger cable networks typically assent to provide advertising as well as money to promote a network at a local level. One basic network agreement, for example, calls for payment of ten cents per subscriber per year by the network, if matched by the system, to promote that particular network. Larger networks such as HBO, MTV, and Discovery also engage in direct national consumer advertising intended to stimulate subscriber demand. Similarly, each party typically desires to receive some fraction—above its marginal costs—of the net revenues generated by each additional subscriber as compensation for the risk of a changing environment. Without mutual ownership, then, the double marginalization problem cannot be entirely banished.[10]

Benefits to Cable Firms and Consumers

One could easily expand those examples of arms-length contracting problems. As detailed in chapter 6, such factors can explain empirical effects that vertical integration appears to have on the carriage and marketing behavior of integrated cable systems. Such efficiencies are likely to result in lower consumer prices or higher subscribership for vertically affiliated networks, although not necessarily in greater product diversity or improved access to subscribers by program creators.

---

10. Contingent input-pricing schedules in which both buyer and seller share risks and rewards from changes in demand are typical in media industries. For the motion picture case, *see* R. Cassady, Exchange by Private Treaty (1974) (Bureau of Business Research, Graduate School of Business, University of Texas). The FCC Network Inquiry special staff analyzed broadcast television contracts extensively. 1 FEDERAL COMMUNICATIONS COMMISSION, NETWORK INQUIRY SPECIAL STAFF, NEW TELEVISION NETWORKS: ENTRY, JURISDICTION, OWNERSHIP AND REGULATION (Government Printing Office 1980). Although advertisers usually purchase a television spot for a certain lump sum, a network or station will "adjust" the amount if audience size differs substantially from that expected.

The benefits to cable firms or consumers from transactions efficiencies are limited by the prevalence of minority ownership relationships and also by the relatively small proportion of transactions made within vertically integrated firms. Even a TCI-affiliated cable network, for example, makes only about a quarter of its transactions "internal" to the corporation. A number of networks, such as those associated with Continental Cablevision, Cox Cable, or smaller MSOs, make very few such transactions. The presence of efficiency benefits from those and other sources, however, is consistent with the tendency we observe for the largest MSOs to have greater numbers of vertical ownership affiliations and for the prevalence of equity sharing relationships in the cable industry.

CAPITAL AND CREATIVE RESOURCES OF CABLE OPERATORS

In its 1990 report the FCC notes in defense of vertical integration in cable that "on several occasions, MSO investment has enabled a programming service to remain in operation when it otherwise would have been forced to discontinue its programming."[11] Citing congressional testimony and comments to proceedings from vertically integrated programmers or MSOs, the FCC listed C-Span, the Turner Broadcasting networks, BET, and Discovery as examples of "faltering program services" that were bailed out by MSO financial resources.

MSOs, particularly larger ones, stand to benefit not only from the normally expected returns to such programming investments, but from an increase in the supply of programming they can offer their subscribers. The actual motives behind the particular investments cited by the FCC are not obvious, but the examples do suggest the validity of the commission's general contention that the availability of cable operators' capital resources is beneficial to the quality and diversity of cable programming. Cable operators held more than $100 billion in gross cable system assets in 1995,[12] not to mention the much greater resources of some of their parent corporations.

Abundant capital is undoubtedly most important to the successful launch of cable networks, especially in recent years. A new network usually

---

11. Competition, Rate Deregulation and the Commission's Policies Relating to the Provision of Cable Television Service, Report, MM Dkt. No. 89-600, FCC 90-276, 67 Rad. Reg. 2d (P&F) 1771 (1990) [hereinafter 1990 FCC Cable Report] ¶ 83.

12. On the basis of an average per subscriber price of $1,856 reported for the first eight months of 1995 and a total subscribership base of 60.9 million, total assets would be approximately $113 billion. *See* PAUL KAGAN ASSOCIATES, CABLE TV INVESTOR, Aug. 31, 1995, at 6.

requires substantial funds to sustain itself during the time required to persuade cable operators to carry its programming and become known to subscribers. Of sixteen successful basic network launches from 1985 to 1991 tracked by Paul Kagan Associates, fifteen had negative cash flow for at least one year and eleven for three years or more. Among the larger investments were CNBC ($60 million in losses over three years), VH-1 ($39 million over seven years), the Sci-Fi Channel ($80 million over three years), and Comedy Central ($228 million over six years to date, including losses incurred by The Comedy Channel and HA! TV before they merged to create Comedy Central in 1991).[13] Not included in those amounts were prelaunch outlays, which may run $25 million to $75 million each.[14] In addition, many cable networks fold before reaching profitability; such uncertainty calls for large financial resources to diversify risk.

A similar argument applies to the creative resources of MSOs and their parent companies. The 1990 FCC report mentions the potential benefits from integration of knowledge transfer, since the direct contact that cable operators have with subscribers is likely to stimulate ideas for new or improved cable networks.[15] Product development attributable to customer contact at the retail level is a well-recognized benefit of vertical integration in other industries.[16] Without the possibility of backward integration, ideas developed at the MSO level may never come to fruition because their originators have no other practical means to appropriate the value of those ideas.

Even in the absence of such upstream knowledge transfer, however, executives and managers who are skilled at cable system operation may also be skilled at cable network operation. Such synergies from shared management expertise are probably one reason that media conglomerates such as Time Warner, Viacom, Times Mirror, Capital Cities/ABC, and News Corporation own a wide variety of media production and distribution interests, often both cable systems and cable networks.[17] Drawing on the same specialized management pool, corporate relationships between program suppliers and cable systems are likely to stimulate innovation and thus entry and diversity in programming.

---

13. Calculations by the authors are based on PAUL KAGAN ASSOCIATES, CABLE TV PROGRAMMING, Dec. 27, 1990, at 7; Dec. 26, 1991, at 4; May 23, 1994, at 3.

14. PAUL KAGAN ASSOCIATES, CABLE TV PROGRAMMING, June 23, 1994, at 3; June 17, 1993, at 4.

15. 1990 FCC Cable Report, *supra* note 11, ¶ 84.

16. OLIVER E. WILLIAMSON, MARKETS AND HIERARCHIES: ANALYSIS AND ANTITRUST IMPLICATIONS (Free Press 1975).

17. For a general analysis, *see* Michael E. Porter & M. S. Salter, Diversification as a Strategy (1982) (Harvard Business School).

The benefits of creative and capital resources of MSOs or of their parent companies to the supply of cable programming should not be exaggerated. Concepts for successful cable networks have come from many sources. And as illustrated in table 3-1, several large corporations, including Capital Cities/ABC, Hearst Corporation, and General Electric have made successful major programming investments, including launches of Sci-Fi, fX, America's Talking, and ESPN2, in the absence of any cable system affiliations.[18]

The large percentage of cable networks listed in table 3-1 that were actually launched by operators (or with their equity participation), however, suggests an important role that financial and creative resources of system operators have played in the cable programming industry. Table 3-1 also illustrates that an even larger number of networks—especially the economically most important ones—have been vertically affiliated with systems at one time or another and thus have had access to those financial and creative resources in their development. Prominent examples of cable system operators who were entrepreneurial in programming development during the industry's formative years are apparent in the table, including Warner Communications, Cablevision Systems Development Corporation,[19] and Viacom. Since the late 1980s, TCI and Time Warner have taken a leading role in programming development. Although not shown in table 3-1, many of the regional sports and regional news cable networks now operating were developed and launched by cable operators within the regions of their franchises.

SIGNALING COMMITMENT

A prospective cable network typically spends months or even years obtaining carriage commitments from MSOs before attempting an actual launch. That period is much like the stage in which producers of syndicated broadcast programs work to obtain commitments from local stations. Many cable

---

18. The launches of America's Talking, ESPN2, and fX were by broadcast networks NBC, ABC, and Fox, respectively. Those broadcast networks had earlier made deals with a number of MSOs that guaranteed them channel space for the cable networks in lieu of payments for carriage of the broadcast networks' programming. Those deals were precipitated by the retransmission consent provisions of the 1992 Cable Act. Industry analysts have credited the rapid carriage growth of America's Talking, ESPN2, and fX to those carriage guarantees. PAUL KAGAN ASSOCIATES, CABLE TV PROGRAMMING, June 23, 1994, at 1.

19. Charles Dolan, Cablevision's chief executive officer, originated Home Box Office when he operated Manhattan Cable and independent cable systems.

networks scrap launch plans if MSO commitments prove insufficient to justify entry investments.[20]

Carrying a new network requires a cable system to invest scarce channel space and other resources; subsequent quality deterioration or failure of a network will diminish its profits.[21] Prominent publicity in the cable industry trade press touting MSO commitments to carry prospective or new networks suggests that such deals signal the credibility of the network to other MSOs and reduce that risk. A carriage commitment by an MSO with a financial interest in a network is likely to have more credibility than an arms-length contractual commitment, because an MSO stands to lose not only its original investment but the profits to its systems branch if a network turns sour. Thus, other MSOs are likely to have greater confidence that a network will be adequately financed and otherwise supported in the future. In effect, the vertical affiliation reduces the perceived risk of future opportunistic behavior by a signaling MSO, especially if it has a relatively large number of cable subscribers. Consistent with that model, the first prelaunch commitments routinely come from MSOs having an equity investment in a network.

Signaling commitment is one likely motive for the equity-sharing offers many basic networks make to MSOs and for the formation of consortia among several MSOs in the launch or acquisition of emerging networks. The immediate financing obtained and the implicit commitments to support a network in the future promote diffusion of carriage commitments by additional MSOs. Consider, for example, the 1991 launch of Court TV, which involved equity sharing by Time Warner, Cablevision Systems, and TCI, and the January 1995 launch of The Golf Channel, which involved equity sharing by six major MSOs.[22]

To the extent that signaling commitment to cable networks reduces the risk of an entrant's failure, MSOs' equity sharing and other financial involvement in cable networking increase efficiency. Thus, MSOs' equity ownership should also promote the access of program creators to the market and increase program diversity.

---

20. PAUL KAGAN ASSOCIATES, CABLE TV PROGRAMMING, Sept. 25, 1992, at 1.

21. Signaling commitment in that context can be likened to a firm's investment in specialized assets as a way to signal to a second firm that it will remain in the contractual relationship over a long period because those assets would otherwise have to be sacrificed. *See* OLIVER E. WILLIAMSON, THE ECONOMIC INSTITUTIONS OF CAPITALISM (Free Press 1985); *see also* PAUL KAGAN ASSOCIATES, CABLE TV PROGRAMMING, Sept. 25, 1992, at 1.

22. PAUL KAGAN ASSOCIATES, CABLE TV PROGRAMMING, July 31, 1991, at 5–6; Anita Sharpe, *Golf Channel Faces New Hazards as Cable Climate Shifts*, WALL ST. J., Mar. 23, 1994, at B1.

CONCLUSION

Many examples suggest that cable operators' transactions efficiencies and competitive advantages in providing creative and financial resources to the cable program-supply industry motivate vertical integration between cable system operators and programming networks. The presence of efficiency motives is consistent with the tendency for larger MSOs to have greater numbers of vertical ownership affiliations and also for the prevalence of equity sharing in the industry. Larger MSOs will benefit relatively more from transactions efficiencies, and the risk-reducing effects of signaling commitment in the launch of new networks will be greater if more subscribers are involved.

The prevalence of minority relationships and the comparatively few transactions that are actually made between vertically affiliated firms suggest that vertical transactions efficiencies are of relatively minor significance in cable television. But many economists have emphasized the importance that reduced risks—an evident benefit from the involvement of MSOs in the financing of cable networks—have for market entry and innovation in industry more generally.

An environment of reduced risks takes on special social significance in cable television not only because it enhances efficiency, but because it affects programming diversity and the access of programming suppliers to subscribers. Obviously, vertical integration reduces freedom of access to subscribers by unaffiliated programming suppliers. Extensive integration also limits the diversity of programming ownership sources. Nevertheless, the ownership involvement of MSOs improves the entry possibilities of program creators that choose to accept financial support, and with it, the diversity of programming content available to subscribers.

Our categorization of efficiency-promoting motives or effects of vertical ownership in this chapter is not exhaustive. We suggest other possibilities in the context of our discussion of strategic behavior in the following chapter.

5

Vertical Integration, Strategic Behavior, and the Supply of Cable Programming

IN A RAPIDLY CHANGING INDUSTRY with firms continuously facing competition from new entrants, strategic behavior is important. How might established cable television firms strategically use vertical ownership ties to defend their market positions? A possibility of particular policy interest is that an MSO-network combination will use its cable system ties anticompetitively to disadvantage existing or potential network rivals by foreclosing them from access to the cable subscribers it controls. A second possibility is that such a combination will use its network ties strategically to create barriers to entry or otherwise disadvantage alternative multichannel video programming distributors by denying them access to the programming it controls.

In this chapter we focus on the possible role of vertical ownership in disadvantaging rival programming suppliers and thus affecting the supply of cable programming adversely. While the bulk of our analysis of program access and barriers to entry at the facilities level is discussed in chapter 7, the economic model we develop in this chapter underlies part of that later analysis.

THE POTENTIAL ROLE OF VERTICAL INTEGRATION IN ANTICOMPETITIVE BEHAVIOR

In its 1990 report the FCC related an incident that illustrates how vertical ownership might have anticompetitive effects on the supply of cable programming.[1] NBC president Robert W. Wright testified in congressional

---

1. Competition, Rate Deregulation and the Commission's Policies Relating to the Provision of Cable Television Service, Report, MM Dkt. No. 89-600, FCC 90-276, 67

hearings that CNBC's attempts to obtain prelaunch affiliation commitments in 1988—shortly after TCI, Time Warner, and some other MSOs had acquired their interests in CNN—were met with demands by "a number of the large MSOs" that CNBC make a commitment that it would not provide a general news service. CNBC's subsequent affiliation agreements, in fact, stated:

> [I]t is understood and agreed that it is not the intent of [CNBC] to allow [the service] to become, and the CNBC Service or no segment thereof shall become, a general news service covering events unrelated to [business, financial, consumer, and other specified news events].[2]

The commission concluded that the central purpose of that clause must have been to prevent competition with CNN.[3] After citing other examples and evidence, the FCC report reached its conclusion that vertically integrated MSOs are able to limit competition in the cable programming industry.[4]

To conclude that vertical ownership ties are responsible for raising barriers to entry or reducing competition in cable programming, two conditions must be satisfied. First, an integrated firm's MSO branch or branches must be able to significantly and profitably disadvantage a rival to its network branch by foreclosing its controlled downstream systems to that rival. If the national market share of the MSOs involved in the CNBC instance were too small, for example, CNBC's revenues would be unaffected by their demands.[5] Profitability is also an issue. In our example, excluding CNBC would necessarily reduce short-term profits of CNN's affiliated MSOs; those MSOs would sacrifice the benefit of carrying a presumably more desirable menu of programming.

The second condition is that a network must not be able to implement the same strategy without the benefit of vertical ownership ties. Hence, if

---

Rad. Reg. 2d (P&F) (1990) ¶¶ 120–122 [hereinafter 1990 FCC Cable Report]. *See also* Donna A. Lampert, *Cable Television: Does Leased Access Mean Least Access?*, 44 FED. COMM. L.J. 245 (1992).

2. 1990 FCC Cable Report ¶ 120 (brackets in FCC original).

3. *Id.* ¶ 122.

4. *Id.* ¶ 127.

5. The implication of that logic is that an integrated firm must be able to raise the costs of its rival network. For a general analysis of such models, *see* Steven C. Salop & David T. Scheffman, *Raising Rivals' Costs*, 73 AM. ECON. REV. 267 (1983). For a specific analysis of market foreclosure involving cable networking, *see* Janusz A. Ordover, Alan O. Sikes & Robert D. Willig, *Noncompetitive Behavior by Dominant Firms Toward the Producers of Complementary Products*, *in* ANTITRUST AND REGULATION: ESSAYS IN MEMORY OF JOHN J. MCGOWAN (Franklin Fisher ed., MIT Press 1985).

CNN could have induced the involved MSOs to make the same demands on CNBC in the absence of any ownership connections, the vertical relationship would not have a decisive strategic advantage. The fundamental motive for foreclosure would have nothing to do with vertical integration. The role of integration here can only be to facilitate an anticompetitive strategy that would be more difficult or impossible for a cable network to carry out on its own.

We argue in this chapter that the first condition is plausible: Cost and demand conditions in the cable industry appear conducive to foreclosure. We do not find persuasive evidence, however, that the second condition is fulfilled. It is likely that vertical integration does facilitate instances of anticompetitive foreclosure behavior. The historical record argues, however, that vertical ownership ties are only one among a variety of alternative strategies—some potentially anticompetitive and others procompetitive— that cable networks can employ on their own to establish and defend their competitive positions.

One necessary condition for vertical foreclosure strategies to be effective is the presence of program buying, or monopsony, power at the MSO level. We also show, however, that if MSOs do exert excessive monopsony power in the programming market, vertical integration can positively affect efficiency and diversity by restoring the flow of revenues from subscribers back to the program supply industry.

We now analyze the two conditions under which vertically integrated firms could behave anticompetitively to adversely affect program supply. Throughout the discussion, we presume that the relevant programming market involved is content-specific, for example, news, music video, or movies.[6]

The Plausibility of Vertical Foreclosure in Program Supply

An essential feature of a credible foreclosure model in the cable industry is the presence of economies of scale in cable networking with respect to the subscriber reach of the relevant network. If scale economies are important, then a rival network might be significantly disadvantaged by an MSO's or MSOs' having a sufficiently large national market share of cable subscribers.[7]

---

6. In chapter 8 we discuss the more difficult prospect of dominating the entire cable television programming market. We focus here on the national cable programming market. Local or regional programming suppliers, such as regional sports networks, account for a relatively minor part of all programming industry revenues, but their foreclosure is also a possibility that we consider briefly in chapter 8.

7. Several models of vertical foreclosure have been offered in the general economic literature. *See* Michael A. Salinger, *Vertical Mergers and Market Foreclosure,* 103 Q.J.

Our analysis of vertical foreclosure in cable programming supply requires some elaboration of the economics of cable networking and the business relationship between networks and MSOs. The model we set out, however, offers a foundation for interpreting a wide variety of strategic behavior in the cable industry, including our chapter 7 analysis of the potential for vertical integration to raise barriers to entry to alternative multichannel video programming distributors.

Economies of Scale and Program Quality in Cable Networking. Media product distribution is fundamentally subject to economies of scale with respect to the number of individuals or households that consume a product. The producer-distributors of television programs, newspapers, and magazines face a relatively high first-copy cost of creating (or financing) a product.[8] Once created, however, the incremental physical cost of serving additional viewers or readers is typically low or even zero. Panel A of figure 5-1 illustrates the result for the video case; for a given program investment, a media producer-distributor typically realizes declining average costs as more and more viewers consume the product.

We illustrate the demand side of that model in panel B of figure 5-1. Audience demand for a given program will generally rise with higher production values, more popular stars, or the use of more expensively produced program formats. As the flattening of the curve indicates, however, there are bound to be diminishing returns to such spending.

Finally, in panel C of figure 5-1 we show how those cost and demand conditions interact to determine the programming investment decisions of a video producer-distributor. The forty-five-degree line indicates a firm's breakeven point, where total revenue equals total production investment if we assume that a firm's only cost is the first-copy expense of creating a video product. There are no marginal costs of distribution in that example, and thus pure economies of scale obtain with respect to the number of viewers attracted. Curve *A* in panel C shows how a firm's revenue depends on the

---

ECON. 345 (1987), Oliver Hart & Jean Tirole, *Vertical Integration and Market Foreclosure*, BROOKINGS PAPERS ON ECON. ACTIVITY: MICROECON. 205 (1990), and Janusz A. Ordover, Garth Saloner & Steven C. Salop, *Equilibrium Vertical Foreclosure,* 80 AM. ECON. REV.127 (1990). The model described in this section uses some assumptions that typify those models but primarily relies on the presence of downstream monopsony power and upstream economies of scale.

8. The effects of economies of scale on media product distribution have been explored by a number of economists, beginning with Paul A. Samuelson, *The Pure Theory of Public Expenditure,* 36 REV. ECON. & STAT. 387 (1954). That insight and the relationship of scale economies to product quality are applied empirically to explain market structure

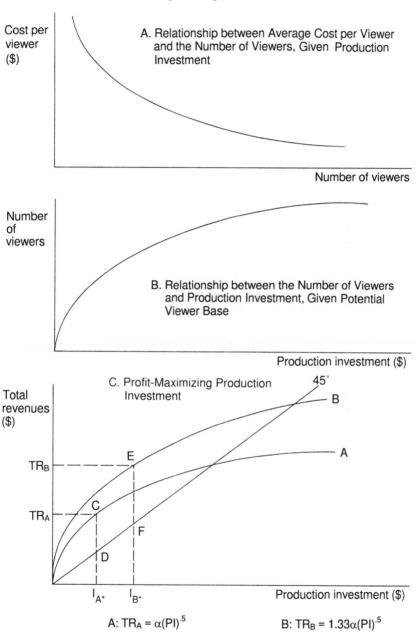

Figure 5-1
Cable Programming Network Model

A. Relationship between Average Cost per Viewer and the Number of Viewers, Given Production Investment

B. Relationship between the Number of Viewers and Production Investment, Given Potential Viewer Base

C. Profit-Maximizing Production Investment

A: $TR_A = \alpha(PI)^{.5}$ B: $TR_B = 1.33\alpha(PI)^{.5}$

Note: TR represents total revenues, α represents an unknown coefficient, and PI represents production investment.

amount of production investment for some given potential geographic market. As panel B suggests, that curve will become flatter as diminishing returns to investment set in. Finally, a firm's point of maximum profits is investment level $I_A{}^*$, where the difference between revenues and costs, *CD*, is maximized.

Curve *B* in panel C indicates the effects on a producer-distributor's total revenues from an increase in the size of its potential geographic market. Since there are no marginal costs, an increase in potential market size simply means an identical increase in potential revenues for the same level of total costs. A firm's profit-maximizing investment level increases to $I_B{}^*$, where *EF* is maximum profit. Basically, programming investments and profits increase because the marginal productivity of a dollar spent on programming automatically rises by the same percentage that a video program's potential audience rises.

That simple model abstracts from the competitive dynamics by which media firms react to one another's investment decisions. Basically, however, the model explains why large cities' newspapers are thicker and more expensively produced than small-town papers, why broadcast TV stations in big cities spend lavishly for local news programs compared with bare-bones productions in small markets,[9] and why production budgets of American movies and TV programs are typically far larger than those of foreign-produced products.[10]

The actual extent of scale economies in cable networking is an empirical question about which we do not have systematic data. It is evident, however,

---

in James N. Rosse, *Daily Newspapers, Monopolistic Competition, and Economies of Scale*, 57 Am. Econ. Rev. Papers & Proc. 522 (1967); James N. Rosse, *The Evolution of One-Newspaper Cities*, in Proceedings of the Symposium on Media Concentration 129 (Federal Trade Commission 1978); Bruce M. Owen, Economics and Freedom of Expression (Ballinger Publishing Co. 1975). Economic models similar to that presented in this section appear in David Waterman, *World Television Trade: The Economic Effects of Privatization and New Technology*, 12 Telecomm. Pol'y 141 (June 1988); Steven S. Wildman & Stephen E. Siwek, International Trade in Films and Television Programs (Ballinger Publishing Co. 1988); Bruce M. Owen & Steven S. Wildman, Video Economics (Harvard University Press 1992).

9. For example, the National Association of Broadcasters reports that average 1990 news expenditures of all stations in the ten largest U.S. television markets were $6.8 million, $1.3 million for markets 41–50, and $.7 million for markets 91–100. National Association of Broadcasters, TV Financial Report, 1991

10. Higher spending on American movies and video products has become a generally accepted economic explanation of why they tend to dominate box office receipts and television schedules around the world. *See* Waterman, *supra* note 8, and Wildman & Siwek, *supra* note 8.

that individual cable systems can, with little more than a flip of a switch, take a network signal from a satellite and relay it to subscribers. Other marginal costs to a network, such as negotiations with operators, billing, and the like, are also relatively small. One analyst estimates that 74 percent of the total operating expenditures made by the twenty-eight largest national basic networks in 1992 were for programming.[11]

A related factor may accentuate economies of scale for advertiser-supported cable networks. In general, advertisers prefer to reach as high a percentage of their target audience as possible. All cable networks are inferior to broadcast technology in that respect because even the most ubiquitous cable networks reach only about two-thirds of all TV households. A 1993 survey of the twenty-six largest cable networks indicated that broadcast stations realized average cost-per-thousand rates that were 24 percent higher than cable networks'—$8.75 for broadcast versus $6.67 for cable, a difference that is widely attributed to cable's coverage handicap.[12] That comparison implies that advertiser-supported cable networks that are unable to reach all potential cable subscribers are at a further competitive disadvantage.

Figure 5-2 shows the net effect of those economic pressures on the basic cable programming industry. The figure shows a positive correlation between potential audience reach and basic network program investments. Eighty-nine percent of those investments was accounted for by networks reaching at least 90 percent of cable subscribers in 1991. Of course, both cause and effect are involved; investing more makes a network more attractive to viewers and widens its distribution. Then, too, some programs cost more than others. Nevertheless, those data are consistent with the economies-of-scale model.

Similar relationships are also apparent in premium cable networking. In 1991 HBO and Cinemax had a combined subscribership of 23.5 million

11. PAUL KAGAN ASSOCIATES, CABLE TV PROGRAMMING, Jan. 29, 1993, at 3. Strictly speaking, of course, those scale economies would apply to cable program producers and not necessarily to networks themselves. If program producers could find comparable outlets where a cable network is not available, then they could simply license to cable networks on a constant fee-per-subscriber basis and distribute through other media elsewhere. Original or exclusively licensed products are the great majority of basic and premium cable fare, however, and the sheer volume of those programs precludes exhibition for all but a fraction of them on local broadcast media. Cable networks compete with local broadcast stations and other media for rights to major theatrical movies and some off-network series, but the next-best options for producers of those programs are not necessarily very attractive.

12. PAUL KAGAN ASSOCIATES, CABLE TV ADVERTISING, Jan. 31, 1994, at 1.

Figure 5-2

Relationship between Basic Cable Networks' Programming Expenditure and
the Potential Audience Reach

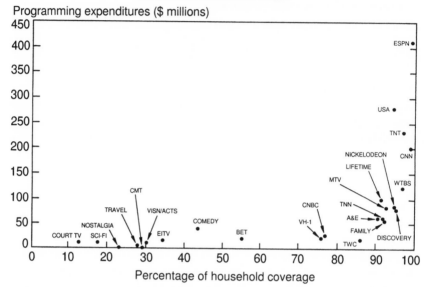

Source: Paul Kagan Associates, *Cable TV Programming*   (Jan. 29, 1993, 3; Feb. 25, 1995, 5).

compared with 9.9 million for Showtime and The Movie Channel.[13] As economies of scale in cable networking would predict, the more widely distributed Time Warner networks appear to offer more attractive programming. In that year HBO/Cinemax exhibited sixty-nine exclusively licensed theatrical films—fifty-seven of them from the eight major studios plus twelve made-for-pay features—in contrast to Showtime/The Movie Channel's exhibition of sixty-one exclusive theatrical movies—eight from the major studios plus six original features.[14] It was also reported in 1989 that HBO's original movies cost $4 million to $6 million each, compared with $3 million to $4 million each for Showtime's.[15]

The implication of those economic conditions—declining costs per subscriber on the cost side and incentives to increase production budgets on the demand side—is that if a network is restricted from access to some cable markets, its average cost per subscriber will increase. That cost increase

13. PAUL KAGAN ASSOCIATES, PAY TV NEWSLETTER, Jan. 31, 1993, at 4.

14. PAUL KAGAN ASSOCIATES, PAY TV NEWSLETTER, Aug. 31, 1991, at 4.

15. PAUL KAGAN ASSOCIATES, PAY TV NEWSLETTER, Apr. 30, 1989, at 3.

could in turn diminish that network's ability profitably to invest as much in programming and thus reduce its competitiveness in all markets. Restricted access is likely to be most important if competition is between relatively similar networks, such as general news channels or premium movie networks. In those cases economies of scale work against survival of all the networks; prices to subscribers or advertisers for essentially the same product could be reduced by a merger.

Another media industry, daily newspapers, offers an analogy. Head-to-head competition between daily newspapers in the United States survives in relatively few markets. Where competition does exist, the competing papers usually segment fairly sharply toward different socioeconomic readerships. Where content differentiation appears to be minor, competing papers are likely to engage in intense price competition until one paper or another loses the edge in readership or advertising. That competition eventually leads to sharper differentiation, the failure of one paper, or a merger. Detroit and Dallas are examples of the apparent results of intense price competition among two relatively similar newspapers. In Detroit a joint operating agreement resulted; in Dallas one newspaper folded.[16]

In addition to scale economies, product differentiation contributes to the vulnerability of rival cable networks in the cable industry. Consumers subscribe to a cable system on the basis of its menu, so a new network with content similar to that of an existing channel is less attractive to potential subscribers than a network with distinctly different fare. That economic motive for an operator to differentiate its menu follows from classic economic models that demonstrate that a monopolist has an incentive, other things being equal, to offer a greater variety of radio or television programming than do firms that compete with one another.[17]

The MSOs' more enthusiastic reception of sharply differentiated recent entrants such as the Cartoon Channel and the Sci-Fi Channel than to NBC's proposed "general news" cable network version may reflect those incentives. In fact, when asked for an explanation of his rejection of NBC Cable News in 1985, Dan Ritchie, chief executive officer of Westinghouse Broadcasting

---

16. Robert A. Rosenblatt, *Meese Approves Rescue Plan for Detroit Papers*, L.A. TIMES, Aug. 9, 1988, § IV, at 1; *Dallas Dies*, ECONOMIST, Dec. 14, 1991, at 28. Joint operating agreements are exemptions from the antitrust laws, codified by the Newspaper Preservation Act, 15 USCA §§ 1801–1804 (1970). That exemption permits "failing" newspapers in the same city to merge their business operations while maintaining separate editorial functions.

17. *See* Peter O. Steiner, *Program Patterns and Preferences and the Workability of Competition in Radio Broadcasting*, 66 Q. J. ECON. 194 (1952); BRUCE M. OWEN, JACK H. BEEBE & WILLARD G. MANNING, JR., TELEVISION ECONOMICS (Lexington Books 1974).

and Cable Co., the third largest MSO, which had minimal programming interests, and none in the news area, at the time, stated: "Cable operators don't need another all-news channel. . . . Basically, it would be taking up extra channel capacity with a duplicated service. . . . [NBC Cable News] would not bring you a single new subscriber."[18] Response to NBC's general news float was reportedly cool throughout the ranks of the top fifty MSOs; the "duplication" theme was reiterated by several others.[19] Those reactions suggest that the MSOs involved in the later incident with CNBC may have had a benign incentive to ensure a differentiation from CNN in the future.[20]

The history of the cable programming industry seems to verify the natural pressures of scale economies and operator incentives. Several pairs or groups of basic cable networks with similar content have competed for a period of time before one has failed or a merger occurred. CBS Cable went out of business after competing with the Arts Channel. Comedy Central was the result of a merger between HA! TV and the Comedy Channel; VISN/ACTS ensued from a consolidation of two religious networks; and, as we discuss below, several networks failed in attempts to compete with CNN, MTV, and the leading home shopping networks.

MSO Monopsony Power and the Profitability of Foreclosure. The implication of our discussion of the economics of cable networking is that large MSOs might be able to use their control of local markets to affect entry and competition between networks. The larger an MSO's national subscriber base, the greater the increase in a network's costs, and thus the greater the decline in its competitive position that a refusal to deal could cause.[21]

How large must MSOs be to have a significant impact on cable programming networks—or in other words, to exert significant monopsony power? Numerous claims have been made in the press, congressional

---

18. *NBC Cable News Project in Jeopardy,* BROADCASTING, Jan. 13, 1986, at 33–34.

19. *Id.*

20. Eventually, NBC started CNBC, whose financial news and business-oriented news service did directly compete with FNN, an unaffiliated network. But following a familiar pattern in the industry, FNN soon proved the weaker network and sold its assets to CNBC, which then became the dominant network in financial and other news.

21. The private antitrust suit involving the two largest integrated premium network operators was based on that theory. *See* Viacom Inc. *v.* Time Inc., Complaint, No. 89-3119 (S.D.N.Y., 1989, unsealed Feb. 7, 1992). In addition to "time-lock" campaigns, Viacom complained that Time employed a range of anticompetitive tactics to limit the Viacom networks' access to programming by limiting their access to cable subscribers.

hearings, and FCC proceedings that TCI has had excessive power over network survival by means of its disproportionate national share of cable subscribers.[22] One widely reported incident involving The Learning Channel typifies those claims.[23] When TLC was put up for sale in 1990, the Lifetime Network reportedly offered a price of $40 million, while TCI made a lower bid through a subsidiary. With the Lifetime deal near closing, TCI reportedly threatened to remove TLC from virtually all its cable systems, which served approximately 20 percent of all U.S. cable subscribers, if the sale was consummated. Lifetime then reportedly withdrew its bid, and TCI's subsidiary purchased TLC a few months later for $32 million.[24] Other reported incidents have involved home shopping networks and ESPN.[25] As one would expect, there are benign versions of those stories. TCI's chief executive officer, John Malone, for example, reportedly characterized TCI's behavior in the TLC incident quite benevolently and attributed TCI's 1990 public statements about carriage of TLC to a rapid decline in the quality of its programming.[26]

The economies-of-scale model suggests, however, the possibility that a single MSO serving a quarter or less of all cable subscribers might exert monopsony control over cable networks. Assume, for example, that a widely distributed cable network suffered a 25 percent fall in its potential subscriber reach. If the elasticity of viewership with respect to programming investment were .5 (that is, a 10 percent fall in program spending leads to an initial 5 percent fall in viewing, other things being equal), then a 43.8 percent fall both in optimal investment and in the network's total viewership would

---

22. *See* J. Roberts, *How Giant TCI Uses Self-Dealing, Hardball to Dominate Market*, WALL ST. J., Jan. 27, 1992, at 1; Laura Landro, *Tele-Communications Sets Cable-TV Agenda*, WALL ST. J., Feb. 11, 1986, at 6; M. Ivey, *The King of Cable TV*, BUS. WEEK, Oct. 26, 1987, at 88. *See also* Cable TV Consumer Protection Act of 1991: Hearing Before the Subcomm. on Communications of the Sen. Comm. on Commerce, Science, and Transportation, 102d Cong., 1st Sess. (1991). Testimony of Roy M. Speer, chairman and chief executive officer of Home Shopping Network, Inc., at 422; and Examining the Effects of Megamergers in the Telecommunications Industry, Opening Statement of Hon. Howard M. Metzenbaum to the Hearings Before the Subcomm. on Antitrust, Business Rights, and Competition of the Sen. Comm. on the Judiciary, 103d Cong., 1st Sess. (1993).

23. Roberts, *supra* note 22.

24. A private antitrust suit making basically the same allegations was dismissed on procedural grounds. Data Broadcasting Corporation *v.* Tele-Communications, Inc., No. 92-4840 (S.D.N.Y. dismissed Nov. 5, 1992). *See* 63 ANTITRUST & TRADE REG. REP. (Nov. 26, 1992), at 656.

25. Landro, *supra* note 22; Ivey, *supra* note 22.

26. Ken Auletta, *John Malone: Flying Solo*, NEW YORKER, Feb. 7, 1994, at 59.

result from that 25 percent foreclosure.[27] The net effect is cumulative. An initial fall in audience causes a reduction in spending, which in turn reduces viewership in other markets and again reduces optimal spending. The actual extent to which such a foreclosure action could threaten a cable network's viability would vary, of course, with how well-established a network was, the substitutability of rival networks, and alternative distribution routes that the affected network or the producers of its programming might have.

The power to foreclose also implies the ability to force down the license fees that an MSO pays to networks.[28] Some anecdotal evidence suggests the possibility that larger MSOs hold significant monopsony power in the programming market. A 1988 National Telecommunications and Information Administration report on the cable industry, for example, cited a number of input price differentials larger than one would expect from transactions costs savings for large versus small MSOs.[29] A more recent study offers suggestive econometric evidence that larger MSOs exert monopsony power over programming suppliers.[30] Persistent complaints by independent cable operators in FCC proceedings that they pay substantially greater prices for programming than do the major MSOs are further consistent with monopsony power, although costs could also account for those differences.[31]

In summary, cost and demand conditions in the cable industry, combined with suggestive evidence of MSO monopsony power, imply the possibility of vertical foreclosure strategies in cable networking. Note, however, that such strategies are not necessarily profitable. The uncertain

---

27. Those are the particular percentage changes that are shown in panel C of figure 5-1. The elasticity of audience size with respect to production investment was estimated by Robert W. Crandall, *FCC Regulation, Monopsony, and Network Television Costs*, 3 BELL J. ECON. 483 (1972), by using British public television data to be approximately .5 to .7. A point estimate of .77 was made by Rolla Edward Park in *New Television Networks*, 6 BELL J. ECON. 607 (1975), by using U.S. broadcast network data for 1971.

28. See the appendix to this chapter for a model of the effect of MSO size on input prices.

29. Among specific examples cited by NTIA are a $.02 per subscriber monthly rate for CNN paid to MSOs with more than five million subscribers compared with $.29 for MSOs with fewer than 500,000 subscribers, and $.90 per subscriber paid for HBO by the largest MSO, TCI, Inc., compared with $5.00 paid by "small" MSOs. Note that those data may be incomplete descriptions of more complex pricing structures. NATIONAL TELECOMMUNICATIONS AND INFORMATION ADMINISTRATION, VIDEO PROGRAM DISTRIBUTION AND CABLE TELEVISION: CURRENT POLICY ISSUES AND RECOMMENDATIONS 80–82 (1988).

30. Tasneem Chipty, *Horizontal Integration for Bargaining Power: Evidence from the Cable Television Industry*, 4 J. ECON. MGMT. STRATEGY 375 (1995).

31. 1990 FCC Cable Report, *supra* note 1, ¶ 114.

long-term gains to a firm's network branch from lessened competition must be weighed against the certainty of a short-term sacrifice in profits to an integrated firm's MSO branch from excluding or disadvantaging an unaffiliated rival. Under certain conditions, however, foreclosure may be profitable. For example, an unaffiliated rival network might be poorly financed—not an uncommon circumstance in the cable industry.[32] Or two entering networks in a certain programming category might engage in a war of attrition in which economies of scale dictate that only one can survive. A credible threat by network A to foreclose its vertically affiliated cable systems from an unaffiliated rival network B will increase B's expected cost of entry relative to A's, at a potentially low short-term sacrifice to network A. Network B might then make a rational decision to exit the market.

We turn now to the second condition required for anticompetitive behavior to be attributed to vertical integration—that vertical ties are necessary for such an anticompetitive strategy to be implemented.

Vertical Integration as a Facilitator of Anticompetitive Behavior

One way vertical integration could facilitate anticompetitive behavior is analogous to our discussion of transactions efficiencies in chapter 4. Affiliation contracts are inherently incomplete, unable to insure against opportunistic behavior by either party in the absence of mutual ownership. A network's foreclosure strategy might require unstated future cooperation, such as an MSO's continuing refusal to carry a rival network on its systems. In the absence of ownership ties, it would be hard to maintain such cooperation. Cooperation would be particularly difficult without ownership if more than one MSO were involved, as Robert Wright's testimony suggested may have been the case in the CNBC incident.

Vertical integration helps to overcome such contracting difficulties and thus might play an important role in implementing anticompetitive behavior. History, however, shows a variety of strategies unrelated to vertical integration that established cable operators can employ to discourage or prevent entry and to otherwise defend their competitive positions. Such strategies— which may or may not be anticompetitive in their intent or their effects— include input price reductions, the launching of "companion" networks, and exclusive contracting with program producers.

---

32. *See* Janusz Ordover & Garth Saloner, *Predation, Monopolization, and Antitrust in* 2 HANDBOOK OF INDUSTRIAL ORGANIZATION 537 (Richard L. Schmalensee & Robert D. Willig eds., Elsevier Science Publishers 1989) for a survey of predatory pricing models that rely on a "long purse" available to a predator.

Strategic Alternatives to Vertical Foreclosure. The pre-1987 history of CNN—before any ownership affiliations had been established between that network and MSOs—suggests the potential of both aggressive input pricing and the launch of companion networks to deter entry. In the fall of 1981, Group W/Westinghouse, then the third largest cable operator in the United States, and ABC announced that they would launch Satellite News Channel (SNC), a general cable news channel, to compete with CNN. They offered to pay cable operators to carry SNC, rather than to charge fees as CNN and most other networks were doing.[33]

Turner Broadcasting, CNN's parent company, then sharply reduced its fees to cable operators. Further, three days after SNC's announcement, Ted Turner declared that by January 1, 1982, he would begin a second general news service, CNN2 (later Headline News), for no extra charge to cable operators. CNN2 launched on schedule, and SNC soon followed.[34] SNC, though, failed to obtain enough system affiliations, and within a year its owners had shut it down, sold their assets to Turner Broadcasting, and agreed to a three-year no-competition clause.[35] Then, within a month of SNC's demise, Turner announced that he would more than triple CNN's fees to cable operators.[36]

In mid-1985, two years before CNN became vertically affiliated, NBC first floated its idea of starting a general cable news service to compete with CNN. The trade press reported that TCI, ATC, and some other MSOs encouraged NBC to proceed. TCI's Malone cited "a lot of grumbling" about recent CNN rate hikes as a reason for that encouragement.[37]

By December 1985, however, the tide had turned against the prospective NBC Cable News:

> One reason odds are getting long is Ted Turner, who views the NBC cable venture as a threat to his CNN and CNN Headline News. In an effort to keep affiliates happy, Turner is offering volume discounts [for MSOs serving over 100,000 subscribers] for news services starting [new launches of CNN or CNN2] in 1987. Another is loss of Tele-Communications, Inc., largest MSO, as customer. TCI encouraged NBC to get into business, but it has become among first to tell NBC "no sale." According to TCI executive, NBC showed little flexibility in negotiations. What's more, he

---

33. John A. Quelch, Cable News Network (1983, rev. July 1985) (Harvard Business School).

34. *Id.*

35. PAUL KAGAN ASSOCIATES, CABLE TV PROGRAMMING, Oct. 14, 1983, at 1.

36. PAUL KAGAN ASSOCIATES, CABLE TV PROGRAMMING, Dec. 16, 1983, at 1.

added, Turner showed himself to be "cable friendly" by shucking plans for programmers-only C-band direct venture [a medium-powered direct broadcast satellite venture] and extending C-band direct rights to TCI.[38]

A month later, the trade press reported that among fourteen of the top fifty MSOs that had by then rejected NBC Cable News were TCI and ATC, "both of which [had] reportedly cut special sweetheart deals with CNN (calling for [additional] discounts of 20 percent or more)."[39] As a result of that discouraging reception, NBC withdrew from the market until its 1987 attempts to obtain prelaunch commitments for CNBC.

A possible interpretation of those stories is that CNN engaged in predatory pricing and other anticompetitive behavior to thwart the entry of competitors. The launch of CNN2, in particular, might be interpreted as an anticompetitive strategy of brand proliferation intended to increase barriers to entry into general news networking.[40]

Anecdotal evidence of such potentially anticompetitive strategies in cable networking has not been confined to news networks. For example, MTV, a basic cable network, has successfully dominated rock music video networking since its launch in 1981. The press and other observers have reported a history of timely license fee cuts made by MTV in response to competitive threats.[41] In 1984 MTV launched its companion network, VH-1, in evident response to the anticipated entry of Cable Music Television, a short-lived competing music channel launched late that year by Ted Turner.

A recurring subject of antitrust litigation in cable networking has been exclusive contracting between networks and program suppliers, notably involving theatrical movies and cable music. Exclusive contracts between HBO and certain major movie studios were one subject of the 1989 private antitrust suit filed by Viacom against the Time Inc. networks alleging the latters' attempt to monopolize premium cable networking.[42] Several private suits have alleged that MTV entered into exclusive contracts with several major record companies with the intent of preventing entry at the networking

---

37. *NBC Ponders Plan for Cable News Service*, BROADCASTING, Aug. 26, 1985, at 33.

38. *Glimmering Hopes,* BROADCASTING, Dec. 16, 1985, at 7.

39. *NBC Cable News Project in Jeopardy*, BROADCASTING, Jan. 13, 1986, at 182.

40. For a comparable analysis in the ready-to-eat breakfast cereal industry, *see* Richard L. Schmalensee, *Entry Deterrence in the Ready-to-Eat Breakfast Cereal Industry*, 9 BELL J. ECON. 305 (1979).

41. Landro, *supra* note 22; R. SERGE DENISOFF, INSIDE MTV (Transaction Publishers 1988).

42. *Viacom, supra* note 21.

level.[43] Of course, in pursuing those strategies, MTV may have benefited from its initial upstream affiliations with Warner Records, the largest distributor of recorded music. MTV may also have benefited from its downstream affiliation with Warner-Amex Cable, then the fifth largest MSO, and later with Viacom, which bought MTV in 1985. MTV did enter into exclusive contracts with several record companies, however. Then, too, most of the antitrust litigation in music video networking has concerned exclusive contracting with music producers after 1984, for which vertical affiliation with Viacom offers no apparent advantage.

The point of those examples is not that the pricing, product introduction, or exclusive contracting strategies employed were anticompetitively motivated: All that behavior has benign interpretations. Price reductions are not anticompetitive if they reflect a movement of price toward cost by a firm confronted with competition. As we discuss at greater length in chapter 7, exclusive contracting has procompetitive explanations. Finally, the common practice of creating "spinoff" cable networks is reported to create on-air promotion opportunities and to benefit from shared marketing, sales, and overhead expenses. QVC Fashion, for example, was reported to comprise only 5 to 6 percent of QVC's operating costs.[44] Similar incentives exist for the acquisition of similar "companion" networks by a single firm, for example, the common ownership of The Nashville Network and Country Music Television by Gaylord Broadcasting. An advantage to a cable operator of commonly owned networks within a single programming category is that owners have an incentive to counterprogram their networks to minimize duplication of content.

The main point of the news, music, and movie examples is that if entry deterrence or other anticompetitive foreclosure behavior in cable networking is profitable, it can be accomplished without the benefit of vertical integration. A second point is that the presence of horizontal market power is crucial to interpreting the examples as anticompetitive behavior. With the obvious exception of exclusive contracting between networks and program producers,[45] foreclosure strategies in cable networking could not be effective without cooperation of an MSO or MSOs having a combined national market share sufficiently large to disadvantage a rival network. To the extent that

---

43. *See* Peter Newcombe, *Music Video Wars*, FORBES, Mar. 4, 1991, at 68; Edmund L. Andrews, *Plan to Create MTV Rival Is Under Antitrust Scrutiny*, N.Y. TIMES, July 23, 1994. None of the legal challenges has succeeded in court.

44. PAUL KAGAN ASSOCIATES, CABLE TV PROGRAMMING, Apr. 30, 1992, at 1.

45. To be anticompetitive in those cases, exclusive contracting would have to rely on horizontal control at the program production level.

CNN (or its MSO stockholders) may have behaved anticompetitively in the CNBC instance, success depended on rejection of the general news version of CNBC by an MSO or MSOs controlling enough subscribers on the margin to make or break the new network. The same is true for CNN's earlier pricing or product introduction strategies.

The Effects of Vertical Foreclosure on Consumers

If vertical integration facilitates anticompetitive strategic behavior, the result can be higher barriers to entry, reduced efficiency, and impaired First Amendment objectives. The economic effects of vertical foreclosure on consumers are not necessarily negative, however. The role of integration may be simply to influence an eventual outcome of a competitive network rivalry in which only one, or a relatively few networks under common ownership, can survive. Consumers may end up with substantially the same menu of programs in the long term with or without integration. That point, as well as the fundamentally ancillary role that vertical integration can play within the range of alternative cable networking strategies, is illustrated by a final example: the development of home shopping networks.[46]

The first national shopping channel, Home Shopping Network (HSN), was launched in 1985 without any ownership affiliations with cable operators. HSN quickly became a "made-for-television cultural phenomenon,"[47] earning a 20 percent operating profit on sales of $107 million in its first nine months and reaching about fifteen million subscribers on cable by 1986.

Amid projections that cable home shopping would reach sales of $800 million within another year, competition rapidly followed. Cable Value

---

46. The home shopping network narrative to follow was assembled from Edmund L. Andrews, *After Delay, FTC Allows QVC's Takeover*, N.Y. TIMES, Feb. 4, 1995, at 17; John M. Higgins, *The Heat Is Rising in Home Shopping Wars*, MULTICHANNEL NEWS, Mar. 28, 1993, at 40; John M. Higgins, *FTC Seeks More Antitrust Data on Shopping Nets*, MULTICHANNEL NEWS, Sept. 13, 1993, at 40; J. Lippman, *Home Shopping Rivals Prepare for Merger*, L.A. TIMES, July 13, 1993, at D1; PAUL KAGAN ASSOCIATES, CABLE TV PROGRAMMING, May 31, 1992; Apr. 30, 1991; Feb. 28, 1991; 1990 FCC Cable Report, *supra* note 1, at app. G; L. Zinn, *Home Shoppers Keep Tuning In—But Investors Are Turned Off*, BUS. WEEK, Oct. 22, 1990; L. Brown, *Home Shopping Is Forever*, CHANNELS, Apr. 1987; M. Ivey, *Home Shopping*, BUS. WEEK, Dec. 15, 1986; *Teleshopping: TV's Hottest Ticket*, BROADCASTING, Sept. 1, 1986, at 89; Larry Jaffee, *Thrills and Shills: Home Shopping Net Hawks to Viewers*, CABLEAGE, Sept. 16, 1985, at C7; and Rich Zahradnik, *You Better Shop Around*, MARKETING & MEDIA DECISIONS, Aug. 1986, at 6.

47. *Teleshopping: TV's Hottest Ticket*, BROADCASTING, Sept. 1, 1986, at 89.

Network (CVN) was launched in early 1986 as a joint venture between an entrepreneur and several cable operators, including TCI and Warner Cable. Also in 1986, QVC entered as a publicly traded independent network without initial MSO backing, although it offered small equity shares to MSOs that agreed to carry it. In the same year Time Inc. and Comcast began purchasing stock in QVC. Time also began acquiring CVN stock, and Warner expanded its CVN holdings. Then, in 1987, TCI purchased a 22.7 percent block of QVC's stock. By one estimate, as many as thirty-six home shopping cable networks entered in 1986 and 1987, at least four of which—The Fashion Channel, America's Value Network, Sky Merchant, and America's Shopping Channel—had MSO equity involvement at or soon after their launch. A companion network to HSN, HSN II, was also launched in 1986. By late 1987 CVN and QVC had both overcome HSN's initial lead to become, respectively, the first and second most widely distributed cable shopping networks, with HSN in third position.

In 1989 industry consolidation began. Reportedly at the urging of TCI, QVC acquired CVN that year and merged the two into the largest national cable shopping network. By 1990 the QVC Network reached thirty-five million subscribers to second-place HSN's twenty-one million, and third-place J. C. Penney Shopping Network's ten million. The J. C. Penney Network, which had no history of MSO affiliation, failed, sold its assets to QVC in May 1991, and thus further consolidated QVC's market leadership. In the meantime, the other nationally distributed shopping channels had declined, failed, or been acquired by one of the market leaders. QVC launched its own new network, the QVC Fashion Channel, in 1991.

In early 1992 TCI acquired a controlling stake in the still-independent Home Shopping Networks.[48] In July 1993 QVC Networks, Inc., proposed to acquire a majority share in Home Shopping Networks. The move was investigated and approved by the Justice Department but was delayed by allegations of scandal at HSN and later dropped because QVC was attempting to acquire Paramount Pictures. Finally, in early 1995 the Federal Trade Commission approved a different plan with a similar outcome: the acquisition of 57 percent and 43 percent, respectively, of HSN by Comcast, Inc., and TCI.[49]

The result of the eventful history of cable home shopping networks is that by 1993, cable operators had obtained substantial equity control in all

---

48. That acquisition was actually made by Liberty Media, to which TCI had transferred QVC's stock in the 1991 division of TCI's assets. Those assets then reverted to TCI in its 1994 "remerger" with Liberty Media.

49. Andrews, *supra* note 43.

four of the significant surviving national cable shopping networks: HSN, HSN II, QVC, and QVC Fashion.[50] Of most significance, a single cable operator, TCI, had gained a major equity stake in all four of those networks as of early 1995.

Two observations follow from the home shopping network experience. First, the rapid growth of QVC and CVN, which surpassed that of the market's first and independent entrant, suggests that vertical integration may have had strategic value to QVC and CVN and thus to the MSOs holding equity in those networks.[51] If so, however, that strategic advantage had to be derived from the horizontal market power of the MSOs that supported them. Without such market power, TCI would not have had the leverage to affect the fortunes of QVC and HSN. The home shopping story thus illustrates the fundamentally ancillary role that vertical integration plays in cable networking, as well as the necessity of program buying power at the MSO level for vertical relationships to have any impact on network competition.

The second observation is that although the behavior of TCI, other MSOs, or their vertically affiliated networks might have been anticompetitive, the end result was not necessarily economically harmful to consumers. Of course, the involvement of MSOs in cable home shopping might have reduced competition in that program category below what it otherwise would have been. If so, the net effect of integration would be inefficient as well as detrimental to First Amendment–related objectives.[52] But the pattern of consolidation among competing shopping networks, with survival only of the spinoffs launched by the two existing market leaders, follows the

---

50. QVC Fashion failed, and then another home shopping network, Q2, was launched as a companion network to QVC in 1994.

51. In support of that theory, for example, the chief executive officer of HSN presented numerous examples in congressional testimony of instances in which TCI systems had replaced HSN with QVC before Liberty Media's acquisition of HSN stock. Examining the Effects of Megamergers in the Telecommunications Industry: Hearings Before the Subcomm. on Antitrust, Business Rights, and Competition of the Sen. Comm. on the Judiciary, 103d Cong., 1st Sess. (1988). Testimony of Roy M. Speer, at 422–41. On the other side of that issue were allegations that HSN had been mismanaged.

52. To reach that conclusion, one must also consider the general competitive environment. Cable shopping networks compete with many other retail outlets offering the same or similar products, so one cannot assume that such effects in the cable shopping networking itself are necessarily significant to consumer welfare in general. The Justice Department's approval of QVC's acquisition of HSN and the FTC's later approval of HSN's majority acquisition by Comcast and TCI were apparently based on their conclusions that competition from those other retail outlets was sufficient. Andrews, *supra* note 46.

historical pattern of news, music video, and several other cable programming types. The natural economic forces of economies of scale in networking, cable system preference for dissimilar or counterprogrammed networks, and the cost economies of operating spinoff or companion networks may have made the home shopping outcome largely inevitable.

The main effect of integration may just be to help pick the winners and losers. To that extent, integration's net effects on economic efficiency and the diversity of programming would be minor. Such effects may still, however, have important First Amendment consequences—a subject we consider in chapter 8.

MSO MONOPSONY POWER, FREE RIDING, AND VERTICAL INTEGRATION

If MSOs are able to exert excessive monopsony power, then vertical integration can also have a beneficial effect on consumers by promoting efficiency as well as First Amendment–related objectives. That can occur because vertical integration increases the flow of revenues back to program production, a flow that would otherwise be constricted by the exertion of downstream monopsony power.[53]

Consider the negotiation process by which cable networks and MSOs arrive at input price terms. At least in the absence of vertical ownership, we can expect input price outcomes to vary from MSO to MSO and from network to network according to the relative bargaining power of the negotiating parties. Assume hypothetically that a network has all the bargaining power. In that case an MSO would be willing to pay the full marginal value of adding a given network to its systems. If the bargaining power were entirely with the MSO, however, economic theory predicts that the network would be willing to accept some price as long as that price would at least cover the network's marginal costs of distributing the programming to its local markets. Because there are economies of scale in networking, however, the network's marginal cost of distributing to the MSO would necessarily be below its average cost. Hence, the network would on average have to collect revenues above its marginal sales and distribution costs to cover its first-copy program production costs. It follows that if a particular MSO were to force the input prices of a number of networks below their average costs of distribution, the flow of subscriber revenues to the production

---

53. The following narrative is based on David Waterman, *Local Monopsony and Free Riding*, 8 INFO. ECON. & POL'Y 4 (1996). *See also* the appendix to this chapter.

industry would be significantly constrained, thus reducing the supply of programming.

Assume, to illustrate, that a cable network just covers its total production cost of $1,000 by collecting $10 each from individual cable systems in 100 separate local markets and that the marginal costs of delivering the network by satellite are zero. If the cable systems in ten of those markets formed an MSO and made a credible threat to refuse carriage of the network, it would still be worthwhile for the network to make a deal as long as it could get at least some amount over its $0 marginal cost from the MSO. If the MSO managed to exert that bargaining power over a number of networks, either they would all have to reduce their production costs, or some would have to exit the market, which would reduce the supply of programming available to all other cable markets.

In that sense an MSO can become a free rider on the contributions of other cable systems to the first-copy costs of production. The essence of the free-rider problem is that a price-making MSO ignores an externality effect that its localized exercise of monopsony power imposes on other cable operators, whose profits will fall with the decline in attractiveness of programming that they can offer to consumers. Of course, that monopsonist also suffers a decline in the attractiveness of its programming, but the decline is only in proportion to its share of the national market. In the example, total production investments would fall by only 10 percent. The MSO and the other cable operators could theoretically benefit by restoring the network's programming investment to its former level, but their diffuse ownership affords them no practical mechanism to accomplish that. We illustrate the logic of the free-rider model, which differs in significant respects from the standard textbook monopsony model, in the appendix to this chapter.

An MSO monopsonist has a more profitable alternative to free riding: vertical integration with networks over which it has monopsony power. By integrating, an MSO can effectively internalize the negative externality effect on program supply. By increasing the amount and quality of affected networks' programming back to an optimally profitable level for all MSOs, an integrated MSO benefits in one part from increasing the programming that its own systems have available. By also improving the amount and quality of programming available to other systems to an optimal level, an integrated firm creates value to them, at least some of which the integrated firm can extract in the bargaining process.

In terms of our criteria, the potentially negative effects of MSO monopsony power on social welfare and thus the positive effects of vertical integration are evident. Monopsonistic reduction of input prices in some markets would reduce the quality and quantity of cable programming in all markets and as a consequence program diversity and the access of program-ming suppliers to subscribers. The net effects of MSO monopsony power on economic efficiency are uncertain because local monopsony could, up to a point, countervail excessive market power at the network level and reduce the input prices of programming. Those reductions might in turn be passed on to consumers in the form of lower prices.[54] In the presence of excessive MSO monopsony power, however, vertical integration not only would increase programming investments and diversity, but would result in a more efficient allocation of resources to program production.[55]

We noted in chapter 4 that the tendency for vertical ownership to be more prevalent among larger MSOs was consistent with the greater benefits that those MSOs can derive from transactions and other efficiency benefits of vertical integration. The free-rider model also suggests a rationale for the acquisition strategies Time Warner and TCI have followed since the 1980s: accumulating relatively large national market shares at the facilities level, and at the same time, forming vertical relationships with relatively large numbers of cable networks. Similarly, MSOs' sharing equity in some networks could also be an attempt to limit the incentives by some individual MSOs to exert local monopsony power myopically at the expense of other cable operators.

OTHER STRATEGIC ADVANTAGES OF VERTICAL INTEGRATION

Strategic bargaining is one of the other strategic, though not necessarily anticompetitive, advantages of vertical integration between cable networks and MSOs. An ownership tie between an MSO and one of two relatively similar networks competing for access to an operator's systems, for example, probably gives the MSO an advantage in bargaining with the unaffiliated network. If we assume that an affiliated network implicitly becomes avail-able on the most favorable possible terms after an ownership tie is estab-lished, the unaffiliated network may perceive that if no deal is struck with

---

54. To the extent that two-part tariffs are employed at the input level, a fall in retail prices will not necessarily occur. Both buyer and seller have an incentive to maintain the marginal input price at an efficient level and to bargain over the lump-sum portion of the tariff. Most cable programming supply contracts have specific sliding scales that depend on subscribership volume, an arrangement that can simulate a two-part tariff.

55. That statement presumes that the original "efficient" flow of funds back to production created optimal consumer welfare in terms of program diversity and prices. That is not necessarily the case, however, because of the ambiguous tradeoff between product variety and price.

it, the MSO has less to lose. That obviously increases the MSO's bargaining power over the unaffiliated network.[56]

A likely example of such a strategy is the formation of Spotlight, a premium theatrical movie service, by a consortium of five MSOs in 1980. Spotlight was relatively undifferentiated from HBO, which at that time dominated premium cable networking with a 70 percent market share. Until its demise in 1983, Spotlight was never marketed outside the consortium's systems, a policy that suggests its primary advantage as a bargaining device.

The net effects on program supply of a vertically integrated MSO's strategic bargaining advantages are uncertain. On one hand, reduced revenues and profits of unaffiliated program suppliers would reduce program investment. For reasons discussed above, however, the implicit increase in the flow of revenues back to the production branch within an integrated firm should increase programming investments.[57]

Another strategic motive for MSOs to vertically integrate may be access to programming. MSOs might accumulate programming interests to gain the power to raise barriers to entry by alternative multichannel video programming distributors or to ensure themselves of adequate programming access in the face of competitive challenges by other multichannel video programming distributors. We consider program-access issues more fully in chapters 7 and 8.

CONCLUSION

In this chapter we examined ways in which vertical ownership ties between cable operators and cable programming networks might give cable firms a

---

56. Another way to express the same idea is that if two similar competing networks are able to set input prices so that they earn excess profits before integration, then the duopolistic price coordination necessary to maintain those profits is likely to break down when one of the firms becomes integrated.

57. Michael H. Riordan & David J. Salant, Exclusion and Integration in the Market for Video Programming Delivered to the Home (July 7, 1994; rev. Sept. 12, 1994) (paper presented at AEI Telecommunication Summit), offer a strategic bargaining model of vertical integration between cable systems and cable program packagers (networks) that shows similarly ambiguous effects on the supply of programming owing to the integration. A key difference between their scenario and ours is that in theirs, the strategic bargaining effect is confined to the implicitly reduced input price of programming for an affiliated network because of the elimination of arms-length bargaining, which in turn reduces profits of an unaffiliated network because it then sells less programming to the integrated system. In their model an unaffiliated network does not change its input price in reaction to vertical integration.

strategic advantage in the programming supply industry. Our focus has been on anticompetitive effects that those ownership affiliations could have on the supply of cable programming.

Economic theory and the empirical record suggest that vertical integration is likely to facilitate anticompetitive foreclosure that may occur in the cable networking industry. The history of news, movie, and other cable networking program categories, however, demonstrates that vertical integration is only one among several strategic resources that cable programming networks or their parent companies might employ to establish and defend their market positions in the programming supply industry.

The negative consequences of vertical foreclosure on programming diversity and the access by program suppliers to subscribers are evident. Whatever detrimental effects vertical foreclosure may have are, however, mitigated to the extent that economies of scale in cable networking, incentives toward content differentiation, and other natural economic forces lead over time to the basically similar menus of programming available to consumers.

To be effective, vertical foreclosure in programming supply requires the presence of monopsony power at the MSO level. If monopsony power is excessive, however, vertical integration may have the procompetitive effect of increasing the flow of revenues back to the production industry and thus may increase the supply of cable programming and promote economic efficiency and program diversity.

The analysis in this chapter suggests that any public policies intended to reduce anticompetitive behavior in the programming supply industry should focus on the exercise of monopsony power by MSOs in the programming market rather than on their vertical integration with cable networks.

In the following chapter, we turn to an empirical investigation of how vertical integration affects the programming menus and marketing behavior of cable systems.

APPENDIX: MSO MONOPSONY POWER AND FREE RIDING

This appendix shows graphically how MSOs' exercise of localized monopsony power can negatively affect the supply of cable programming.[58] After setting out some basic assumptions, we define a benchmark model in which

---

58. This appendix is based on Waterman, *supra* note 53, which contains a complete model for the general case of an industry having many of the characteristics of the cable television industry.

no MSOs exist and all cable systems behave as input price takers in the programming market. We then hypothesize a case in which some cable systems become input price makers in the programming market by forming an MSO, an action that allows that MSO to free ride on the payments of other cable systems to the cable program supply industry.

We then describe the bilateral bargaining model that underlies that MSO's presumed ability and incentive to exercise monopsony power with program suppliers. Finally, we show how the localized exercise of monopsony power differs from that of the standard monopsony model.

Assumptions

Let there be M geographically separate local markets, each of which contains a local monopoly cable system. Each of those cable systems offers a menu of N differentiated cable networks to subscribers, at à la carte prices. There is no advertising or basic service.

The cable networks are produced upstream, each at a constant cost, K, but we assume that they can be distributed to local cable systems via satellite at a zero marginal cost. We assume that the networking industry is monopolistically competitive with free entry and exit. Product variety, N^*, is thus determined as an equilibrium condition of the model.

For ease of exposition, we need several symmetry assumptions. Each of the local markets is the same size and has identical demand conditions. Each of the networks, though differentiated, is equally attractive and is distributed symmetrically in some product space.

With respect to consumer demand, the networks are all partial substitutes. Aggregate demand for all networks thus increases as N increases, but we assume that the increase occurs at a decreasing rate. We also assume that the à la carte retail consumer price demands for networks are independent of the number of networks offered.

Initial Equilibrium: Input Price-Taking Behavior of Independently Owned Local Cable Systems

In the initial case, assume that local cable systems, although they have monopoly power in the final market and can make excess profits, are able to exert no market power with program suppliers in the input market.

Panel A of figure 5A-1 describes that industry equilibrium aggregated over all M markets. On the vertical axis is the sum of input payments paid to each network by all M cable systems together. The curve D is the aggregate derived demand for differentiated networks by all M cable systems, given

Figure 5A-1
Initial Equilibrium: Input Price-Taking Behavior by All Local Cable Systems

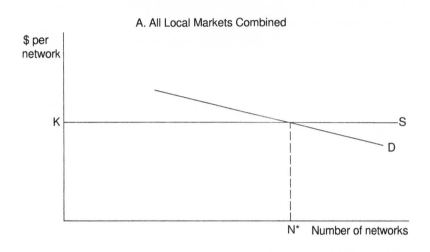

A. All Local Markets Combined

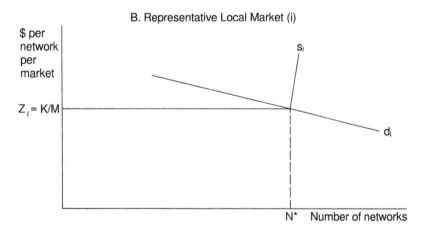

B. Representative Local Market (i)

their costs and the assumed consumer demand conditions. The more substitutable networks are for each other—the more fixed an aggregate subscribership is with respect to N, the steeper D is. Incorporated into D are the monopoly retail prices the system is able to charge subscribers. The supply curve, S, is flat by assumption since new networks can be produced and distributed at constant cost, K.[59] At the aggregate supply-demand equilibrium in panel A, the upstream networking industry produces N^* networks.

Panel B of figure 5A-1 shows the same equilibrium as it is perceived by the ith individual price-taking cable system in a representative local market. The scale of the vertical axis is simply reduced by the factor M so that it indicates the actual input price per network that the cable system pays for each network, labeled Z_i. The per market derived demand, d_i, is identical to D except for the vertical scale. That is, the equilibrium number of networks available in each market is necessarily the same. The supply function, s_i, has a somewhat different shape from that in panel A. As a price taker, the system must pay $Z_i = K/M$ to receive any networks, and so s_i is flat up to N^*. The steep slope upward in s_i after N^* indicates that by offering more than Z_i for each network, system i could theoretically induce entry into networking upstream. That positive effect on network entry would be only in proportion to local system i's share of the national market.

Input Price-Making Behavior by a Single MSO

Imagine now that some number of local cable systems combine into an MSO of size m and that the MSO successfully challenges the price-making behavior of upstream networks. Figure 5A-2 illustrates the negative effect that such behavior would have on the supply of networks available to all cable systems.

Except that the vertical axis scale in panel A of figure 5A-2 is multiplied by a factor of m, the derived demand curve, d_m, is unchanged from d_i. As an input price maker, however, the MSO now perceives a different supply curve for networks, s_m, whose slope is proportional to m/M. If the MSO had all the bargaining power, it could in theory force wholesale price per network down to each network's marginal distribution cost of zero; it is still worthwhile for a network to distribute to the MSO as long as that cost is at least covered. As the curve s_m shows, the MSO's price-making action would negatively affect the supply of networks in proportion to the number of all local cable markets the MSO controls.

The optimal equilibrium input price per network paid by the MSO, Z_m, is determined by the intersection of d_m with MC_m, the curve marginal to s_m. The MC_m function shows the incremental impact on total system outlays for programming as the number of networks purchased by MSO m increases. Optimal input price for the MSO is still greater than zero because the MSO

---

59. That supply curve could slope upward, as is usually assumed, with sacrifice only to the simplicity of the exposition.

Figure 5A-2
Revised Equilibrium: Input Price-Making Behavior by a Single MSO

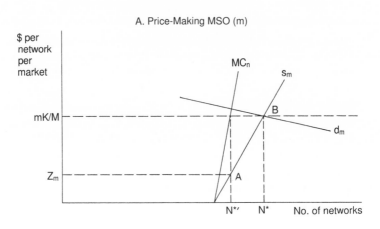

A. Price-Making MSO (m)

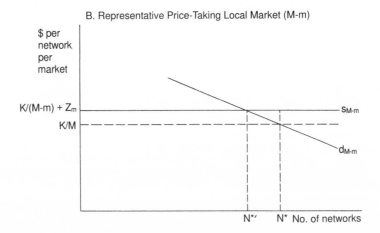

B. Representative Price-Taking Local Market (M-m)

considers the marginal effect of its input price-reducing action on its own supply of programming.

Panel B of figure 5A-2 illustrates the negative externality effect that the MSO's price-making behavior has on all the *M–m* other price-taking cable systems, owing to the fall in the number of networks available to them. For those systems the total input price paid per network by each independent system must rise slightly as N^* falls to N^*. The effective supply curve for those systems thus shifts up to s_{M-m}. It is in that sense that the MSO is a free rider on the larger contributions to production costs made by the independently owned, price-taking cable systems.

If monopsony power were exerted by a number of MSOs in the cable industry, the industry could not function. Each MSO would myopically consider only the slight effect of its own price-making behavior, but the cumulative negative externalities of those actions would essentially put nearly all networks out of business.

At least two factors can mitigate that tendency, however. First, note from panel A of figure 5A-2 that the greater the national market share of an individual MSO, the less is its incentive to free ride; the MSO's perceived supply function, s_m, and with it MC_m, become progressively flatter until 100 percent ownership of all cable systems completely internalizes the externality and eliminates the incentive to exercise monopsony power. If we assume that there are no transactions efficiencies involved, a cartel of vertically integrated MSOs controlling all cable systems and all cable networks will eliminate the free-rider effect.

A second mitigating factor is that the incentive for an MSO to exercise monopsony power does not necessarily imply the ability to do so. We consider that in the following section.

The Role of Bargaining Power

Implicit in the transition between the price-taker and the price-maker models above is the hypothesis that forming coalitions of local monopoly cable systems across geographic markets gives an MSO the necessary bargaining power for it to become a price maker. Specifically:

$$Z^e = Z^{pm} + g(Z^{pm} - Z^{pt}),$$

where $0 < g < 1$, and g is a decreasing function of m/M, the national market share of an MSO, and an increasing function of n/N, the market share of an upstream network or commonly owned networks in a given negotiation. The superscript indicates the equilibrium solution, and p^m and p^t indicate the price-maker and price-taker values, respectively. That model follows from the basic postulate of bargaining theory that a party's bargaining power in a bilateral game is inversely related to how much that party has to lose if no deal is struck. Other things equal, an MSO's bargaining power will increase as its share of the national market rises because the proportion of net revenues or profits that a cable network or commonly owned network group stands to lose if no deal is struck increases, while that of an MSO does not.

The basis for the price-taking model of figure 5A-1 is that although any individual local cable system is the only outlet for networks in its local market area, a cable network would be unlikely to respond to a bargaining threat from that system if its refusal to carry the network would have an insignificant effect on the network's total revenues. Such extreme price-taking behavior is unrealistic, as is the extreme price-making behavior illustrated in figure 5A-2. In effect, the supply function in panel A of figure 5A-2 describes only the potential contract curve that an MSO and a cable network or networks face in their input determination process; the actual input price could range anywhere from point *A* to point *B*.

As an MSO becomes larger, two opposing forces are at work: increased bargaining power—and thus greater ability to force the input price downward—and an increase in its optimal input price, since a larger MSO internalizes a greater proportion of the negative externality that its price-making behavior would have on the supply of programming. The actual balance of those two opposite forces as an MSO becomes larger is an empirical question. It is reasonable, however, that MSOs within a certain size range would have both the incentive and the ability to force input prices, and thus the supply of programming, below a socially optimal level.[60]

Comparison with the Standard Monopsony Model

The free-rider model differs from the standard textbook monopsony model in important respects. Figure 5A-3 shows the standard model. The single buyer of some input, X (assume labor, within a small geographic area), has demand for the input, D_x, which slopes downward simply because the lower the input price (the wage) the firm has to pay, the more workers it can profitably employ. The monopsonist also faces a supply curve for the labor, S_x, which slopes upward because of inelasticity in its supply; the more local workers the firm seeks to employ, the higher the wage required to hire a marginal worker. The curve MC_x is the curve marginal to S_x, and shows the marginal wage the firm must pay for additional workers. In equilibrium the monopsonist will set the marginal input price equal to its demand for the

---

60. Waterman, *supra* note 53, formally shows that the exercise of monopsony power may enhance welfare by moving the level of product variety toward its optimal level, but that after a certain point, its excessive exercise will unambiguously reduce welfare. In the latter case, vertical integration or cartel behavior will increase welfare by restoring the level of product variety toward the welfare optimum.

Figure 5A-3
Standard Monopsony Model

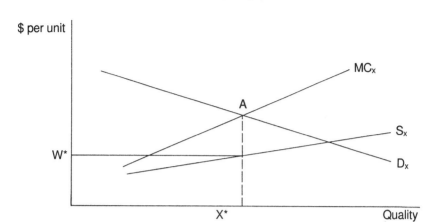

input, indicated by point A. That quantity of workers can be had for only W_x^*, however, as indicated by the supply function, S_x. In the standard model a monopsonist has an incentive to inefficiently restrict the total quantity of the labor purchased because it considers not only the wage paid to the marginal worker but the higher wages that will have to be paid to all its other workers.

In the free-rider model an MSO controlling less than 100 percent of the national market also perceives an upward sloping supply curve for its input, cable programming networks. Unlike the standard model, that supply curve does not slope upward because of higher marginal costs of input resources; as panel A of figure 5A-1 indicates, the supply of programming inputs is assumed to be perfectly elastic. The basic incentive to exercise monopsony power in the free-rider model arises because the average cost diverges from the marginal cost of input distribution and because a geographically localized firm does not bear the full burden of input price reductions.

A second difference between the free-rider model and standard treatments of monopsony is the effects of monopsony on final prices and economic welfare. The appropriate standard model for comparison in that case is one of bilateral monopoly: a market in which a downstream firm with monopsony power faces an upstream firm with monopoly power. Lower prices and higher welfare may result from greater monopsony power in that circumstance to the extent that the upstream firm is forced to reduce marginal input prices below what it would have charged to a competitive downstream firm.[61] Output prices are not necessarily reduced by the exertion of monopsony power, however, if two-part input tariffs are used.[62] In the free-rider model as presented, the exertion of monopsony power does not affect output prices because we assume that perfectly efficient, two-part input tariffs are employed and that output prices are independent of changes in product variety in the demand function. Welfare in the free-rider model is thus changed only by changes in product variety.

---

61. F. M. SCHERER & D. ROSS, INDUSTRIAL MARKET STRUCTURE AND ECONOMIC PERFORMANCE (3d ed., Rand McNally 1990).

62. *See* ROGER D. BLAIR & JEFFREY L. HARRISON, MONOPSONY (Princeton University Press 1993), for a related argument.

6

Empirical Effects of Vertical Integration in Cable

CHAPTERS 4 AND 5 suggest several reasons why cable operators having vertical ownership affiliations with cable networks are likely to behave differently from those that do not. In this chapter we investigate statistically whether vertical integration has an influence on final market outcomes at the cable system level. Specifically, we use econometric techniques, supplemented with some descriptive data, to analyze the effects of integration on the menus of cable networks that systems carry and on how systems price and promote those networks to subscribers. On the basis of the motives for integration we set forth in chapters 4 and 5, we then discuss likely reasons for such effects.

We address the following primary questions.

- To what extent, if any, do integrated systems tend to favor vertically affiliated networks in terms of more frequent carriage or by means of preferential pricing or promotion? Of particular interest, do unaffiliated networks tend to be excluded or otherwise disadvantaged on integrated systems?

- How does integration affect the total number of cable networks offered by systems?

- How do our findings for high-capacity cable systems—fifty-four or more channels—differ when compared with systems as a whole?

We chose to analyze the fifty-four or more channel benchmark separately because it generally represents state-of-the-art cable technology. To the extent that our findings differ for large channel systems, we gain insight into whether the effects of integration are likely to diminish as subscriber choices expand—possibly to hundreds of channels with video compression or to even larger video-on-demand libraries.

The primary database for our econometric analysis is the A. C. Nielsen Cable On-Line Data Exchange. We employ a subset of 1,646 cable systems owned by the largest twenty-five MSOs as of mid-1989. Considering only systems in those MSOs allows us to compare integrated-system behavior with that of a large, presumably comparable group of nonintegrated systems. Those twenty-five MSOs accounted for essentially all vertical ownership relations with substantial nationally distributed cable networks in 1989, as well as for approximately 59 percent of all U.S. basic cable subscribers.

The Nielsen database contains a variety of demand-side, cost-related, and institutional data for franchise areas; carriage and other information for twelve individual integrated cable networks (four premium, six basic, and two hybrid networks);[1] and summary data for how many basic, pay, and PPV networks were carried in total.[2] We augment those data with descriptive information collected in 1993 and 1994.

Answers to the empirical questions we address in this chapter do not provide a complete picture of the differences in cable system menus or in cable firm behavior that may exist. Also, to determine whether differences we do observe are caused by transactions efficiencies or by anticompetitive behavior would require more data than we have available. We are nonetheless able to make useful measurements of the extent to which vertical integration does matter and to determine whether policy makers' concerns about both "favoritism" of affiliated networks and reduced programming diversity have any basis. Those measurements, and our interpretations of their likely causes, complete the basis for our policy discussion of vertical integration and cable programming supply in chapter 8.

Our analysis shows that cable television systems do tend to favor their affiliated cable networks. At least in some cases, that favoritism is at the expense of rival, unaffiliated networks. We also find that integrated systems tend to carry fewer cable networks. Those differences in the numbers of networks carried, however, are mostly small or statistically insignificant. We conclude that the predominant measurable result of vertical integration is that integrated cable systems tend to substitute their own similar affiliated networks for unaffiliated networks on their programming menus. Our results

---

1. Hybrid networks are those offered as a basic service by some systems and as a premium service by others.

2. Details of the database, including variable definitions, averages by MSO, and sources of ownership information, appear in the appendix to this chapter.

suggest that that tendency is likely to persist as system channel capacities expand, although that its extent will diminish.

We consider nationally distributed basic, premium, and PPV networks in our analysis. We begin with premium networks, for which more complete data and analysis are available.

PREMIUM NETWORKS

Our analysis covers the four largest integrated movie-based networks: HBO, Cinemax, Showtime, and TMC. The econometric results we report here combine new analysis with selected findings from an earlier study of ours;[3] all use the Nielsen database.

Those four networks had basically the same vertical affiliations at the time of our 1989 analysis as shown in table 3-1 for 1995.[4] In 1989, ATC accounted for 7.1 percent of U.S. basic subscribers. Paragon, in which Time Inc., ATC's corporate parent, had acquired a 50 percent unconsolidated interest in 1987, had 1.6 percent of subscribers. Viacom, Inc., the sole owner of Showtime and TMC, accounted for 2.5 percent of subscribers. Premium subscription market shares of the four networks were: HBO, 42 percent; Showtime, 16.5 percent; Cinemax, 14.9 percent; and TMC, 6.8 percent.

Our key assumption in choosing to analyze those networks was that since all primarily offered recent theatrical feature films, they were relatively close substitutes in the eyes of subscribers. It is thus of particular interest to learn not only whether ATC, Viacom, and Paragon favored their own affiliated premium networks, but whether any such favoritism was at the expense of rival networks.

Carriage of Premium Networks

The systems in individual MSOs vary substantially in their demographic and other characteristics—notably channel capacities and numbers of homes passed. Higher per capita income or higher channel capacity, for example, can be expected to increase the likelihood of a pay network's carriage on any given system, independent of its ownership. It would thus be misleading

---

3. David Waterman & Andrew A. Weiss, *The Effects of Vertical Integration Between Cable Television Systems and Pay Cable Networks: 1988–1989*, 72 J. ECONOMETRICS 357 (1996).

4. But ATC, the MSO then affiliated with HBO and Cinemax, had not yet come under common ownership with Warner Cable through the late 1989 Time Inc.–Warner Communications merger.

simply to examine descriptive data showing whether integrated MSOs tend to carry affiliates and rivals more or less frequently than does the average nonintegrated MSO. A multivariate model is therefore appropriate.

The basic procedure we use to isolate the effects of system ownership on carriage decisions is as follows. For each network, we estimate the probability that each system in the sample carries the network. Those probabilities are specified as a function of whether Viacom, ATC, or Paragon owned the system as well as relevant exogenous factors such as average per capita income, homes passed, and channel capacity. We then use a form of the estimated models to predict the effects of ownership on the percentage of systems in each MSO that offer each network. The details appear in the appendix to this chapter.

The first column of table 6-1 gives estimates of the percentage of ATC- and Viacom-owned systems that carry the indicated network.[5] The second column gives estimates of the percentage of systems in the MSO that we would expect to carry the network if the MSO were not integrated—given the particular demographics, channel capacities, and other characteristics of the systems. The third column gives the differences between the first two columns as well as the absolute values of the *t*-ratios for those differences. A negative sign for the difference indicates that a network is actually carried by the MSO's systems more frequently than the demographic and other exogenous variables would predict and vice versa. We could make no statistical estimates in cases in which either all or none of the systems in an MSO carried the network.[6]

For ATC and Viacom systems, table 6-1 shows significant differences for all cases for which we could make estimates. The effects are particularly large for the "companion" networks, Cinemax and TMC. The systems of those MSOs thus have a tendency to carry their own networks more frequently and to carry rivals less frequently than does the average noninteg- rated system.[7]

---

5. To calculate statistical margins of error for our results, "actual" carriage is estimated by the model rather than simply reported from the available descriptive data. Since those numbers are typically within 1 percent of the true carriage, there is little practical difference.

6. We indicate such cases with "(n)." Since there was no evidence of carriage differences for Paragon—Time's 50 percent–owned affiliate—we generated no predic- tions for that MSO.

7. Our findings are generally consistent with those of preliminary econometric studies of the effects of vertical integration involving the same premium networks: Michael A. Salinger, A Test of Successive Monopoly and Foreclosure Effects: Vertical Integration

Table 6-1
Effects of Vertical Integration on Premium Network Carriage

	Actual Carriage (%)	Normal Carriage (%)	Difference (%) (2) − (1)	
		All Systems		
ATC (109 systems)				
HBO	98.2	98.2	—	
Cinemax	91.0	77.6	−13.4[a]	(5.2)
Showtime	46.7	85.1	+38.5[a]	(8.1)
TMC	12.2	51.9	+39.7[a]	(13.2)
Viacom (20 systems)				
HBO	98.4	98.4	—	
Cinemax	14.6	74.7	+60.1[a]	(7.8)
Showtime	80.7	80.7	—	
TMC	85.1	49.9	−35.2[a]	(5.0)
		54 plus Channel Systems Only		
ATC (14 systems)				
HBO	100.0	(n)	(n)	
Cinemax	100.0	(n)	(n)	
Showtime	64.9	95.5	+30.5[a]	(2.3)
TMC	21.4	84.5	+63.1[a]	(5.7)
Viacom (2 systems)				
HBO	100.0	(n)	(n)	
Cinemax	0	(n)	(n)	
Showtime	100.0	(n)	(n)	
TMC	100.0	(n)	(n)	

Notes: (n) designates percentages that could not be estimated. A dash indicates that we made no prediction because the model coefficient was statistically insignificant. *t*-ratios are in parentheses.
a. Significant at the .05 level (two-tailed test).

Table 6-1 also shows that on ATC's fifty-four-plus channel systems, carriage of HBO and Cinemax was 100 percent, but those systems had significant tendencies to carry Showtime and TMC less frequently than the average nonintegrated system. There were only two fifty-four-plus Viacom systems in our sample. Both carried HBO, Showtime, and TMC, but neither

Between Cable Systems and Pay Services (1988) (unpublished manuscript, Columbia University Graduate School of Business), using data from the 1987 CABLE TV FACTBOOK; David Waterman, Andrew A. Weiss & T. Valente, Vertical Integration of Cable Television Systems with Pay Cable Networks: An Empirical Analysis (paper presented at the Telecommunications Policy Research Conference, Airlie, Va., Oct. 1–3, 1989), using 1983 data from Paul Kagan Associates.

Figure 6-1

Carriage of Rival Premium Cable Networks on ATC Systems
by Channel Capacity

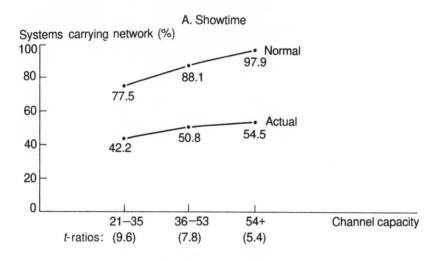

A. Showtime

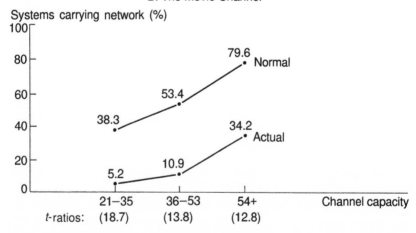

B. The Movie Channel

Notes: Sample includes 109 systems: 29 with 21–35 channels; 64 with 36–53 channels; 14 with 54+ channels; and 2 with 12–20 channels (no estimates made). The *t*-ratios measure the significance of the difference between the normal and actual predictions.

Table 6-2
Carriage of Major Integrated Premium Networks, December 3, 1991

	ATC (106 systems)	Viacom (13 systems)
HBO	100%	100%
Cinemax	100%	30%
Showtime	52%	100%
TMC	9%	92%

Source: Paul Kagan Associates, *Kagan Cable TV Census* (1992) (derived).

carried Cinemax. Figure 6-1 illustrates a more detailed channel-capacity–dependent analysis of Showtime and TMC carriage on ATC systems. We plot separate statistical estimates of actual versus normal carriage of these two networks for three different channel capacity categories, including the fifty-four-plus group.

Although some of the estimates in figure 6-1 are based on relatively small samples, they suggest some important points. First, a substantial difference between actual and normal carriage rates persists as channel capacity expands. The actual percentages of ATC systems carrying Showtime and TMC, however, grow higher for larger capacity systems. Those results suggest that as channel capacities expand, vertically integrated cable systems are likely to increase carriage of all networks, including rivals. The results do not provide evidence, however, that higher channel capacities will eliminate incentives for vertically integrated systems to exclude rival networks. For example, although the predicted normal carriage of Showtime on fifty-four-plus ATC systems had reached virtually 100 percent, little more than half those systems actually carry that rival network.

Finally, available descriptive data in table 6-2, collected just before ATC systems were consolidated with Warner Cable systems after the Time Warner merger, suggest a continuation in carriage rate differences for the four major premium networks on the integrated MSOs.

Pricing and Promotion of Premium Networks

Carriage data provide an incomplete picture of vertical integration's effects on premium networks. In particular, even if both affiliated and unaffiliated networks are carried, an integrated system might price them differently to subscribers. Personal selling and other marketing tactics offer other opportunities for system operators to favor one available network over another.

For example, cable systems frequently offer promotional discounts for certain premium networks to induce consumers to sign up for basic service.

To determine the net effects of any differences in pricing or other marketing behavior, we compare subscribership to the four premium networks on integrated and nonintegrated systems. We make those comparisons by using a prediction methodology similar to that of our carriage comparisons. The basic models are regression equations, and we allow several additional explanatory variables. Those include variables for whether each of the other three subject networks was carried and for the length of time that each of the four subject networks had been carried.[8]

Table 6-3 reports actual and normal subscribership penetration predictions for ATC and Viacom systems, where penetration is subscribership divided by the number of homes passed. In six of the eight cases, subscribership is significantly higher for affiliated networks and lower for unaffiliated networks than we would expect if the systems in question were not integrated. In the other two cases the effects are minor and are based on very small samples because of both the infrequency of carriage events and data limitations. For the most part, those subscribership results suggest that integrated systems also tend to favor their affiliated premium networks in pricing and promotion behavior.

BASIC AND HYBRID NETWORKS

For each of the six basic and two hybrid networks for which we had data, we followed a statistical procedure similar to the one we used for the premium networks. A central difference between the present analysis and that for premium networks is that we make no a priori assumptions about which other networks might be close substitutes for the networks at hand. Hence, while the models for the premium networks included variables for ownership of presumed rivals, those for the basic and hybrid networks included only variables for MSOs having a 5 percent or greater equity

---

8. We also directly estimated the effects of vertical integration on published à la carte subscription prices of each of the four premium networks on ATC, Viacom, and Paragon systems. Except in one case, however, we did not find statistically significant differences in those prices. (The prices charged by ATC systems for TMC were significantly lower than would be expected if they had behaved as the average nonintegrated system, but that result was based on data from only four systems.) One explanation for the neutral price results is that vertical integration has little effect on prices. The more frequently significant results for subscribership that we report, however, suggest either that published à la carte prices do not reflect true prices or that nonprice marketing behavior is more important.

Table 6-3
Subscribership Penetration Model Predictions

	Actual Penetration (%)	Normal Penetration (%)	Difference (%)		Number of Systems
ATC (109 systems)					
HBO	20.7	14.9	−5.8[a]	(3.8)	50
Cinemax	9.3	6.4	−2.9[a]	(12.9)	45
Showtime	5.1	6.0	1.0[a]	(4.7)	18
TMC	4.1	3.9	−0.2[a]	(2.5)	4
Viacom (20 systems)					
HBO	12.8	15.7	2.9[a]	(2.0)	10
Cinemax	7.5	7.0	−0.5	(0.1)	2
Showtime	9.1	6.9	−2.2[a]	(4.8)	10
TMC	4.7	3.4	−1.3[a]	(6.1)	8

Note: *t*-ratios are in parentheses.
a. Significant at the .05 level (two-tailed test).

ownership in a network. Thus, we are comparing carriage of the subject networks on systems in MSOs having equity ownership with carriage on all other systems.

We report predictions of actual and normal carriage rates by the vertically affiliated MSOs for each network in table 6-4. In two of the fifteen cases considered, there was 100 percent carriage of the network obtained. In the thirteen testable cases, nine showed significantly higher actual carriage than the normal; two differences were insignificant; and in the remaining two cases, carriage by the integrated MSO was significantly lower than the normal. The last differences, however, were among the least extreme of the group.

Our available data are neither a complete nor a random sample of integrated basic cable networks. In 1990 the FCC noted that thirteen of the twenty-four most widely available commercial basic cable networks as of May 1990—including AMC but not Bravo and CVN[9]— had vertical ownership ties to MSOs.[10] A comparison of those data with our sample suggests that the seven listed by the FCC for which we did not have data tended to be

9. CVN had merged with QVC into a single network by that date.

10. Competition, Rate Deregulation and the Commission's Policies Relating to the Provision of Cable Television Service, Report, MM Dkt. No. 89-600, FCC 90-276, 67 Rad. Reg. 2d (P&F) 1771 (1990), app. G, at 8.

Table 6-4
Carriage of Basic and Hybrid Networks by Vertically Affiliated MSOs

Network/MSO	Number of Systems	Actual Carriage (%)	Normal Carriage (%)	Difference (%)	
CVN					
TCI	406	72.3	26.4	−45.9[a]	(18.3)
Warner	89	78.2	33.0	−45.2[a]	(11.2)
AMC					
TCI	406	64.6	21.7	−42.9[a]	(15.3)
Cablevision Systems	24	91.7	32.0	−59.7[a]	(11.3)
BET					
TCI	406	18.0	22.4	4.4[a]	(2.3)
ATC	109	56.1	38.8	−17.3[a]	(4.1)
QVC					
Comcast	33	100.0	(n)	(n)	(n)
ATC	109	9.8	16.4	6.6[a]	(2.3)
TCI	406	17.2	12.9	−4.3[b]	(1.9)
Discovery					
Cox	27	100.0	(n)	(n)	(n)
Metrovision	22	76.9	84.1	7.2	(0.8)
TCI	406	86.1	71.8	−14.3[a]	(7.7)
MTV					
Viacom	20	90.0	85.4	−4.6	(1.3)
VH-1					
Viacom	20	80.5	47.4	−33.1[a]	(5.7)
Bravo					
Cablevision Systems	24	71.1	21.6	−49.5[b]	(7.0)

Notes: (n) designates percentages that could not be estimated. *t*-ratios are in parentheses.
a. Significant at the .05 level (two-tailed test).
b. Significant at the .10 level (two-tailed test).

larger and more commonly carried on cable systems.[11] Our analysis is likely to overstate the integrated versus nonintegrated carriage differences for basic networks in general, since more widespread basic networks would be less

---

11. The seven integrated networks not included in our analysis, with their subscriber percentage reach in parentheses, were: CNN (97.0), WTBS (96.0), Nickelodeon/Nick at

Table 6-5
MSO Carriage of Owned Networks

Network	MSO with Ownership Interest in Network	Carriage % by Systems with Network Ownership Interest	Carriage % by Systems without Network Ownership Interest	Difference in Carriage (%)
AMC	CVS, TCI	85.1	73.0	12.1
BET	TCI, T/W	47.1	47.0	0.0
CNN	(a)	99.5	98.2	1.4
Discovery	TCI, Cox, Newhouse	99.0	95.1	4.0
USA	Viacom	100.0	97.3	2.7
TNN	Gaylord Broadcasting[a]	—	—	—
Family	TCI	96.2	95.6	0.6
WTBS	(a)	95.9	96.7	−0.9
Nickelodeon	Viacom	100.0	92.3	7.7
TNT	(a)	99.1	92.3	6.7
MTV	Viacom	100.0	86.9	13.1
HLN	(a)	82.0	73.7	8.3
VH1	Viacom	100.0	72.5	27.5
QVC	(b)	84.4	64.9	19.6
Encore[b]	TCI	84.8	15.8	69.0
Bravo[b]	CVS	86.7	21.4	65.2

Notes: Group (a) includes Time Warner, TCI, Cablevision Systems, Comcast, Continental, Jones, Lenfest, Sammons, Times Mirror, TKR, Viacom, Telecable, and Scripps Howard. Group (b) includes Comcast, TCI, Time Warner, Cablevision Systems, Colony, Continental, Newhouse, Sammons, Times Mirror, and Viacom.
a. According to the 1994 *Jerrold Television and Cable Factbook*, Gaylord Broadcasting Co. owns cable systems serving approximately 63,000 subscribers in Riverside, California, Lenoir, North Carolina, and Greer, South Carolina. None of those three systems was in the commission's random sample.
b. Hybrid services (offered both as basic and as premium).
Source: Economists, Inc. (1994, app. G, table 13).

likely to have significantly different carriage rates on vertically affiliated than on unaffiliated cable systems.

In table 6-5 descriptive data for a group of sixteen integrated basic and hybrid networks collected in 1993 and 1994 suggest the same general pattern

Nite (90.6), The Family Channel (87.5), Lifetime (83.8), TNT (79.3), and Headline News (74.5). The reported reach of those we included were: MTV (89.8), Discovery Channel (88.6), VH-1 (61.7), QVC (60.4), BET (48.0), and AMC (46.4).

of higher carriage rates for integrated networks. In fourteen of the sixteen cases, systems having a vertical affiliation carried the network more frequently. Those data also suggest a tendency for higher total carriage rates to be associated with lower carriage differences between MSOs with and without ownership affiliations. In seven of the eight cases in which table 3-1 indicates a network had at least 90 percent cable household coverage overall, carriage rates exceeded 90 percent on both the affiliated and unaffiliated MSOs.[12] Conversely, the four networks having the largest carriage differences—VH-1, QVC, Bravo, and Encore—had among the lowest total carriage rates.

Although the data are less complete than for premium networks, the weight of evidence is that MSOs integrated with basic and hybrid networks also tend to favor those networks by carrying them more frequently than the average nonintegrated system. The differences appear to be very minor, however, for more widely distributed basic networks.

THE NUMBER OF NETWORKS CARRIED

We also used the Nielsen data sample to investigate the relationship between the extent of an MSO's vertical integration into networking and the total number of networks offered on its systems. We statistically estimated separate models for the number of nationally distributed basic, premium, and PPV networks, and for the combined total of those three network types.

The basic indicators of ownership are the actual number of networks in which an MSO had at least a 5 percent equity interest and a yes-or-no indicator of whether it had a 5 percent or greater interest in any network. In the basic and total models we also used a variable indicating whether an MSO had a 20 percent or greater interest in any network. We used linear regression models for the basic and total variables and ordered probit models for the premium and PPV variables.

The results appear in table 6-6. We report the estimated marginal effects of network ownership on carriage, with separate estimates for all systems and for fifty-four-plus channel systems only. Consider, for example, the effect of the total number of cable networks owned on the total number of networks carried. The −.05 statistic for all systems indicates that, other things being equal, each additional cable network with which a cable system is vertically integrated leads, on average, to a decline in the number of cable networks carried of one-twentieth of a network. The −.97 effect for fifty-four-

---

12. Those eight networks were CNN, Discovery, USA, Family Channel, WTBS, Nickelodeon, TNT, and MTV, which is the exception.

Table 6-6
Marginal Effects of Vertical Integration on the Numbers of Networks Carried

	All Systems		54-Plus Channel Systems Only	
Basic networks (advertiser supported)				
Number of network affiliations	.01	(0.7)	−.07	(1.3)
Affiliated with any basic network	.17	(1.1)	−.59	(1.7)[a]
Affiliated with any basic networks (20% or more)	−.05	(0.3)	−.46	(1.4)
Premium networks				
Number of premium network affiliations[b]	−.27(4.2)[c]/−.23(5.4)[c]		−.36(2.2)[c]/−.29(2.5)[c]	
Affiliated with any premium networks	−.32	(4.2)[c]	−.28	(1.3)
PPV networks				
Affiliated with any PPV networks (5% or more)	−.01	(0.3)	−.14	(1.2)
All cable networks (basic + pay + PPV)				
Total number of network affiliations	−.05	(2.5)[c]	−.15	(2.6)[c]
Affiliated with any cable networks	−.23	(1.2)	−.97	(2.1)[c]
Affiliated with any cable networks (20% or more)	−.19	(1.1)	−.79	(2.0)[c]

Notes: We include all affiliations 5% or more, except where noted. *t*-ratios are in parentheses.
a. Significant at the .10 level (two-tailed test).
b. Marginal effect of 0 to 1 affiliation / 1 to 2 affiliation.
c. Significant at the .05 level (two-tailed test).

plus channel systems of the yes-or-no, 5 percent or more equity affiliation with any network means that when demographics, channel capacity, and all other things are equal, large integrated systems as a group tended to carry about one less network than did nonintegrated large systems as a group.

For premium and PPV networks, we estimate the marginal effects of affiliation by a method similar to that in the carriage equations for individual networks. As a result of the inherent nonlinearity of the underlying ordered probit models, the effects differ according to the actual number of affiliated networks. For the fifty-four-plus channel systems, affiliation with one premium network leads to an average decline of .36 in the number of premium networks carried and affiliation with a second network leads to a further decline of .29.

Several points emerge from table 6-6. First, the signs of nearly all coefficients are negative. Although only some of the coefficients are statis-

Table 6-7
Mean Numbers of Networks Carried by the Systems in the Nielsen Sample

	Full Sample (1,604 systems)	54-Plus Channel Systems Only (269 systems)
Basic (advertiser supported)	17.0	21.8
Premium	4.3	5.9
PPV	.3	1.0
Combined cable networks	21.6	28.7

tically significant and the signs and magnitudes of insignificant coefficients should not be taken as definitive, the generally negative pattern of those signs is of interest. The data thus suggest that integration tends to reduce cable network carriage.

The magnitudes of the negative effects on cable network carriage, however, are mostly quite small. As table 6-7 shows, the average total numbers of cable networks carried for all 1,604 systems and for all 269 systems with fifty-four-plus channels in the sample were 21.6 and 28.7, respectively. Yet an average system would have to have twenty network affiliations to reduce that total by one network. The effects appear to be smallest for basic cable networks as a group and insignificant for the relatively sparsely offered PPV networks.

The effects were largest for premium networks. For example, systems in MSOs affiliated with two premium networks carried an average of .5 fewer premium networks in total. Those data are consistent with findings of our earlier econometric study that both Viacom and ATC cable systems carried significantly fewer of the four major movie-based premium networks than the average nonintegrated cable system.[13]

Another point of interest from table 6-6 is that the marginal effects of ownership on carriage are consistently negative for systems with fifty-four-plus channels, as well as for the sample as a whole. One might expect higher channel capacity to have the opposite effect.[14] Again, however, keep in mind

13. We found Viacom systems to carry, on average, .27 fewer of the four major movie-based networks (3.05 normal versus 2.78 actual; $t = 3.4$) and ATC systems to carry .63 fewer of those four (3.13 normal versus 2.50 actual; $t = 12.0$). *See* Waterman & Weiss, *supra* note 3.

14. The more negative effects on total network carriage in larger systems may occur because on larger capacity systems, the marginal profit to a system from carrying any individual network is lower, which increases the likelihood that marginal networks will be excluded owing to a change in carriage costs or other factors.

that other things being equal, the probability of carrying all networks still increases with higher channel capacity. Those results nevertheless show no tendency for channel abundance to eliminate the incentives of vertically integrated cable systems to reduce the number of available cable networks.

SUMMARY OF RESULTS

While our data are incomplete, we find that vertically integrated cable systems tend to favor the programming with which they have ownership ties, either by more frequent carriage of those networks than would otherwise be expected or, at least in the case of premium networks, by lower pricing or more vigorous marketing of their affiliated programming. For the four integrated premium networks our results suggest that integration also tends to disadvantage rival premium networks—the relatively close substitutes— either because of relatively infrequent carriage of rival networks or, if rivals are carried, because of less advantageous marketing of them. Available data suggest that carriage differences are relatively minor for many basic and hybrid networks, especially those better established in the market.

We also find that vertically integrated cable systems tended to offer fewer numbers of cable networks to subscribers. Those differences were small for all cable networks as a group, however, and were largely insignificant for affiliated basic and PPV networks. Although we did not directly determine that more frequent carriage of affiliated basic networks results in less frequent carriage of unaffiliated basic networks, the marginally negative or neutral effects of integration on the total numbers of basic networks carried imply that conclusion.

Finally, we did not find evidence that higher channel capacities eliminate the tendency for vertically integrated cable systems either to exclude rival networks or to carry fewer cable networks overall. The probabilities of carriage of all cable networks on integrated systems, including rival networks, do, however, increase as channel capacity expands.

INTERPRETATIONS

What do those results imply about the effects vertical integration has on consumers with regard to efficiency and First Amendment–related objectives? One could attribute the general pattern of network carriage and subscribership observed to the foreclosure models discussed in chapter 5. That is, we might observe an integrated MSO to carry its affiliated networks more frequently and rivals less frequently if integrated networks were using their vertical ties with one or more MSOs anticompetitively. Such behavior could also explain why integrated cable systems that do carry rivals' networks tend to favor their own programming by means of preferential pricing or promotion. A likely outcome of such strategic behavior would also be that integrated systems carry fewer networks in total.

Our findings have other explanations, however, that are positive for consumers. In particular, the results are consistent with the pursuit of transactions efficiencies and thus greater economic efficiency.

Transactions Efficiencies

To show that transactions efficiencies could be responsible for the effects of vertical integration we observe, consider the following abstract example. Two comparable premium cable networks, A and B, are partial substitutes—one or both of them candidates for carriage by a certain local cable system. As table 6-8 illustrates, the initial, nonintegrated case posits a hypothetical equilibrium in which each network charges the system $3 per subscriber and the system faces a $2 per subscriber marketing and billing cost. We hypothesize that given subscriber demand and those costs, $10 is the system's optimal retail price for both networks. Profits for both networks are positive, even after subtracting a $400 per network carriage cost. We assume that total system profits would not be increased by eliminating either network. The per channel cost is fixed with respect to the number of subscribers and represents the cost of maintaining and marketing an extra channel and contracting with the network, plus the opportunity costs of not carrying some third network that is also available.

Now imagine that the system integrates with network A and that because of transactions efficiencies, the real, implicit input price for A falls to $1.[15] The system then has an incentive to lower the retail price of A since its marginal profits are higher on sales of that network. We hypothesize that the system's optimal strategy is to lower the price of A to $8 but that the optimal price for B remains $10. The other data for the integrated case in table 6-8 show the results. Subscribers shift to A, some from network B and some from other sources. Profits from A rise, but profits from B become negative. It is thus profitable for the system to exclude B altogether.[16]

Of course, our example shows only one possible result of integration. Practically anything could happen because of the initial $2 fall in input price.

---

15. In effect, any reduction of risk, asymmetric incentives, or contracting effort can be thought of as a fall in that input price.

16. That will, of course, shift more demand from B to A and increase the profit attributable to A in table 6-8.

Table 6-8
Hypothetical Illustration of Efficiency Motives for Network Exclusion

	Initial Case		After Integration	
	A	*B*	*A*	*B*
Network				
Retail price	$10	$10	$8	$10
Subscribers	100	100	150	75
Total system revenue	$1,000	$1,000	$1,200	$750
Input price per subscriber	$3	$3	$1	$3
System selling cost per subscriber	$2	$2	$2	$2
Total system cost per subscriber	$500	$500	$450	$375
Carriage cost per network	$400	$400	$400	$400
Total system profit	$100	$100	$350	($25)

The operator, for example, might also want to change the retail price of *B*, which would have secondary effects on price and subscribership of *A*, and so forth. Or the rival network might react to the system's integration with *A* by also reducing *B*'s input price.[17] In fact, one can construct examples in which integration serves to increase the amount of programming carried by making it profitable to carry certain networks that are otherwise excluded because of the higher costs of arms-length transactions.[18]

The numerical example nevertheless illustrates a consistent, transactions efficiencies–based explanation for our main empirical results. Under reasonable assumptions, an initial increase in efficiency due to integration can increase the likelihood that integrated cable operators will carry affiliated networks and can reduce the likelihood of unaffiliated network carriage as well as the total number of networks offered.

---

17. In a formal analysis of the effects of partial vertical integration by a multiproduct monopolist, Salinger shows that few end results can be ruled out theoretically, including "Edgeworth's paradox," a condition in which there is an increase of both final prices resulting from an initial decline in the input price of one of two substitute products sold by a monopolist. Michael A. Salinger, *Vertical Mergers in Multiproduct Industries and Edgeworth's Paradox of Taxation*, 5 J. INDUS. ECON. 545 (1991). For the origins of Edgeworth's paradox, *see* FRANCIS Y. EDGEWORTH, PAPERS RELATING TO POLITICAL ECONOMY (Macmillan 1925).

18. Suppose, for example, that a third possible network, *C*, is a very poor substitute for *A* and *B*, and thus would draw negligible demand from them. Suppose *C*, if it were unaffiliated, would charge an optimal $3 input price and that the system would again set a $10 optimal retail price and attract seventy-five subscribers. The system would then collect only $750 in total revenues for network *C*. Such a network would be unprofitable to carry: $750 − $375 − $400 = −$25. If integration reduced the effective input price to $1, however, *C* would be profitable, even at the same $10 retail price: $750 − $225 − $400 = $125.

How might transactions efficiencies also explain the tendency for higher channel capacities to diminish, but not eliminate, Viacom and ATC's exclusion of unaffiliated pay networks? One factor is reduced substitution effects. Adding networks to a system's menu to some extent dilutes the demand interrelationship between any two of them and thus reduces the benefits to the integrated operator from excluding any unaffiliated network.

A second factor is reduced carriage costs in larger systems. Consider the role of the per network carriage cost in the example. If it were not for that $400 expense, the system could profitably continue to offer both network *A* and network *B*, though at different price levels. Our data are insufficient for measuring actual carriage costs, but the strong statistical relationship we found between the total number of homes passed by a system and the number of networks it carries suggests that they must be significant. Other things being equal, carriage costs are likely to be smaller for larger channel systems because opportunity costs decline. That is, the marginal value of additional networks should diminish as more attractive networks are added to systems' menus. The probability of carrying any given network thus increases.

Network carriage costs are unlikely to disappear, however, regardless of channel capacity. A system will always incur some incremental cost in offering an additional network to subscribers. It is unlikely to carry premium networks and PPV events, for example, unless it can achieve some minimum penetration that warrants the necessary advertising and promotion or personal selling costs.[19] Those incremental costs, in fact, are apparently the basis for some expectations that direct broadcast satellite operators will eventually be able to offer more narrowly focused niche programming, such as live performing arts events, than can cable systems.[20]

Also, the existence of carriage costs is not a necessary condition for exclusion of unaffiliated networks. In theory, if two premium networks are

---

19. *See* HERBERT S. DORDICK & DAVID WATERMAN, ARTS AND CULTURAL PROGRAMMING ON NON-BROADCAST MEDIA: PAST EXPERIENCE AND FUTURE PROSPECTS (Corporation for Public Broadcasting 1984); PAUL KAGAN ASSOCIATES, PAY TV NEWSLETTER, July 31, 1992, at 9. Marketing-related carriage costs are also suggested by substantial variations in the number of cable systems that have the technical capability and choose to carry major pay-per-view sporting events. PAUL KAGAN ASSOCIATES, PAY TV NEWSLETTER, Nov. 30, 1992, at 5.

20. T. Kerver, *Hubbard's World*, CABLEVISION, May 18, 1991, at 24; R. Brown & S. McClellan, *Programming DBS: Still a Long Way to Go*, BROADCASTING, Feb. 22, 1993, at 36. *See also* LELAND L. JOHNSON & DEBORAH R. CASTLEMAN, DIRECT BROADCAST SATELLITES: A COMPETITIVE ALTERNATIVE TO CABLE TELEVISION? (RAND Corporation 1991).

partial substitutes and per channel costs are zero, it would always be profitable to carry both of them at some set of retail prices. But in practice charging a relatively low price for an affiliated network could carry a negative quality signal or otherwise be inexplicable to subscribers. A comparable solution for the integrated system in that case would be to carry both networks at the same retail price, but to promote vigorously only the affiliated network.

For those reasons, we would expect to see integrated cable systems' excluding rival networks, though less frequently in larger capacity cable systems.

Efficiency versus Strategic Effects of Vertical Integration

While our statistical research does not resolve the causation issue, it seems very likely that the observed differences reflect both efficiency and strategic factors.[21] Cable television programming is a dynamic industry in which market entry, growth, and exit by programming suppliers constantly occur. Our cross-sectional study thus shows snapshots of strategic behavior in which MSOs or their parent companies attempt to influence outcomes in favor of networks in which they have equity interests. Such behavior may have negative effects on consumers. But we also find theoretical support and anecdotal evidence that vertical contracting problems motivate carriage and marketing decisions of vertically affiliated cable systems, presumably to the benefit of subscribers in the cost and quality of cable service.[22] Moreover, the tendency for carriage differentials to be smaller for better established, more widely distributed basic cable networks again suggests that in terms of programming content, the end result of the strategic behavior we do encounter is probably not much different from what we would observe in the absence of integration.

---

21. Distinguishing between a transactions-efficiency and a cost-raising model would require estimating the per channel carriage costs (actual plus opportunity) of various networks to determine the threshold beyond which a profit-maximizing cable system would be expected to eliminate a rival network for efficiency-related reasons.

22. Strictly speaking, economic welfare as measured by producers' and consumers' surplus could rise or fall because of transactions efficiencies at the programming input level. Michael Salinger's analysis of the general two-product partial vertical integration problem shows that welfare by that measure may fall because of an initial fall in the price of one product, depending on the values of elasticities and cross-elasticities of demand. Salinger, *supra* note 17. When we also consider the possibility of a change in product variety, the result is further complicated by the classic ambiguity in welfare effects in industries with economies of scale and product differentiation.

Programming Diversity

The empirical evidence suggests that in some cases programming diversity decreases the amount of cable network programming available. Diversity is likely to increase on other dimensions, however. First, our results likely overstate any decline in the total amount of programming available to cable subscribers owing to integration. An increase in carriage of other types of programs, such as local and distant broadcast stations and locally originated programs, could offset a lower number of cable networks. Second, any programs that replace unaffiliated cable networks on a menu may improve the diversity of program content or audience appeal. That is, eliminated cable networks are likely to be closer substitutes for affiliated networks than any new additions that replace them.[23]

Cable Systems of the Future

Perhaps the most significant technological development that will affect cable systems over the coming decade is digital video compression. Compression typically requires computer equipment at the cable headend and a set-top box for each subscriber to convert the digital signals to a form that a television set can process. Although the profitability of compression will depend on subscriber demand, many believe that its use to expand cable system capacities to several hundred channels will be a cost-effective investment.[24]

The essential economic effect of video compression is simply to lower a cable operator's marginal physical cost of providing additional channels of programming to subscribers. Engineering cost estimates suggest that compression can reduce those costs to very low levels.[25] As channel-carriage costs fall, the opportunity costs of carrying alternative programming options decrease. As more programming is added, substitution effects among par-

---

23. We acknowledge Tasneem Chipty for that point.

24. Digital compression systems are now being installed in some cable systems, although the pace of installation has fallen well short of announcements in 1993 and 1994. Compression of only a subset of a cable system's channels is an option. DirecTV and USSB already employ digital compression to expand their 32-channel FCC allocation to more than 150 channels of DBS service. The cable industry has recently focused attention on internet access and other two-way services, rather than additional video channels, as potential usages for large-capacity systems.

25. A recent trade report estimated that without compression, the upgrade of a cable system's physical transmission plant from 330 to 550 MHz, which generally allows an increase from about forty-five to about eighty channels, costs between eleven and twenty

ticular program services on a menu will also diminish. Therefore, the effects of vertical integration on program menus or other operator behavior are likely to decrease.

It is difficult, however, to predict the degree to which such capacity expansion would mitigate integration's influence. For several reasons, significant effects of integration are likely to persist, even if physical carriage costs were negligible. First, the weakening of subscriber demand substitution effects among cable networks as options increase is likely to taper off quickly. A common assumption among industry observers is that a large proportion of the video programming on very high capacity systems will be devoted to time-shifted program repetition or to other offerings with relatively marginal subscriber demand. Table 6-9 shows a 500-channel cable system prototype advanced by one cable executive. "Traditional" or basic cable services occupy seventy channels, and distinct monthly subscription premium services occupy six slots. The majority of remaining channels are devoted to various time-shifted versions of those same channels and to a near video-on-demand system that, if similar to many of those now in trial stages, would repeat the more popular programs at regular intervals. Such increases in program choices would seem unlikely to significantly affect demand substitution, for example, between competing cable news or music video networks. A second consideration is that a system operator's behavior is driven by the extent to which unaffiliated networks may subtract from demand for all its affiliated networks as a group. For example, if premium networks A and B are both multiplexed onto five channels as in the table 6-9 prototype, the relevant substitution effect simply takes place between the groups of five A channels and five B channels. Similar effects may be expected for jointly owned groups of networks having distinct programming. A variable is thus the extent to which programming ownership may become more diffuse as channel capacity expands. Finally, marketing considerations and nonphysical costs of channel carriage (such as billing or transactions costs) also seem likely to persist for many types of programming on very large capacity cable systems.

---

cents per channel, per subscriber, per month when amortized over a five-year period. PAUL KAGAN ASSOCIATES, CABLE TV PROGRAMMING, Feb. 28, 1994, at 1. The high rate of cable system rebuilding to 550 MHz and greater is evidence of the profitability of those rebuilds in many markets. Assuming an $80 additional cost for an addressable converter that is digital rather than analog (AUGUST E. GRANT & KENTON T. WILKINSON, COMMUNICATIONS TECHNOLOGY UPDATE: 1993–1994 (Technology Futures 1993), at 16) and an average four-to-one signal compression ratio, the cost per channel, per subscriber, per month would fall to between one and two cents for an eighty-channel system when amortized over the same period.

Table 6-9
Applications of 500-Channel Platform

Program Category	Number of Channels
Traditional cable service	70
Basic service multiplex (15 x 4)[a]	60
Commercial-free top-20 basic package	20
Pay service multiplex (6 x 5)[b]	30
Near video on demand (recent hits)	100
Special event PPV	10
Home shopping	40
Party-line interactive platform (games)	100
Downstream data transmission	20
HDTV, new technologies	50
Total	500

a. Fifteen basic networks each time-shifed four times.
b. Six different premium services each time-shifted five times.
Source: Encore Media (reported in *Cable TV Programming*, August 31, 1993, p. 2; material from original table deleted).

A similar analysis applies to more sophisticated true video-on-demand systems. These systems require video servers that store libraries of movies or other programming. In response to a subscriber's electronic request, such a server can transmit any video choice. Potentially, video-on-demand technology can make a subscriber's program choices virtually unlimited. Currently, video server technology appears to have relatively high marginal physical costs to maintain a library, but those are widely expected to drop. Other things equal, we would expect the effects of ownership ties between a library's owner and certain of the software products it might carry to diminish along with those costs. But for reasons similar to those advanced for the case of channel-capacity expansion, it seems likely that the effects of vertical integration on program menus and marketing behavior will persist in video-on-demand systems.

CONCLUSION

We observe significant tendencies for vertically integrated cable systems to favor their affiliated networks in carriage or marketing. That behavior can be at the expense of relatively similar rival networks. It can also reduce the amount of cable programming available to subscribers. A comparison of our results for both the full sample and larger capacity systems alone suggests that those effects of vertical integration, though they will diminish in importance, are likely to persist as cable systems expand the program choices they offer subscribers.

Although we cannot be sure of the reasons for the observed outcomes of vertical integration, and evidence of the benefits of integration to consumers remains ambiguous, an overall empirical pattern emerges: The relatively minor effects on the total amount of programming made available suggest that the main result of vertical integration is the substitution of one similar network for another or, perhaps, more advantageous marketing of one rather than another. We discuss the policy implications of those empirical findings in chapter 8.

APPENDIX: DATA COLLECTION AND MODELING METHODOLOGY

This appendix supports the statistical results reported in this chapter. Additional details may be found in an earlier study[26] covering the four largest vertically integrated premium networks, some results of which are summarized in tables 6-1 and 6-3. All other results reported in this chapter are original to this book.

General Methodology

All the econometric results reported in this chapter are based on reduced-form models arising from a structural simultaneous equations model of the carriage, pricing, and output decisions of cable system operators. The primary database we used to make those estimates is the A. C. Nielsen Cable On-Line Data Exchange (CODE). Those data are for a subset of 1,646 systems owned by the twenty-five largest MSOs as of August 19, 1989. We supplemented the Nielsen data with ownership information from approximately mid-1989 from a variety of sources.

Table 6A-1 lists and defines the primary variables employed in our models. Those include CODE data items (*MEDIANY* through *LHPASS*) and ownership data (*AFFIL* through *PPVAFL*). Table 6A-2 shows average values for those variables, by MSO, for the twenty-five largest MSOs. We excluded three of those MSOs (United Cable, Paragon, and Storer) from the models for the present study because of their minority ownership relationships with other MSOs in the group. We combined three other MSOs (United Artists, Westmarc, and Heritage) with TCI, because TCI had a majority ownership of them.

---

26. Waterman & Weiss, *supra* note 3. More complete references to previous relevant work may be found in that article.

Table 6A-1
Variable Names and Definitions

MEDIANY	median household income, 1988 ($10,000s)
LMEDIANY	logarithm of *MEDIANY*
RENTERS	percentage of households that are renters, 1988
AGE3554	percentage of households with head aged 35–54, 1988
MULTIFAM	percentage of households that live in multifamily units, 1988
CHILDREN	percentage of households with one or more children
CHANCAP	system channel capacity
LCHANCAP	logarithm of *CHANCAP*
TV	number of commercial broadcast stations in a market
FRANTIME	number of months since a system was originally franchised (before 10/71 set to 10/71)
LFRANTIME	logarithm of *FRANTIME*
DENSITY	total miles of cable plant divided by total number of homes passed
DMA1	= 1 if system is in one of the 25 largest broadcast television markets, = 0 otherwise
DMA2	= 1 if system is in broadcast markets 26–50, = 0 otherwise
DMA3	= 1 if system is in broadcast markets 51–100, = 0 otherwise
ADDRESS	= 1 if system has one- or two-way addressability, = 0 otherwise
54+	proportion of systems in an MSO with 54-plus channel capacity
HPASS	homes passed by a cable system (10,000s)
LHPASS	logarithm of *HPASS*
AFFIL	number of networks a system's MSO is affiliated with (5% or greater equity)
AFFILDV	= 1 if *AFFIL* > 0, = 0 otherwise
AFFIL20	number of networks a system's MSO is affiliated with (20% or greater equity)
AFFIL20DV	= 1 if *AFFIL20* > 0, = 0 otherwise
BAFFIL	number of basic networks a system's MSO is affiliated with (5% or greater equity)
BAFFILDV	= 1 if *BAFFIL* > 0, = 0 otherwise
BAFFIL20	number of basic networks a system's MSO is affiliated with (20% or greater equity)
BAFFIL20DV	= 1 if *BAFFIL20* > 0, = 0 otherwise
BAFFILDV14	= 1 if a system's MSO is affiliated with 1–4 basic networks, = 0 otherwise (5% or greater equity)
BAFFILDV5	= 1 if a system's MSO is affiliated with 5 or more basic networks, = 0 otherwise (5% or greater equity)

Table 6A-1 (continued)

PAYAFL	number of premium networks a system's MSO is affiliated with (5% or greater equity)
PAYAFLDV	= 1 if *PAYAFL* > 0, = 0 otherwise
PPVAFL	number of pay-per-view networks a system's MSO is affiliated with (5% or greater equity)

We first discuss the reduced-form models and prediction methodology that underlie the carriage results for the twelve individual integrated networks reported in tables 6-1 and 6-4. Then we discuss the premium network subscribership models that are the basis for table 6-3. Finally, we turn to the predictions of the total numbers of basic, premium, and PPV networks that we report in table 6-6.

Individual Network Carriage Models

To model the carriage decisions, we introduce the latent variable, NET^*_{ij}, to represent the propensity of system i to carry network j. We assume that NET^*_{ij} can be written as

$$NET^*_{ij} = X_i \beta_j + A_{ij}, \qquad (6A\text{-}1)$$

where the X_i vector contains demand, cost, and other system-specific factors, plus dummy variables to represent integration between the networks and MSOs, and the A_{ij} are normally distributed. $VIACOM_i$, for example, is the dummy variable used to represent integration between Viacom systems and networks. It is equal to one if system i is owned by Viacom and equal to zero otherwise. We also define the observed dummy variables for carriage, NET_{ij}, such that $NET_{ij} = 1$ if network i is carried on system j and $NET_{ij} = 0$ otherwise. Including intercepts in (6A-1) means that $NET_{ij} = 1$ if $NET^*_{ij} > 0$ and $NET_{ij} = 0$ if $NET^*_{ij} < 0$. The normality assumption on A_{ij} implies that the carriage dummy variables are modeled by probit maximum likelihood.

A brief discussion of the explanatory variables included in the carriage equations follows. The first set of variables—median household income (*MEDIANY*) and the percentages of households that are renters (*RENTERS*), that are headed by a person aged 35–54 (*AGE3554*), that live in multifamily units (*MULTIFAM*), and that have one or more children (*CHILDREN*)—are franchise-region-specific demographic variables. *MEDIANY*, *AGE3554*, and *CHILDREN* are usually associated with high cable demand. We enter

Table 6A-2

Means of Independent Variables by MSO

MSO	# Systems	MEDIANY	RENTERS	AGE3554	MULTIFAM	CHILDREN	HPASS	TV	FRANTIME	DENSITY
Adelphi	57	28,039.5	0.25	0.24	0.18	0.42	11,932.6	8.0	205.5	0.020
ATC	109	26,310.7	0.32	0.24	0.24	0.41	36,831.2	6.9	212.0	0.014
Cablevision Industries	90	23,418.1	0.28	0.23	0.17	0.44	10,592.3	6.2	157.7	0.019
Cablevision Systems	24	29,684.2	0.29	0.24	0.29	0.40	21,546.6	8.5	135.5	0.020
Centel	94	25,211.0	0.24	0.23	0.17	0.43	7,320.8	7.1	138.4	0.017
Continental	105	31,756.6	0.33	0.25	0.32	0.41	29,231.6	10.4	124.7	0.014
Comcast	33	28,989.2	0.31	0.24	0.30	0.40	35,666.5	7.6	196.6	0.016
Cooke	85	23,712.1	0.31	0.24	0.17	0.43	7,300.5	6.0	235.7	0.020
Cox	27	28,120.3	0.35	0.25	0.31	0.40	87,015.4	5.9	189.9	0.012
Heritage	40	26,848.0	0.26	0.23	0.20	0.43	21,929.1	6.5	138.7	0.017
Jones	101	30,101.3	0.27	0.25	0.23	0.45	16,250.7	8.5	129.2	0.015
KBL	6	31,628.0	0.39	0.26	0.41	0.40	108,784.8	10.7	122.0	0.007
Metrovision	22	31,175.7	0.31	0.24	0.27	0.42	28,513.5	7.4	186.7	0.011
Paragon	26	22,782.7	0.40	0.22	0.35	0.38	34,701.4	8.7	243.3	0.014
Post	54	24,363.1	0.29	0.22	0.18	0.40	10,781.1	7.9	271.1	0.014
Sammons	67	26,706.9	0.29	0.24	0.19	0.42	16,814.7	8.7	236.1	0.014
Storer	72	26,345.1	0.29	0.24	0.20	0.42	32,486.4	7.2	180.1	0.017
TCI	225	25,446.9	0.29	0.23	0.20	0.42	14,999.1	6.5	189.8	0.017
Telecable	23	27,394.0	0.34	0.25	0.27	0.44	35,227.6	7.2	171.2	0.014
Times Warner	45	27,266.6	0.30	0.24	0.25	0.40	32,297.6	8.0	254.4	0.016
United Artists	78	25,655.5	0.30	0.24	0.21	0.43	20,488.5	7.0	170.1	0.017
United Cable	49	29,735.2	0.31	0.24	0.24	0.42	36,022.6	7.6	184.0	0.013
Viacom	20	28,838.9	0.35	0.26	0.29	0.39	66,235.8	10.1	236.3	0.011
Warner	89	24,279.4	0.31	0.23	0.21	0.41	28,249.4	7.4	253.0	0.017
Westmarc	63	24,879.9	0.26	0.22	0.20	0.39	8,675.1	6.2	182.0	0.016

	CHANCAP	DMA1	DMA2	DMA3	ADDRESS	54+	BAFFIL	BAFFIL20	PAYAFL	PPVAFL	AFFIL	AFFIL20
Adelphi	41.9	0.49	0.18	0.33	0.47	0.28	0	0	0	0	0	0
ATC	39.6	0.17	0.35	0.24	0.29	0.13	3	0	2	2	7	2
Cablevision Industries	35.9	0.08	0.32	0.33	0.12	0.08	0	0	0	0	0	0
Cablevision Systems	43.2	0.50	0.08	0.08	0.42	0.33	3	3	1	0	4	4
Centel	38.6	0.18	0.34	0.32	0.29	0.11	0	0	0	0	0	0
Continental	49.1	0.60	0.10	0.20	0.46	0.47	1	0	0	2	3	0
Comcast	40.0	0.48	0.06	0.18	0.39	0.21	1	0	0	2	3	0
Cooke	31.0	0.18	0.18	0.27	0.32	0.04	0	0	0	0	0	0
Cox	41.9	0.19	0.19	0.26	0.44	0.30	2	1	0	2	4	1
Heritage	38.0	0.23	0.10	0.33	0.15	0.15	*	*	*	*	*	*
Jones	41.8	0.45	0.14	0.22	0.25	0.25	1	1	0	0	1	1
KBL	77.0	0.67	0.17	0.00	1.00	0.83	0	0	0	0	0	0
Metrovision	43.7	0.36	0.14	0.45	0.23	0.32	1	1	0	0	7	3
Paragon	46.8	0.65	0.04	0.04	0.42	0.27	0	0	0	0	0	0
Post	39.8	0.39	0.13	0.17	0.22	0.15	0	0	0	0	0	0
Sammons	35.0	0.45	0.09	0.34	0.27	0.05	0	0	0	0	0	0
Storer	35.7	0.39	0.06	0.08	0.15	0.07	0	0	0	0	0	0
TCI	35.6	0.24	0.20	0.22	0.26	0.09	10	8	0	0	10	8
Telecable	46.0	0.17	0.30	0.22	0.96	0.22	0	0	0	2	2	0
Times Mirror	36.7	0.42	0.22	0.22	0.02	0.16	0	0	0	2	2	0
United Artists	38.3	0.27	0.31	0.21	0.38	0.18	*	*	*	*	*	*
United Cable	45.2	0.43	0.02	0.22	0.59	0.39	0	0	0	0	0	0
Viacom	33.9	0.70	0.15	0.00	0.35	0.10	5	5	2	2	9	7
Warner	40.7	0.22	0.28	0.28	0.37	0.21	6	1	0	0	6	1
Westmarc	36.1	0.24	0.06	0.37	0.17	0.11	*	*	*	*	*	*

Note: * indicates data consolidated with TCI in the statistical analysis.

MEDIANY in logarithmic form (*LMEDIANY*) to allow for decreasing marginal effects. We have no prior expectations about how *RENTERS* and *MULTIFAM* affect cable markets; those two variables may proxy for factors affecting cable demand, or they may represent cost factors.

The rest of the included variables describe various aspects of each system. *CHANCAP* gives a system's channel capacity; we assume that large systems are more likely to carry each network. Again, we enter that in logarithmic form (*LCHANCAP*).[27] *TV* gives the number of competing broadcast stations in a market. More competition should encourage operators to offer more services, but successful competition may limit the number that can be profitably offered. The same applies for the three *DMA* dummy variables; larger markets tend to offer a wider range of other entertainment alternatives, but the net effect on network carriage could be positive or negative.

The natural logarithm of the number of homes passed by the system (*LHPASS*) indirectly represents a cost factor. If there are economies of scale in offering and marketing networks, then greater product differentiation is optimally offered with a larger subscriber base. We include $LHPASS^2$ to allow for further nonlinear effects, although we expect the total effect from *LHPASS* to be positive. Note, however, that the coefficients on *LHPASS* and $LHPASS^2$ in some models imply that, above some level of homes passed, the probability that a network is carried actually starts to decline. But those levels are typically very large—approximately 102,000 homes passed in the case of CVN—and the coefficients on the squared terms show that the declines above those levels are slow. Hence, the results should be taken as simple approximations to the results that would be obtained from models in which the marginal effects of the number of homes passed decline toward zero but remain nonnegative as the number of homes passed increases.

DENSITY gives a measure of how densely the homes passed are arranged. Higher density could cause lower marginal costs of operation, or, like *MULTIFAM* or *RENTERS,* that variable might proxy for demand characteristics. Several previous authors estimating demand functions for cable[28] have found *LFRANTIME*, the natural logarithm of the elapsed time since a system's original franchise was awarded, to be significant. *LFRANTIME* may proxy for unknown characteristics such as system management philosophy that can influence carriage decisions.

---

27. We used the variable *CHANCAP-TV*, which represents discretionary channel capacity, in the premium models.

28. *See, e.g.,* W. Mayo & Y. Otsuka, *Demand, Pricing, and Regulation: Evidence from the Cable Television Industry*, 22 RAND J. ECON. 396 (1991).

The final system variable we include is *ADDRESS*, a dummy variable equal to one if the system has one- or two-way addressability and zero otherwise. As we noted, addressability is particularly likely to affect the carriage of PPV networks. We did not use that variable in the premium network results taken from our earlier study.

The MSO dummies in the premium models were for ownership by ATC, Viacom, and Paragon. Assuming that premium networks are close substitutes, we included all three variables in each model. Higher carriage of HBO by ATC systems, for example, may be associated with lower carriage of Showtime. We did not presume that the basic and hybrid networks are close substitutes, so in the model for each of those networks we included only the dummy variables for the MSOs with ownership affiliations to the network. The network MTV, for example, is owned by Viacom, so that X_i in the MTV equation would include $VIACOM_i$.

Table 6A-3 shows ownership details by MSO in mid-1989. We show the maximum likelihood estimates of the probit models for the six basic and two hybrid networks in table 6A-4. Asymptotic *t*-ratios are in parentheses. Variables other than the MSO dummies are sporadically significant, although their signs and patterns of significance are not always consistent. But while we can expect at least some of the demographic variables, such as *LMEDIANY*, *AGE3554*, and *CHILDREN*, to increase cable demand in general, substitution effects among various networks make it difficult to interpret signs in the individual equations.

The coefficients on the MSO dummies in table 6A-4 represent the effects of affiliation on the probabilities of carriage of the eight individual basic and hybrid networks and are significant in a number of cases. We obtained similar results for premium networks in our earlier study.

Individual Carriage Model Predictions

To estimate the effects of integration on the actual numbers of systems that will carry networks, we develop predictions from the reduced-form carriage models. First, we find the number of systems in each relevant MSO expected to carry the relevant network. We then set the coefficient on the relevant MSO dummy to zero and hence find the expected number of systems in the MSO that would carry the network if those systems behaved like the average nonintegrated system in the sample. The difference between those numbers represents the implied effect of vertical integration.

The number of systems that carry the network is given by

$$\sum_{i=1}^{n_k} NET_{ij},$$

Table 6A-3
Ownership Details by MSO, Mid-1989
(equity shares of 5% or greater)

MSO	Affiliations
ATC	Basic: BET (16%); Movietime (11%); QVC (9%)[a] Premium: HBO (82%); Cinemax (82%) PPV: Viewers Choice I, II (17%)
Cablevision Systems	Basic: AMC (50%); CNBC (50%); Sports Channel America (50%) Premium: Bravo (50%)
Continental Cablevision	Basic: Movietime (11%) PPV: Viewers Choice I, II (12%)
Comcast	Basic: QVC (13%)[a] PPV: Viewers Choice I, II (12%)
Cox	Basic: Movietime (11%); Discovery (25%) PPV: Viewers Choice I, II (13%)
Jones	Basic: Mind Extension University (100%)
Metrovision (Newhouse)	Basic: Movietime (11%); Discovery (25%); Video Jukebox (17%); Eastern Microwave (WWOR, WSBK common carrier) (100%) PPV: Viewers Choice I, II (11%)
TCI	Basic: BET (14%); AMC (50%); Discovery (49%); QVC (23%)[a]; CVN (17%)[a]; Prevue Guide (20%); Turner Broadcasting (CNN, Headline News, TBS, TNT) (22%)
Telecable	PPV: Viewers Choice I, II (minority)
Times Mirror	PPV:Viewers Choice I, II (minority)
Viacom	Basic: MTV (100%); VH-1 (100%); Nickelodeon/ Nick at Nite (100%); Lifetime (33%) Premium: Showtime (100%); The Movie Channel (100%) PPV: Viewers Choice 1, 11 (11%); Viewers Choice (11%)
Warner	Basic: Movietime (44%); CVN (22%)[a]; Turner Broadcasting System (CNN, Headline News, TBS, TNT) (18%)

a. CVN and QVC merged in June 1989. Data in this table reflect ownership before the merger.
Sources: FCC, *1990 Cable Report* (appendix G); letters to the FCC from Cox Cable, Comcast, Continental, Cablevision Systems, NewChannels (Newhouse), TCI, and Viacom, dated early 1990 in Dkt. 89-600; Paul Kagan Associates, *Cable TV Programming* (December 20, 1989, 2–3).

where n_k is the number of systems in MSO k and i runs over those systems. Hence, since A_{ij} is normally distributed and

$$E[NET_{ij}] = P(NET_{ij} = 1) = \Phi \left(X_i \ \beta_j \right),$$

Table 6A-4
Probit Models for Eight Basic/Hybrid Networks

	CVN		BET		QVC		Discovery		VH1		MTV		AMC		Bravo	
C	-12.5	(5.3)	1.8	(.6)	-11.2	(4.1)	-12.2	(4.7)	-8.7	(3.6)	-10.9	(2.8)	-7.7	(3.2)	-31.7	(5.9)
LMEDIANY	-.00	(.0)	-1.2	(4.7)	.29	(1.1)	.073	(.3)	-.23	(1.0)	-.66	(2.1)	-.32	(1.4)	2.1	(4.7)
RENTERS	-1.4	(2.4)	3.3	(4.9)	-.81	(1.2)	.39	(.6)	-.94	(1.6)	.44	(.5)	-.99	(1.7)	2.0	(2.0)
AGE3554	-3.6	(2.3)	.38	(.2)	-1.9	(1.1)	3.4	(1.9)	3.1	(2.0)	8.0	(3.2)	1.0	(.7)	2.0	(.7)
MULTIFAM	-.52	(1.0)	-1.2	(5.9)	.00	(.0)	-.94	(1.7)	1.6	(3.1)	2.2	(2.5)	.30	(.6)	.69	(.8)
CHILDREN	1.6	(2.8)	4.1	(.8)	-.50	(.8)	.69	(1.1)	1.5	(2.7)	1.7	(1.9)	-.63	(1.1)	-.024	(2.3)
TV	.033	(1.7)	.008	(.4)	-.033	(1.6)	-.027	(1.1)	-.017	(.9)	.005	(.1)	-.035	(1.8)	-.007	(.2)
LFRANTIME	.33	(4.1)	-.16	(1.8)	-.11	(1.3)	-.00	(.1)	-.025	(.3)	-.22	(1.8)	-.015	(.2)	-.24	(1.7)
DENSITY	-3.4	(2.8)	2.5	(.6)	3.0	(.7)	-2.0	(10.2)	1.2	(.3)	1.5	(.3)	-3.5	(.9)	7.5	(1.3)
LCHANCAP	4.3	(.9)	2.5	(7.0)	.93	(4.9)	-2.9	(.8)	2.2	(11.1)	1.6	(6.7)	1.1	(6.3)	2.6	(7.7)
DMA1	-.39	(2.3)	-.29	(1.5)	.38	(2.0)	-.07	(.4)	.00	(.0)	.09	(.3)	.12	(.7)	-.32	(1.0)
DMA2	-.14	(1.1)	.12	(.9)	-.06	(.4)	-.13	(.9)	.08	(.6)	.11	(.6)	.13	(1.0)	-.35	(1.2)
DMA3	-.15	(1.3)	.011	(.1)	-.16	(1.1)	-.23	(1.8)	.05	(.5)	.16	(1.0)	-.11	(.9)	-.13	(.5)
ADDRESS	-.091	(1.0)	.018	(.2)	.22	(2.3)	.16	(1.4)	.11	(1.2)	.68	(2.7)	.19	(2.1)	.24	(1.5)
LHPASS	1.3	(4.9)	.25	(.8)	1.03	(3.2)	.86	(3.2)	.18	(.7)	2.1	(3.5)	1.3	(4.6)	-.41	(.7)
LHPASS²	-.057	(3.9)	-.013	(.7)	-.047	(2.7)	-.040	(2.6)	.00	(.1)	-.091	(2.4)	-.054	(3.7)	.032	(1.1)
TCI	1.5	(15.7)	-.22	(2.1)	.21	(2.1)	.61	(5.9)					1.4	(15.1)		
WARNER	1.4	(8.3)														
ATC			.60	(4.1)												
METRO					-.35	(1.9)	-.30	(.9)								
VIACOM									1.5	(3.2)	1.5	(1.6)				
CBLSYS															3.6	(7.5)
N	1,457		1,457		1,457		1,457		1,457		1,457		1,457		1,457	
L	-763.7		-616.8		-561.1		-568.2		-751.5		-301.7		-742.3		-185.5	

Notes: The absolute value of the t-ratios are in parentheses. N is the number of observations. L is the value of the log-likelihood function.

117

where Φ is the cumulative distribution function of the standard normal, the estimated number of systems is

$$\sum_{i=1}^{n_k} \Phi\,(X_i\,\hat{\beta}_j),$$

where $\hat{\beta}_j$ is the maximum likelihood estimate of β_j. The predicted change in the number of systems is given by

$$\sum_{i=1}^{n_k} \Phi\,(X_i\,\hat{\beta}_j) - \sum_{i=1}^{n_k} \Phi\,(X_i\,\tilde{\beta}_{jk}),$$

where $\tilde{\beta}_{jk}$ is $\hat{\beta}_j$ but with the coefficient on MSO dummy k set to zero. The standard error of the change is given by

$$\sum_{i=1}^{n_k} \phi\,(X_i\,\hat{\beta}_j)\ s.e.\,(\hat{\beta}_{jk}), \qquad \text{(6A-2)}$$

where ϕ is the probability density function of the standard normal and $s.e.$ $(\hat{\beta}_{jk})$ is the standard error of the estimated coefficient on MSO dummy k from the probit estimation.

Tables 6-1 and 6-4 show the results for those predictions.

Subscribership Models for Premium Networks

Because the sizes of the cable systems in our sample vary widely in numbers of homes passed, we model penetration as a fraction of homes passed, rather than subscribership directly. Furthermore, the distribution of penetration is skewed to the right, so we also take natural logarithms of the dependent variable.

Next, recall that subscribership and penetration of a particular premium network will be observed only if the network is carried on a system. We define PEN^*_{ij} as the latent penetration of network j on system i and let

$$PEN_{ij} = PEN^*_{ij}\ \text{if}\ NET^*_{ij} > 0$$
$$= 0\ \text{otherwise}$$

denote the corresponding observed variable. Similarly, let $LPEN^*_{ij} = \log$ (PEN^*_{ij}), and $LPEN_{ij} = \log(PEN_{ij})$ when $NET^*_{ij} > 0$ and zero otherwise. The model for $LPEN^*$ is given by

$$LPEN^*_{ij} = X_i\,a_j + \sum_{k=1;\,k\neq j}^{4} b_{jk}\,NET_{ik} + \sum_{k=1}^{4} c_{jk}\,LTIME_{ik} + \xi_{ij}, \qquad \text{(6A-3)}$$

where ξ_{ij} are assumed to be independent over i.

The variables in X in equation (6A-3) are the same as those in the premium carriage equations, under the assumption that the penetration equation is derived from the same structural model. The *NET* variables account for the fact that penetration of a given network will be affected by the combination of other networks offered. ATC systems, for example, are likely to have higher penetration of HBO than will the average nonintegrated system simply because they carry rival networks less frequently. The endogeneity of the *NET* variables also means that the *LPEN* equations are not true reduced forms. But as the discussion to follow shows, it is straightforward to allow for the endogeneity.

The *LTIME* variables, defined as the natural logarithms of the number of months since a system began carrying the relevant network, are included to reflect the likelihood that consumer switching costs will advantage subscribership to a network that the system started carrying before others or that has simply had a longer time to develop subscriber loyalty. The logarithmic form again reflects an expectation of diminishing effects over time.

To estimate our equation, we follow Heckman's two-stage procedure[29] and take the expected value of $LPEN^*_{ij}$, conditional on $NET_{ij} = 1$. That gives $LPEN_{ij}$ as a function of the explanatory and MSO dummy variables in X, the time variables, and variables corresponding to the inverse Mills's ratio. The variables corresponding to the inverse Mills's ratio depend in turn on probabilities from the carriage probit equations. We use ordinary least squares to estimate the equations.

We then use the estimated equations to predict the total effects of vertical integration, as shown in table 6-3. The actual penetrations are the average penetrations predicted by the models. The normal penetrations are the average penetrations when the coefficients on the MSO dummy variables in the penetration and carriage equations are set to zero. We obtain the standard errors of the differences by a method similar to that leading to equation (6A-2).

Numbers of Networks Carried

To model the effects of vertical integration on the number of networks carried, we hypothesize the existence of latent variables representing the propensities of systems to carry basic, premium, and PPV networks. Those propensities can be thought of as arising from the aggregation of the

---

29. *See* TAKESHI AMEMIYA, ADVANCED ECONOMETRICS (Harvard University Press 1985), § 10.7.

individual carriage equations across networks. The corresponding observed variables are the numbers of basic, premium, and PPV networks carried. Further aggregation gives the total number of cable networks carried. Again, assuming normality, we use ordered probit models.[30]

It turns out that the maximum number of basic networks carried is twenty-nine and the total ranges up to thirty-nine. Those numerical ranges imply that it is impractical to estimate ordered probit models for those variables. Linear regression models with the numbers of basic networks and the total number of networks as dependent variables should, however, be close approximations to the corresponding ordered probit models. For the premium and PPV variables, the maximum numbers of networks carried are ten and four, respectively, so it is feasible to estimate ordered probit models. We combined the two systems that carried ten premium networks with the systems carrying nine networks.

The explanatory variables are basically the same as in the carriage probit models except that, rather than the MSO dummy variables, we use variables describing total affiliations of a system's MSO with basic, pay, and PPV networks. In the basic network equation, for example, we include the variable *BAFFIL*, which gives the number of networks with which a system's MSO is affiliated (5 percent or greater equity). We estimated specifications with various affiliation variables. To investigate the possibility that vertically integrated systems also vary channel capacity in the long run to accommodate a desired increase or reduction in programming offered, we estimated some models without the channel capacity variable.

We present ordinary least squares estimates for the basic and total models and maximum likelihood estimates for the premium and PPV models in tables 6A-5 through 6A-10. We obtained the ordinary least squares standard errors from the heteroskedasticity consistent estimate of the covariance matrix.[31] Table 6A-11 gives the ordinary least squares results in models with channel capacity omitted.

Signs for the statistically significant demographic variables were generally in expected directions. Channel capacity and homes passed are consistently positive and strongly significant, although as we would expect, channel capacity is less significant in the more than fifty-four channel system models. Also as expected, addressability is particularly important in the PPV models. The MSO affiliation variables (for example, *BAFFIL* for the basic equation and *TOTAFFIL* for the total equation) are all negative, although

---

30. *Id.*, § 9.3.2.

31. *See* Halbert L. White, *A Heteroskedasticity-Consistent Covariance Matrix and a Direct Test for Heteroskedasticity*, 48 ECONOMETRICA 817 (1980).

Table 6A-5
Number of Basic Networks Carried: All Systems

C	−30.6	(6.6)	−30.5	(6.5)	−30.0	(6.4)	−30.3	(6.5)
LMEDIANY	−.66	(1.4)	−.68	(1.5)	−.72	(1.6)	−.66	(1.4)
RENTERS	−2.6	(2.0)	−2.6	(2.0)	−2.5	(1.9)	−2.6	(2.0)
AGE3554	6.0	(1.9)	5.9	(1.9)	5.6	(1.8)	6.0	(1.9)
MULTIFAM	5.0	(5.1)	5.0	(5.0)	4.9	(5.0)	5.1	(5.1)
CHILDREN	1.9	(1.7)	1.9	(1.6)	1.8	(1.6)	1.9	(1.6)
TV	−.095	(2.6)	−.097	(2.6)	−.10	(2.8)	−.10	(2.6)
LFRANTIME	−.53	(3.8)	−.52	(3.8)	−.51	(3.6)	−.53	(3.8)
DENSITY	22.9	(2.6)	23.1	(2.6)	22.9	(2.5)	22.6	(2.5)
LCHANCAP	7.7	(26.0)	7.7	(25.9)	7.6	(25.9)	7.7	(25.9)
DMA1	−.24	(.7)	−.22	(.7)	−.19	(.6)	−.24	(.7)
DMA2	.18	(.7)	.19	(.8)	.21	(.9)	.17	(.7)
DMA3	.08	(.4)	.09	(.4)	.10	(.4)	.07	(.3)
ADDRESS	.33	(1.9)	.35	(2.0)	.37	(2.1)	.33	(1.9)
LHPASS	4.9	(9.6)	5.0	(9.6)	4.9	(9.6)	4.9	(9.5)
LHPASS²	−.21	(7.6)	−.21	(7.8)	−.21	(7.7)	−.21	(7.5)
BAFFIL	.013	(.7)						
BAFFILDV			.17	(1.0)				
BAFFILDV14					.38	(2.0)		
BAFFILDV5					.034	(.2)		
BAFFIL20DV							−.046	(.3)
N	1,457		1,457		1,457		1,457	
R^2	.66		.66		.66		.66	
F	176.5		176.6		166.6		176.4	

Notes: The absolute values of the *t*-ratios are in parentheses. *N* is the number of observations. *F* is the test statistic for the hypothesis that all slope coefficients are zero.

they are significant only in some cases. There was virtually no change in the results for the models without channel capacity.

We summarize the effects of vertical integration on the numbers of networks carried through estimates of the marginal effects of vertical integration on the numbers of networks carried. The results appear in table 6-6. In the linear regression models, the marginal effects are given by the coefficients on the MSO affiliation variables. In the ordered probit models, we follow a prediction methodology comparable to that in the individual probit models, as described above.

Table 6A-6
Number of Basic Networks Carried: 54-Plus Channel Systems

C	−53.7	(4.3)	−53.7	(4.4)	−53.5	(4.3)
LMEDIANY	.96	(1.0)	1.0	(1.0)	.95	(1.0)
RENTERS	−3.3	(1.1)	−3.2	(1.1)	−3.2	(1.1)
AGE3554	−7.2	(1.1)	−6.7	(1.0)	−6.8	(1.1)
MULTIFAM	6.1	(2.6)	6.2	(2.8)	5.9	(2.6)
CHILDREN	.10	(.0)	−1.9	(.1)	.19	(.1)
TV	.027	(.4)	.032	(.5)	.026	(.4)
LFRANTIME	−.75	(2.8)	−.88	(3.2)	−.82	(3.1)
DENSITY	41.4	(2.8)	41.9	(3.0)	39.5	(2.7)
LCHANCAP	5.7	(5.6)	5.4	(5.3)	5.5	(5.7)
DMA1	−.10	(.1)	−.15	(.2)	−.12	(.2)
DMA2	1.0	(1.5)	.90	(1.5)	.93	(1.5)
DMA3	.75	(1.1)	.79	(1.3)	.73	(1.2)
ADDRESS	.24	(.6)	.13	(.4)	.22	(.6)
LHPASS	8.6	(4.6)	8.8	(4.9)	8.7	(4.8)
LHPASS^2	−.40	(4.4)	−1.41	(4.6)	−.40	(4.6)
BAFFIL	−.065	(1.3)				
BAFFILDV			−.59	(1.7)		
BAFFIL20DV					−.46	(1.4)
N	238		238		238	
R^2	.47		.47		.47	
F	12.3		12.3		12.3	

Notes: N is the number of observations. F is the test statistic for the hypothesis that all slope coefficients are zero.

Table 6A-7
Number of Premium Networks Carried

	All Systems		54-Plus Channel Systems		All Systems		54-Plus Channel Systems	
C	−14.7	(8.4)	−14.7	(8.3)	−13.9	(2.6)	−14.6	(2.7)
LMEDIANY	.43	(2.5)	.42	(2.4)	.62	(1.3)	.66	(1.3)
RENTERS	.35	(.9)	.30	(.8)	.75	(.8)	.97	(1.0)
AGE3554	−.16	(.1)	−.27	(.2)	−4.3	(1.5)	−3.9	(1.3)
MULTIFAM	.45	(1.2)	.48	(1.3)	−.95	(1.0)	−1.0	(1.1)
CHILDREN	.47	(1.1)	.48	(1.1)	−1.3	(1.3)	−1.4	(1.4)
TV	.066	(4.2)	.065	(4.1)	.13	(3.5)	.13	(3.5)
LFRANTIME	−.13	(2.2)	−.14	(2.3)	−.35	(2.5)	−.34	(2.5)
DENSITY	6.4	(3.9)	6.6	(4.0)	−8.3	(.6)	−5.9	(.4)
LCHANCAP	1.8	(15.0)	1.8	(14.8)	1.2	(2.1)	1.2	(2.2)
DMA1	−.26	(1.9)	−.25	(1.8)	−.37	(1.0)	−.41	(1.1)
DMA2	−.28	(2.8)	−.29	(2.9)	−.23	(.7)	−.27	(.8)
DMA3	−.12	(1.4)	−.11	(1.4)	−.22	(.8)	−.24	(.8)
ADDRESS	.45	(5.9)	.46	(5.9)	.78	(4.2)	.76	(4.1)
LHPASS	1.7	(9.5)	1.7	(9.6)	1.6	(2.1)	1.6	(2.2)
$LHPASS^2$	−.075	(7.7)	−.077	(7.9)	−.075	(2.0)	−.075	(2.0)
PAYAFL	−.27	(5.1)					−.32	(2.3)
PAYAFLDV			−.34	(4.1)	.27	(1.3)		
N	1,457		1,457		238		238	
L	−2,016.1		−2,025.2		−355.7		−353.7	

Notes: The absolute values of the *t*-ratios are in parentheses. N is the number of observations. L is the value of the log-likelihood function.

Table 6A-8
Number of Pay-per-View Networks Carried

	All Systems		54-Plus Channel Systems	
C	−15.8	(5.9)	−28.0	(3.5)
LMEDIANY	.43	(1.5)	.88	(1.7)
RENTERS	.91	(1.6)	1.7	(1.3)
AGE3554	.38	(.2)	−1.7	(.5)
MULTIFAM	−.42	(.8)	−.96	(.9)
CHILDREN	1.4	(2.4)	−.69	(.7)
TV	.022	(1.1)	.034	(1.0)
LFRANTIME	.023	(.2)	−.020	(.1)
DENSITY	−9.5	(1.0)	.74	(.0)
LCHANCAP	1.9	(9.7)	.72	(1.3)
DMA1	.056	(.3)	−.13	(.3)
DMA2	−.045	(.3)	− .01	(.0)
DMA3	.027	(.2)	−.16	(.5)
ADDRESS	1.0	(10.0)	.86	(4.4)
LHPASS	.26	(.7)	3.0	(2.8)
LHPASS²	−.00	(.1)	−.14	(2.7)
PPVAFL	−.014	(.3)	−.11	(1.1)
N	1,363		228	
L	−635.6		−227.9	

Notes: The absolute values of the *t*-ratios are in parentheses. *N* is the number of observations. *L* is the value of the log-likelihood function.

Table 6A-9
Total Number of Networks Carried (Basic, Premium, and PPV Combined):
All Systems

C	−43.8	(8.2)	−44.5	(8.3)	−44.3	(8.3)
LMEDIANY	−.17	(.3)	−.16	(.3)	−.18	(.3)
RENTERS	−2.1	(1.4)	−2.2	(1.4)	−2.2	(1.4)
AGE3554	5.8	(1.6)	5.9	(1.7)	5.9	(1.7)
MULTIFAM	5.6	(4.9)	5.6	(4.9)	5.6	(4.9)
CHILDREN	2.4	(1.8)	2.5	(1.9)	2.6	(1.9)
TV	−.013	(.3)	−.006	(.1)	−.009	(.2)
LFRANTIME	−.77	(4.6)	−.78	(4.7)	−.77	(4.6)
DENSITY	27.7	(2.8)	28.3	(2.8)	28.1	(2.8)
LCHANCAP	9.8	(28.2)	9.8	(28.2)	9.8	(28.2)
DMA1	−.52	(1.3)	−.52	(1.4)	−.52	(1.3)
DMA2	−.20	(.7)	−.20	(.7)	−.19	(.7)
DMA3	−.10	(.4)	−.08	(.3)	−.07	(.3)
ADDRESS	1.2	(6.0)	1.2	(5.9)	1.2	(6.0)
LHPASS	5.8	(9.6)	5.9	(9.6)	5.9	(9.6)
LHPASS^2	−.24	(7.4)	−.24	(7.4)	−.24	(7.4)
AFFIL	−.051	(2.5)				
AFFILDV			−.23	(1.2)		
AFFIL20DV					−.19	(1.1)
N	1,457		1,457		1,457	
R^2	.74		.74		.74	
F	252.6		251.5		251.4	

Notes: The absolute values of the *t*-ratios are in parentheses. *N* is the number of observations. *F* is the test statistic for the hypothesis that all slope coefficients are zero.

Table 6A-10
Total Number of Networks Carried (Basic, Premium, and PPV Combined):
54-Plus Channel Systems

C	−75.9	(5.2)	−77.2	(5.3)	−75.6	(5.1)
LMEDIANY	2.2	(2.0)	2.2	(2.1)	2.1	(2.0)
RENTERS	−2.0	(.6)	−1.6	(.5)	−1.5	(.5)
AGE3554	−12.1	(1.5)	−11.0	(1.4)	−10.4	(1.3)
MULTIFAM	5.3	(2.0)	4.7	(1.8)	4.5	(1.8)
CHILDREN	−2.2	(.8)	−2.3	(.9)	−2.0	(.8)
TV	.20	(2.4)	.21	(2.6)	.19	(2.3)
LFRANTIME	−1.1	(3.2)	−1.3	(3.7)	−1.3	(3.6)
DENSITY	37.9	(2.3)	35.9	(2.3)	35.4	(2.2)
LCHANCAP	7.4	(4.8)	7.3	(4.9)	7.3	(5.0)
DMA1	−.78	(.1)	−.80	(.9)	−.77	(.8)
DMA2	.67	(.9)	.61	(.8)	.63	(.9)
DMA3	.42	(.6)	.48	(.7)	.43	(.6)
ADDRESS	1.6	(3.5)	1.4	(3.0)	1.6	(3.4)
LHPASS	10.7	(5.1)	11.3	(5.3)	10.9	(5.1)
LHPASS^2	−.49	(4.8)	−.52	(5.0)	−.50	(4.8)
AFFIL	−.15	(2.6)				
AFFILDV			−.97	(2.1)		
AFFIL20DV					−.79	(1.0)
N	238		238		238	
R^2	.59		.59		.59	
F	20.1		19.7		19.7	

Notes: The absolute values of the *t*-ratios are in parentheses. *N* is the number of observations. *F* is the test statistic for the hypothesis that all slope coefficients are zero.

Table 6A-11
Total Number of Networks Carried (Basic, Premium, and PPV Combined):
All Systems, Channel Capacity Omitted

C	−28.3	(4.3)	−29.3	(4.4)	−29.0	(4.4)
LMEDIANY	.61	(.9)	.60	(.9)	.60	(.9)
RENTERS	−3.4	(2.0)	−3.5	(2.0)	−3.5	(2.1)
AGE3554	4.6	(1.1)	4.6	(1.1)	4.7	(1.1)
MULTIFAM	8.2	(6.0)	8.1	(6.0)	8.1	(6.0)
CHILDREN	4.0	(2.4)	4.2	(2.5)	4.2	(2.5)
TV	.063	(1.1)	.072	(1.3)	.071	(1.2)
LFRANTIME	−2.1	(9.1)	−2.1	(9.1)	−2.1	(9.1)
DENSITY	4.9	(.5)	6.2	(.6)	5.8	(.5)
DMA1	−.43	(.8)	−.40	(.8)	−.41	(.8)
DMA2	−.29	(.8)	−.28	(.8)	−.28	(.8)
DMA3	.25	(.8)	.31	(1.0)	.30	(1.0)
ADDRESS	2.2	(8.9)	2.2	(8.9)	2.2	(8.9)
LHPASS	9.1	(15.0)	9.3	(15.2)	9.3	(15.1)
LHPASS^2	−.39	(11.9)	−.40	(12.1)	−.40	(12.0)
AFFIL	−.068	(2.6)				
AFFILDV			−.030	(.1)		
AFFIL20DV					−.13	(.6)
N	1,457		1,457		1,457	
R^2	.58		.58		.58	
F	131.4		130.3		130.4	

Notes: The absolute values of the *t*-ratios are in parentheses. *N* is the number of observations. *F* is the test statistic for the hypothesis that all slope coefficients are zero.

7

Vertical Integration and Alternative Multichannel Video Delivery Systems

Does VERTICAL INTEGRATION between cable systems and program suppliers result in the foreclosure of competitors to local monopoly cable systems such as MMDS, HSD, SMATV, DBS, LECs, or competing over-built cable systems? In earlier chapters, we discussed the potential for a competitive market in multichannel video distribution to resolve numerous cable television policy issues. We also noted the abundant complaints made by competitors that they have been denied access to programming or charged discriminatory prices by vertically integrated cable program suppliers.

While the FCC's 1990 report on the industry expressed a favorable view of cable industry vertical integration in general, its consideration of the evidence on program access was less sanguine. The report concluded:

> [V]ertically integrated cable operators often have the ability to deny alternative multi-channel video providers access to cable programming services in which such cable operators hold ownership interests, and there is considerable anecdotal evidence that some have used this ability in anticompetitive ways.[1]

The singling out of vertically integrated cable programmers in the 1992 Cable Act indicates that Congress reached a similar, if not stronger, conclusion regarding the role of integration in limiting access to programming by alternative MVPDs.

---

1. Competition, Rate Deregulation and the Commission's Policies Relating to the Provision of Cable Television Service, Report, MM Dkt. No. 89-600, FCC 90-276, 67 Rad. Reg. 2d (P&F) ¶ 128 [hereinafter 1990 FCC Cable Report].

Unfortunately, there is no available database on program access comparable to that we employed in chapter 6 to study the effects of integration on programming supply. We can, however, review the economic logic of foreclosure claims and consider the available evidence.

We argue in this chapter that there are viable economic models that can explain foreclosure attempts by established cable operators.[2] The singling out of vertically integrated firms for blame, however, is not justified for two reasons.

First, both integrated and nonintegrated firms have engaged in the same potentially anticompetitive behavior. Vertical integration is likely to facilitate any foreclosure behavior by established cable operators that may take place. Its basic source, however, must again be horizontal market power at the cable system or MSO level in the market for programming. To the extent that horizontal market power exists, the empirical record suggests a conclusion parallel to the one we reached in chapter 5 regarding foreclosure in programming supply: Foreclosure of alternative MVPDs can be accomplished either in the presence or in the absence of vertical ownership ties.

Second, there is neither a plausible theoretical case nor empirical evidence that variations in input prices that programmers charge to different MVPDs are attributable to vertical integration. To the extent that cost factors fail to explain those price differences, the record suggests that simple variations in outcomes of the bilateral network-distributor bargaining process are likely to be responsible. Unlike a foreclosure strategy, bargaining outcomes are determined by the horizontal market power of the network seller vis-à-vis that of the downstream buyer. Those outcomes have relatively little to do with whether a seller is vertically integrated.[3]

VERTICAL FORECLOSURE THEORY AND THE ROLE OF INTEGRATION

To the extent that local cable operators enjoy monopoly profits, they have an obvious incentive to protect those profits by restricting entry. Leaving aside vertical integration, one can construct a variety of models that show conditions under which established cable operators might profitably retard

---

2. An earlier version of the material in this chapter was published in David Waterman, *Vertical Integration and Program Access in the Cable Television Industry*, 47 FED. COMM. L.J. 3, 511 (1995).

3. The argument that differences in input prices can be explained as variations in bilateral bargaining outcomes could also be explained from a seller's point of view as unilateral price discrimination. We frame the argument in bargaining outcomes, since neither the buyer nor the seller is necessarily a price maker.

the entry of competing MVPDs at either the local or the national level, by inducing program suppliers to limit those entrants' access to programming.

The essential feature of one such model, for example, is that an established cable operator has made a sunk-cost investment in constructing a physical plant on the expectation that over time operating revenues will cover not only operating expenses, but also amortization of the plant.[4] Assume, however, that a potential multichannel competitor later arrives on the scene. Because its existing plant is otherwise useless, the established operator will find it worthwhile to expend resources to prevent entry all the way up to the point that only its operating costs are covered. The result is that even if the potential entrant has superior technology and program suppliers could expand their subscribership with that new technology, the established operator may still be able to compensate program suppliers for a grant of exclusive rights by more than the entrant could profitably bid for those rights and thus prevent the entry.[5]

One could also posit a reprisal model of entry deterrence at the system level. In that case an incumbent cable system does not compensate networks to refuse sales to competing delivery systems. Rather, the system keeps networks in line by establishing a reputation for punitive action (by moving channel position or refusing to promote) against any network that might do business with an entrant.[6] A necessary condition in such foreclosure models is that an entrant cannot substitute programming from alternative sources. Although clearly an empirical question, there seems to be a consensus in the industry that the lack of more than one or two of the most well-known networks would seriously handicap a multichannel competitor to an established cable system.[7]

What, then, are the roles of vertical integration in such models? One could be to facilitate the contracting process necessary to accomplish the foreclosure objective. For reasons comparable to those discussed in chapter 4, compensating or coercing a supplier to refuse to deal with an entrant is probably easier to carry out if ownership is involved; the risk of a network's

---

4. LELAND L. JOHNSON, COMMON CARRIER VIDEO DELIVERY BY TELEPHONE COMPANIES 45–47 (RAND Corporation 1992).

5. An implicit assumption in the model is that the prospective entrant cannot hold out until the established firm has to replace its plant.

6. The model is based on David Kreps & Robert Wilson, *Reputation and Imperfect Information*, 27 J. ECON. THEORY 253 (1982), and Paul Milgrom & John Roberts, *Predation, Reputation and Entry Deterrence*, 27 J. ECON. THEORY 280 (1982).

7. *See* FCC Los Angeles Cable Television Field Hearing (Feb. 12, 1990); Testimony of Robert Thompson, senior vice president of TCI; Comments of the Wireless Cable Association International, Inc., to FCC MM Dkt. 92-265 (Jan. 25, 1993).

or an MSO's reneging on an agreement is probably reduced, and there may be less risk of legal jeopardy. Also, if a written exclusive dealing contract is involved, ownership is likely to smooth its dissolution if it should later become adverse to the interest of one party. Such anticompetitive advantages of integration are especially plausible if majority ownership of the network or networks in question is involved.

Another role of vertical integration could be to coordinate collusion among networks when more than one network is involved in an attempt to deter entry. Assume, for example, that an established cable system with a potential MMDS competitor in its local market area believes it needs to enlist refusals to deal from at least five networks to prevent or retard entry. The cable system might simply choose five networks and compensate them for that exclusivity. But any perception among the five that the foreclosure strategy might fail, especially if there are first-mover advantages in signing on with the entrant, implies a risk of defection. If the established cable system is vertically affiliated with at least some of the five networks, however, then the risks of defection perceived by nonintegrated networks among them are likely to be reduced, thus facilitating the strategy.

Vertical integration might also facilitate collusion among MSOs to enforce foreclosure attempts carried out on either a local or a national basis. For local entrants such as MMDS and SMATV, colluding MSOs could instigate a general policy against dealing with any program supplier that did business with entrants in any local market the MSOs control. DBS, in contrast, is a national technology and threatens all cable operators simultaneously. National MSO collusion could be facilitated if two or more MSOs are common owners of the same network or networks, or if equity in a sufficiently large number of separately owned networks is concentrated in the hands of relatively few MSOs.

Concerns about nationally coordinated collusion among vertically integrated MSOs are implicit in the 1992 Cable Act and the FCC's blanket prohibition against any non-cost-based pricing by vertically integrated program suppliers. Similar concerns were the basis for the 1994 settlements of federal and state antitrust suits against Primestar Partners, a ten-firm joint venture formed in 1990 to offer medium-power DBS services in the United States.[8] Some provisions of those settlements parallel the cable act by

---

8. United States *v.* Primestar Partners, L.P., No. 93-3913 (S.D.N.Y. Apr. 4, 1994), Competitive Impact Statement. Another consent decree filed in 1994 by the Justice Department, United States *v.* Tele-Communications, Inc. & Liberty Media Corp., Proposed Final Judgment and Competitive Impact Statement, 59 Fed. Reg., No. 91 (May 12, 1994), approves the remerger of those two firms but constrains the program services in which they have ownership interests from similar pricing and exclusivity practices.

enjoining the defendant's majority-owned programming services from engaging in various exclusive contracting and discriminatory pricing practices.

In summary, the theoretical role of vertical integration in the above foreclosure models is to facilitate the exercise of horizontal market power at either the network or facilities level. At the facilities level, such power might be exercised by an established cable system or through coordinated action by one or more MSOs, involving numerous systems.

THE EMPIRICAL RECORD

The question becomes, then, whether those foreclosure models, and vertical integration's role in them, are plausible in the cable industry. As the FCC and many others have pointed out,[9] the motives and effects of exclusive dealing between cable operators and cable networks can often promote efficiency. In its 1990 report, for example, the FCC cited complaints by SMATV, MMDS, and overbuilt cable operators that TNT's policy of granting exclusive rights to established cable operators diminished the complainants' ability to compete with those established operators. But the FCC also noted TNT's claim that the exclusivity offer was designed to induce skeptical cable operators to accept the network during the year following TNT's 1987 launch and thus reduced their uncertainty of TNT's market value to them.[10] The commission further noted a policy of Cablevision Systems, a large MSO having equity interests in several networks. That MSO's programming subsidiary required wireless cable operators to renegotiate their affiliation agreements with its vertically integrated networks to impose areawide marketing responsibilities on the operators once their market penetration reached 2 percent. Such requirements, Cablevision Systems stated in its defense, were intended to prevent, among other things, free riding on the marketing efforts of cable systems in the same market area.

Those counterclaims about cable network marketing practices reflect classic economic arguments that exclusive contracting generally promotes efficiency.[11] Given the evident incentives of established cable systems to

---

9. 1990 FCC Cable Report, *supra* note 1, ¶ 116 .

10. *Id.* ¶ 114.

11. For a survey of those arguments, most of which rely on the free-rider marketing problem or other moral-hazard problems in the relationship between manufacturers and dealers, *see* Michael L. Katz, *Vertical Contractual Relations*, 1 HANDBOOK OF INDUSTRIAL ORGANIZATION 655 (Richard Schmalensee ed., Elsevier Science Publishers 1989). For a recent survey of the economic justifications for exclusivity in antitrust cases, *see* GREGG FRASCO, EXCLUSIVE DEALING: A COMPREHENSIVE STUDY (University Press of America 1991); Howard P. Marvel, *Book Review*, 8 REV. INDUS. ORG. 127 (1993) (book

retard competitive entry if they can, however, it would be surprising not to observe attempts at foreclosure behavior involving program access. In fact, established firms have a long history of attempts to stop the advance of technology by restricting access. In the 1920s some newspapers tried to prevent radio stations from buying news information from the Associated Press.[12] In the 1950s trade associations for motion picture theater operators repeatedly tried to organize boycotts against movie studios that sold old films to broadcast television stations.[13] Broadcast stations and theater operators later joined forces to pressure studios not to supply movies to experimental subscription television (STV) and pay-cable systems in the 1960s and 1970s.[14] Among examples of possible foreclosure involving competing firms in the same industry is extensive antitrust litigation, much of it resulting in plaintiff victories, which has been directed at alleged attempts by motion picture theater chains to prevent independently operated movie theaters from obtaining the films of major studios.[15] Some of those instances have involved vertical integration; others have not.

It is speculative to assess the actual extent of foreclosure behavior involving program access that has occurred in the cable industry. Our review of the record shows, however, that both integrated and nonintegrated cable firms have engaged in the same potentially anticompetitive behavior.

Charging higher prices to an existing or potential entrant can be essentially equivalent in motive and effect to an exclusive contract or outright refusal to deal. The role of vertical integration in exclusive dealing may be

---

review of FRASCO, *supra*). Some recent economic models challenge efficiency justifications for exclusive dealing. *See, e.g.,* Michael H. Riordan & David J. Salant, Exclusion and Integration in the Market for Video Programming Delivered to the Home (July 7, 1994; rev. Sept. 12, 1994) (paper presented at the AEI Telecommunications Summit). The authors specifically argue that exclusive dealing in the cable television industry may have negative welfare consequences, in part because economies of scale in distribution of single products are not realized.

12. D. ROSEWATER, HISTORY OF COOPERATIVE NEWS-GATHERING IN THE UNITED STATES 292–94 (D. Appleton & Co. 1930).

13. W. Lafferty, *Feature Films on Prime-Time Television, in* HOLLYWOOD IN THE AGE OF TELEVISION (T. Balio ed., Unwin Hyman 1990); M. Hilmes, *Pay Television: Breaking the Broadcast Bottleneck,* HOLLYWOOD IN THE AGE OF TELEVISION (*supra*).

14. Subscription Television: Hearings on H.R. 12435 Before the Subcomm. on Communications and Power of the House Comm. on Interstate and Foreign Commerce, 90th Cong., 1st Sess. (1967); R. A. Gershon, *Pay Cable Television: A Regulatory History,* COMMUNICATIONS & L. 3 (June 1990).

15. MICHAEL CONANT, ANTITRUST IN THE MOTION PICTURE INDUSTRY: ECONOMIC AND LEGAL ANALYSIS (University of California Press 1960).

quite different from that of differential pricing, however, so we consider those practices separately, beginning with the former.

The analysis to follow is primarily based on the empirical record established by congressional hearings and FCC proceedings leading up to the 1992 Cable Act. Since October 1993, several complaints and petitions to the FCC involving program access have been filed, and in June 1994, the commission began to rule on some of those cases. In chapter 8 we discuss that more recent regulatory activity.

Vertical Integration and Exclusive Dealing in Cable

Many of the program-access claims cited in the 1990 FCC report alleging exclusivity or refusals to deal involved vertically integrated firms. Those included TNT, Bravo, AMC, and a number of the regional sports networks.[16] Among nonvertically affiliated networks, however, the report cited ESPN contracts prohibiting wireless cable operators from distributing ESPN within any cable franchise area. Also cited were assertions by Telesat, an operator of overbuilt cable systems in Florida, that the Nashville Network (then nonintegrated) refused to renew affiliation agreements with Telesat in its overbuilt markets.[17] The cases cited in the report were both local and national, the latter concerning contracting policies of vertically affiliated networks such as TNT. Because the MSOs that owned equity in TBS, the parent company of TNT, serve much less than 100 percent of U.S. cable subscribers, for example, many of TNT's transactions were with unaffiliated MSOs.

Other evidence corroborates the involvement of both integrated and nonintegrated networks in claims of programming unavailability. In a 1988 report on the cable industry, the National Telecommunications and Information Administration cited data provided by the Wireless Cable Association on the availability of twenty-nine national cable networks. Of seventeen vertically affiliated networks, seven were available and ten unavailable; of twelve unaffiliated networks, eight were available and four unavailable.[18] Virtually all the major unaffiliated and affiliated national networks, in fact, have been mentioned in complaints about program access at one time or another. Examples of such complaints involving unaffiliated networks in-

---

16. 1990 FCC Cable Report, *supra* note 1, ¶ 114.

17. *Id.*

18. NATIONAL TELECOMMUNICATIONS AND INFORMATION ADMINISTRATION, VIDEO PROGRAM DISTRIBUTION AND CABLE TELEVISION: CURRENT POLICY ISSUES AND RECOMMENDATIONS (1988).

clude The Disney Channel, Cable Video Store, A&E, The Weather Channel, Home Shopping Network, USA, ESPN, and FNN.[19]

By the time the 1992 Cable Act became law, the prevalence of exclusive contracts and claims of other outright refusals to deal with alternative MVPDs had apparently diminished. In its March 1993 comments to the FCC, for example, the Wireless Cable Association noted that "[a]lthough TNT and many regional sports services remain holdouts . . . most other programming services now will do business with wireless cable."[20] As the Wireless Cable Association also noted, political or legal pressures were probably responsible for that shift. Such pressures, for example, are suggested by an instance involving HBO. In the mid-1980s, HBO announced that it would offer cable operators the right of "wireline exclusivity" within their local market areas for a rate surcharge of twenty-five cents per subscriber. HBO's announcement was met with a letter from Senator John F. Kerry (D-Mass.) questioning its effects on potential competitive video providers. The offer was later dropped.[21]

The legal proceedings leading up to the FCC's program-access regulations nevertheless showed no apparent diminution in claims that many programmers charge higher prices to MMDS, SMATV, overbuilt cable systems, HSD owners, and HSD program distributors.[22]

Vertical Integration and Input Price Differentials in Cable

While data are not conclusive, some rate comparisons submitted in earlier congressional and FCC proceedings suggest the extent of input price differentials between MSOs and MVPDs. The 1990 FCC report cites data provided by the Wireless Cable Association for seven networks serving MMDS systems. Those data, reproduced in table 7-1, indicate that certain MMDS systems paid 36.4 percent to 78.6 percent more for programming than did

---

19. *Id.* at 103 (The Disney Channel); Comments of Telesat Cablevision to FCC, MM Dkt. No. 89-600, at 26–27, 30 (Cable Video Store, A&E, The Weather Channel, Home Shopping Network); FCC Los Angeles Field Hearings, Feb. 12, 1990 (USA, ESPN); Reply Comments of National Cable Television Cooperative to FCC, MM Dkt. 89-600, at 2 (FNN).

20. Comments of Wireless Cable to MM Dkt. No.89-600, at 17–18 (Jan. 29, 1993).

21. Competitive Issues in the Cable Television Industry: Hearings Before the Subcomm. on Antitrust, Business Rights, and Competition of the Senate Comm. on the Judiciary, 100th Cong., 2d Sess. 152–74 (1988).

22. *See* Comments and Reply Comments to FCC, MM Dkt. No. 92-265, by the Wireless Cable Association, Peoples Choice TV, National Rural Television Cooperative, and the National Private Cable Association.

Table 7-1
Input Price Comparisons Using Public Data

Panel A. Table XI
Sample Rate Comparison between Wireless Cable and Cable[1]
(cents per subscriber)

	Top Wireless Rate	Top Cable Rate	Wireless Premium
CNN*	$.50	$.28	78.6%
USA	.38	.23	65.2%
Nickelodeon*	.35	.22	59.1%
MTV*	.35	.22	59.1%
Nashville	.35	.20	75.0%
A&E	.15	.11	36.4%
Headline News*	.50	.00	—

[1]Information obtained in the comments of the Wireless Cable Association.
*Indicates presence of a vertical ownership relationship with a cable operator.

Panel B. Table XII
Rate Comparisons: Mid-Atlantic Communications' Cable Systems vs. SMATVs[1]

Programmer	SMATV	Cable System	SMATV Premium
HBO*	$6.25 per sub**	$4.00/mo. per sub[a]	56.2%
Cinemax*	6.50 per sub**	3.86/mo. per sub	94.5%
Nick*	0.29 per sub	0.17 per sub	70.5%
MTV*	0.29 per sub	0.17 per sub	70.5%
USA	0.18 per passing	0.18 per sub	not comparable
FNN	0.17 per sub	0.055 per sub	209%
HTS	1.50 per sub	0.75 per sub	100%
CNN*	0.33 per sub	0.25 per sub	32.0%
ESPN*	0.47 per sub	0.32 per sub	46.9%

[1]Information obtained from the comments of the National Satellite Programming Network, Inc., et al.
[a]sub=subscriber
*Indicates that network has vertical relationship with an MSO.
**Sold by cable operator.

Panel C. Wireless Cable vs. MSO Prices

Network	Wireless	MSO
Basic Services		
American Movie Classics[a]	$0.300	$0.136
Arts & Entertainment	$0.110	$0.070
Black Entertainment[a]	$0.060	$0.060
CNN[a]	$0.360	$0.195
Discovery[a]	$0.185	$0.045
ESPN/NFL	$0.560	$0.260
Family Channel[a]	$0.080	$0.040
Lifetime[a]	$0.140	$0.035
MTV[a]	$0.350	$0.050
Nashville	$0.200	$0.065
Nickelodeon[a]	$0.350	$0.100
Prime Ticket	N/A	$0.450
TNT[a]	N/A	$0.200
USA	$0.380	$0.157
VH-1[a]	$0.350	$0.000
The Weather Channel	$0.200	$0.036
WGN	$0.150	$0.030
WOR	$0.100	$0.030
WTBS[a]	$0.100	$0.010
Premium Services		
HBO[a]	$5.080	$4.100
Cinemax[a]	N/A	$2.900
Showtime[a]	$5.050	$2.900
The Disney Channel	$4.000	$2.500

Note: Prices are prices Cross Country Cable chairman and chief executive officer "believed to be charged by the largest cable MSOs compared with prices [for MSOs] supplied to us by the Wireless Cable Association."

a. Network has a vertical relationship with a cable operator.

Sources: Panels A and B are reproduced from FCC, *1990 Cable Report*, appendix G. The authors added an indication of a vertical relationship in panel A. Data for panel C come from a letter from George Remy, chairman and CEO of Cross Country Cable, to the Hon. Alfred C. Sikes, chairman, FCC, Apr. 4, 1990, p. 4 (FCC MM Dkt. 89-600). Indications of a vertical ownership relationship added by authors.

comparably sized cable systems. Data from the National Satellite Programming Network, Inc., a trade organization for SMATV systems, reported premiums ranging from 32 percent to 209 percent for nine networks available to certain SMATV systems. The FCC report also noted claims by the National Rural Telecommunications Cooperative, a distributor of cable programming to HSD owners, that while all networks were available to it, NRTC had to pay rates 233 percent to 780 percent higher than did cable operators for access to eighteen basic cable networks.[23] Finally, Cross Country Cable, Inc., an MMDS operator, submitted data indicating that a package of seventeen basic cable networks available both to MMDS systems and to "the largest cable MSOs" cost the MMDS systems approximately 200 percent more than it did the MSOs.

In nearly all cases in table 7-1, both affiliated and unaffiliated networks reportedly charged lower rates to cable systems than to alternative MVPDs. But while those input price differences seem substantial, the data indicate no discernible tendency for integrated programmers to be more inclined than nonintegrated programmers to charge higher prices to alternative MVPDs.

Program suppliers generally did not dispute that and similar evidence of price differentials in the FCC and other policy proceedings. A main reason for the differences cited by both integrated and nonintegrated programming suppliers was that serving noncable system customers is more costly, primarily because of a higher frequency of bad debts, higher marketing costs, higher advertising costs, and poor signal quality.[24]

While such factors are clearly plausible contributors to input price differences, two other explanations are possible. The first is that established cable operators are attempting to prevent entry or to raise the costs of existing rivals by inducing program suppliers to charge rivals higher prices than they otherwise would. That might be to prevent a fringe competitor such as an MMDS system from gaining a stronger foothold or to force it to exit the market. Or it could be a short-term strategy to raise rivals' costs. In the latter model, higher programming costs paid by a fringe competitor create a price umbrella under which an established firm can continue to charge monopoly prices to consumers.[25] That is, higher consumer prices charged by a fringe

---

23. 1990 FCC Cable Report, *supra* note 1, ¶ 114; National Rural Telecommunications Cooperative Comments to FCC MM Dkt. 89-600, at 24–25.

24. 1990 FCC Cable Report, *supra* note 1, ¶ 116–17.

25. For a general analysis, *see* Thomas G. Krattenmaker & Steven C. Salop, *Anticompetitive Exclusion: Raising Rivals' Costs to Achieve Power over Price*, 96 YALE L.J. 206 (1986). The relevant model in this case is the "cartel ringmaster." *Id.* at 238–40.

competitor then reduce the competitive pressure on an established cable operator to lower its own subscription prices.

While that is a possible explanation for the cable network price differentials we observe, the policing of input price collusion among numerous networks, even in the presence of the fairly extensive vertical relationships in the cable industry, seems very problematic for the model. In addition to being complex, network-affiliate contracts specify confidentiality. The likelihood of undetected discounts to an entrant under those circumstances is high. Of course, an individual MSO should have little difficulty controlling the input price terms charged by a network in which it has a majority ownership investment. The minority ownership relationships prevalent between MSOs and many networks, however, would be less conducive to such price control, as would the absence of any ownership control over other cable networks. Even if only a single MSO or cable system attempted to orchestrate collusion among networks in a localized area, those coordination problems would seem forbidding. It would be even more difficult for several MSOs to coordinate the process.

The 1994 Primestar decrees provide some perspective. The Primestar Partners' original contract contained a clause that required the involved program suppliers to offer their programming to the Primestar DBS system at prices no higher than were charged to any other entity. The government interpreted that clause to be conducive to input price collusion for the possible purpose of preventing entry of a competing DBS system. While that theory recognizes the incentive those firms would have to coordinate input prices, the government's reason for the decrees' prohibition of such price clauses is that even though all the participants were vertically integrated firms, a written document would be instrumental in coordinating collusion. Obviously, such written documents have not been the rule in the cable industry.

A second, alternative explanation for the input price differences we observe is variations in outcomes of bargaining between individual networks (or commonly owned network-groups) and various MVPDs. Just as operators of different delivery systems are likely to have different credit risks, it is also apparent that they have different degrees of bargaining, or monopsony, power in the input market. Less established services such as SMATV and MMDS can be expected to hold relatively little sway over cable networks since their retail distribution of those networks accounts for a relatively marginal share of those networks' profits. The larger MSOs, however, are able to threaten a given program supplier with the loss of a relatively large share of its potential revenues and would thus be likely to negotiate programming price terms that are relatively favorable.

The record of congressional testimony and comments to the FCC is consistent with the theory that input price differences reflect differential bargaining power. As we mentioned in chapter 5, small cable operators make essentially the same complaints about discriminatory pricing by program suppliers as do SMATV, MMDS, and HSD owners. In its 1989 comments to the FCC, for example, the National Cable Television Cooperative, a cooperative formed to secure bulk programming for small cable operators, complained of the "lack of good terms" for cable network programming.[26] In its 1993 comments to the commission, the Community Cable Television Association, a trade association of rural cable operators, complained of unfair terms and practices from both integrated and nonintegrated cable networks.[27]

One could respond to the explanation that bargaining power determines input price differentials by arguing that the entry-retarding effect on emerging technologies of higher prices determined by different degrees of bargaining power is basically the same as that of foreclosure behavior. For our purposes, however, the distinction is important because vertical integration has little to do with bilateral bargaining over input prices. The role of integration in that context is limited to providing contracting efficiencies or providing to a program buyer integrated with one network a strategic advantage in negotiating with another. The effect of those factors on input prices is obviously minor compared with the large differences we have reported here.

CONCLUSION

It is evident that vertical integration can facilitate foreclosure attempts involving program access in the cable industry. The record has shown, however, that both integrated and nonintegrated cable program suppliers engage in the same potentially anticompetitive foreclosure behavior involving exclusive dealing. Empirical evidence that program suppliers charge consistently higher input prices to alternative MVPDs appears to be unre-

---

26. 1990 FCC Cable Report, *supra* note 1, ¶ 114.

27. Comments of the Community Cable Television Association to MM Dkt. 92-265 (Jan. 25, 1993). Specifically: "However, many of CCTA's member operators, who tend to be smaller operators in rural areas, have found that certain of the practices of certain video programming suppliers, whether integrated or not, result in unfair competition or unfair or deceptive acts or practices, the effect of which has been to hinder significantly (and in some instances to prevent) cable television operators from providing satellite programming and satellite broadcast programming to their subscribers at reasonable cost," at 2.

lated to vertical integration. To the extent that cost factors are not responsible for those input price differences, they can be explained by variation in outcomes of the bilateral input price-setting process between program suppliers and MVPDs having varying degrees of bargaining power in the programming market.

The ancillary role of vertical integration in restricting entry at the facilities level is illustrated by the Justice Department's theory underlying the Primestar decrees. Whatever the particular merits of the department's interpretation of Primestar, the decrees rely on a plausible theory of how vertical integration might be employed to coordinate horizontal collusion at either the MSO or program-supplier level.

Vertical integration might contribute to less elaborate foreclosure attempts, particularly at the local level, than the Primestar decrees address. Whether simple or elaborate, however, horizontal market power, especially at the cable system operator level, is the basic ingredient for successful foreclosure of other MVPDs. If that power does exist, the empirical record suggests that foreclosure could be accomplished by other strategies, such as exclusive programming contracts, without the aid of vertical ownership ties.

8

Summary and Policy Conclusions

VERTICAL INTEGRATION between cable networks and cable systems is extensive, and the prevalence of those relationships has grown since the mid-1980s. According to the criteria we set out in chapter 2—economic efficiency, access to the public by program creators, and program diversity—those vertical relationships, unrestrained until the 1992 Cable Act, benefit the social welfare in some respects and detract from it in others.

First, our statistical analysis in chapter 6 confirms that at least to some extent, integrated cable systems do behave as many critics of integration have contended: They tend to favor their vertically affiliated networks through carriage or marketing behavior, and in at least some cases, that conduct appears to be at the expense of unaffiliated, rival networks. Moreover, we observe a tendency for integrated systems to offer somewhat fewer cable networks than do nonintegrated systems.

On the basis of those results, one could argue that vertical integration, given the limited competition from other MVPDs that most cable systems face, reduces the diversity of programming available to the public and limits the access that non-MSO–affiliated program creators have to those media users. One could further argue that any favoritism by a cable system—even of an affiliated network whose programming content is very similar to that of a disadvantaged unaffiliated network—implicitly violates the spirit of the First Amendment. Those arguments may seem especially compelling when applied, for example, to news rather than to entertainment channels. And finally, our comparisons of vertical integration's effects in systems of different capacities suggest that as system bandwidths expand, and near or true video-on-demand systems are developed, such effects of integration, though diminished, will remain significant.

142

Economic theory and the historical experience of the cable industry also suggest that at least to some degree, vertical integration increases barriers to entry into cable networking by unaffiliated program suppliers, regardless of whether those barriers arise from anticompetitive or more innocent motives. It is reasonable to suppose that integration into cable networking by MSOs— at least by those with large national market shares—enhances any ability that established cable operators might have to prevent or retard the entry of alternative multichannel video providers.

Particularly on economic grounds, however, other findings of this study provide counterpoint to those arguments. Under reasonable assumptions, relatively unfavorable marketing of unaffiliated networks, or the exclusion of those networks from a menu altogether, can simply reflect transactions efficiencies that integrated firms realize by carrying and promoting their affiliated networks. The tendency for integrated cable systems to offer fewer networks of certain types than do nonintegrated systems can be attributed to the same efficiency effects. In economic terms it is reasonable to presume that subscribers are better off for those changes. Even if vertical integration provides the strategic advantage that allows one network rather than another to survive, the incentives of cable operators and other natural economic forces are likely to ensure that the array of programming content eventually made available to consumers is substantially the same as if no ownership ties had been involved.

Vertical integration also appears to facilitate entry of new networks by reducing the high risks inherent in their launches. In our view, the main case for vertical integration should be made in terms of the financial resources and other risk-reducing advantages, as well as the creative resources, that cable operators can contribute to the programming industry. In themselves, those advantages of integration undoubtedly promote economic efficiency and the diversity of programming content. By facilitating the entry process, they also promote the access of program suppliers to cable subscribers in an important sense.

Ambiguities in evaluating benefits and costs of vertical integration in cable thus remain. Our findings have more definite implications, however, for the key policy issues involving vertical integration in cable. We begin with the three central issues set out in chapter 2.

RESTRICTIONS AGAINST DISADVANTAGING UNAFFILIATED PROGRAM SUPPLIERS

Should there be regulations intended to prevent or restrict integrated cable system operators from disadvantaging unaffiliated program suppliers? Assuming that to be a desirable goal, the most general way to achieve it is some type of nondiscriminatory access guarantee for unaffiliated networks. The experience with commercial leased-access requirements in cable, however, suggests little promise for such provisions as a way to end unfavorable treatment of nonvertically integrated networks. Given the complexity of contracts, as well as variations in program content and quality, it would be very difficult for regulators to set lease terms comparable to those of the private market. Alternatively, a cable operator might be required to provide nondiscriminatory access at its average incremental cost per channel. In theory, that access price would be defined as an operator's cost of providing a channel, plus the opportunity cost of using the channel for other purposes. Essentially, such a policy would be comparable to an efficient component-pricing rule, which some advocate for local telephony because of the bottleneck access to telephone subscribers that LECs typically control.[1] At least in the case of the cable industry, however, it would also be very difficult to determine what those costs are. Furthermore, even if input prices were ideally regulated, an unaffiliated competitor could not likely match a system operator's control over promotion, pricing, channel positioning, and other marketing variables.

What results can we expect for the 40 percent limit, set by the FCC in 1993, on the number of channels that a cable system can fill with programming in which it has an attributable interest? It is unclear how many cable systems the limit affects, but it would appear to affect only smaller capacity systems of the two largest MSOs, TCI and Time Warner. Also, the FCC grandfathered the existing menus of all cable systems as of December 1992, so the 40 percent rule affects only new additions of programming.[2] The practical effects of the FCC's chosen limits thus appear to be slight. Apart from those particulars, our analysis suggests that channel-occupancy limits set at any level would not accomplish their purpose: They could have little effect on the incentives of cable operators to disadvantage unaffiliated programming, except to the extent that they may induce vertical divestiture. In fact, we argue that channel limits are likely to be detrimental to consumers.

------

1. *See* WILLIAM J. BAUMOL & J. GREGORY SIDAK, TOWARD COMPETITION IN LOCAL TELEPHONY 95 (MIT Press and AEI Press 1994).

2. A cable system violating the limit as of that date can add unaffiliated programming only until its full menu falls below the limit. Implementation of Section 19 of the Cable Television Consumer Protection and Competition Act of 1992: Annual Assessment of the Status of Competition in the Market for Delivery of Video Programming, First Rep., CS Dkt. No. 94-48, FCC 94-235 (1994) ¶¶ 187–90 [hereinafter 1994 FCC Cable Report].

Channel limits rely on the theory that the mere availability of more capacity will provide the needed opportunities for unaffiliated networks, existing or entering, to compete on equal terms for carriage on integrated systems. As our analysis suggests, however, the primary incentives for integrated firms to disadvantage unaffiliated networks, whether benign or anticompetitive in origin, apply only to those that are good substitutes for affiliated networks. We have little reason to believe that the amount of channel capacity the FCC forces a system to reserve for unaffiliated networks will significantly affect such incentives.

For example, assume that there are no channel limits and that the manager of a cable system that carries a vertically affiliated network called the Public Affairs Channel has refused carriage of the unaffiliated Issues and Answers Channel because he believes the latter would largely split viewership with Public Affairs and would not attract any new subscribers. Now assume that channel limits are imposed and the cable system chooses to keep Public Affairs on its menu. As the system adds new, unaffiliated networks to its menu over time, Issues and Answers is no more likely to be among them than before, because, apart from the fact that substitution effects among all networks will diminish somewhat with larger capacities, Issues and Answers' negative economic effect on the audience for Public Affairs is unchanged. Our finding that the exclusion of unaffiliated networks on integrated systems tends to persist in large capacity systems supports that reasoning. Thus, channel limits are unlikely to facilitate the entry of unaffiliated networks that promise to compete with well-established networks having vertical ties. Conversely, a system manager would have little initial incentive to exclude a new unaffiliated network that is well differentiated from his current menu, so that channel limits would not seem to ease entry much in those cases either.

Channel slots reserved for networks having no ownership affiliation with a given cable system will, of course, contribute to the fortunes of those networks in general and promote access to subscribers by the suppliers of those programs. Measured by ownership affiliation, programming diversity will thus be promoted. The unaffiliated networks most helped, however, are likely to be those facing the least intense competition or the lowest barriers to entry in the first place. Also, because the limits restrict a system from carrying only programming in which its particular operator has an ownership interest, the benefits to "independent" program suppliers—those unaffiliated with any MSO—are likely to be minor. A TCI system, for example, can still offer an unlimited number of Time Warner–owned networks and vice versa.

Channel limits are also likely to have certain negative effects on consumers. If we assume that system operators do not choose to divest of programming interests or that they do not choose to forgo investment opportunities in new networks to avoid the channel limits, those regulations will necessarily induce the operators to replace popular affiliated networks with less popular unaffiliated networks. That will reduce efficiency and not meaningfully improve programming diversity. Furthermore, the affiliated networks that a system chooses not to carry owing to channel limits will be those that contribute the least to its total revenues. Such networks are likely to be the least established in the marketplace.

The likely effects of channel limits are complicated by the fact that MSOs typically include systems with a wide variety of channel capacities. If channel limits affect relatively few of an MSO's systems, it can simply endure the costs of having less desirable program menus on those systems. An MSO significantly affected by channel limits, however, is more likely to divest some of its network interests or to refrain from equity participation in entering networks.

The channel-limits provisions thus highlight a contradiction in FCC policy. The commission has repeatedly acknowledged the beneficial effects of vertical affiliation with MSOs on the financial viability of new entrants in program supply and thus on the diversity of programming. Channel limits have the opposite effect because they discourage MSOs from offering financial and other support for new entrants.

Such vertical separation would obviously reduce the tendency for favoritism of affiliated networks simply because an operator would have fewer affiliated networks to favor. While that might be desirable, such a method of achieving divestiture would again tend to remove MSO financial and other support from the least established networks.

In general, our analysis suggests that using regulation to prevent integrated cable operators from disadvantaging unaffiliated networks is simply not practical. Whatever its motives, such behavior can be carried out in a variety of different ways beyond the regulators' control. To the extent that channel-occupancy limits affect certain cable systems, they are likely to decrease both efficiency and the diversity of cable programming. Consequently, the FCC should direct any efforts toward controlling cable system operator behavior elsewhere.

Nondiscriminatory Access to Programming

Should alternative multichannel distributors (such as overbuilt cable systems, SMATV, MMDS, and DBS) be given nondiscriminatory access to programming distributed by suppliers that are vertically integrated with established cable operators?

As outlined in chapters 1 and 2, the 1992 Cable Act mandates that vertically integrated program suppliers observe nondiscriminatory program access; the act requires vertically integrated firms to justify any differences between prices charged to established cable systems and those charged to other media to ensure that they are cost-related.[3] While nonvertically integrated cable networks are prohibited from certain "unfair" behavior, the program-access provisions fall basically on vertically integrated programming suppliers.[4]

One can question the merit of the FCC's program-access regulations on several grounds. The rules may cause inefficient behavior or increase administrative costs; appropriate judgments in access cases may require information and expertise beyond the commission's resources. If the regulations do help establish effective competition, however, consumer prices should fall, and if alternative delivery systems sufficiently expand total consumer demand, program supply and program diversity should increase as well.[5]

The main point of the analysis in chapter 7 is that whether program-access regulations are good public policy, one cannot make a reasonable case for separate treatment of vertically integrated and nonintegrated firms. Both integrated and nonintegrated suppliers engage in the same pattern of behavior with respect to program availability and pricing to cable systems and alternative MVPDs. Although vertical integration might facilitate anticompetitive foreclosure, it is substantially unrelated to the outcomes of bargaining over input prices.

If the FCC's program-access regulations prove effective in constraining the marketing behavior of vertically integrated program suppliers, then vertical divestiture—or in the case of an entering program service, avoidance of MSO affiliations—is again likely to result.[6] Any benefits from the rules

---

3. Implementation of Sections 12 and 19 of the Cable Television Consumer Protection Act of 1992: Development of Competition and Diversity in Video Programming Distribution and Carriage, First Rep. & Order, MM Dkt. No. 92-265, 8 F.C.C. Rcd. 3359 (1993).

4. *Id.* at 4–7 (mimeo pagination).

5. The generally favorable response that cable program suppliers reportedly had to the FCC's program-access provisions suggests that they have confidence in this model. *See, e.g.*, Harry Jessell, *Biondi Sees Net Benefit in Cable Act*, BROADCASTING, Oct. 26, 1992, at 38; R. Granger, *Distributors See Program-Access Rules as a Plus*, MULTICHANNEL NEWS, May 10, 1993, at 6A.

6. While the program-access regulations could have been a factor in the sale by Paramount-Viacom of its cable system interests, the need for cash to finance the merger was widely reported to be a primary motive. *See, e.g.,* John M. Higgins, *TCI Eyes Viacom*

would thus be undermined, their enforcement would be arbitrarily unbalanced, and the widely acknowledged efficiency benefits of vertical integration diminished.[7]

We therefore conclude that any program-access requirements should apply equally to integrated and nonintegrated program suppliers. With that modification, the program-access rules would require all programming suppliers that contract exclusively with cable operators to demonstrate that those contracts are in the public interest. The nondiscriminatory pricing provisions would apply to pricing by all programming suppliers to any MVPD.

FCC Program-Access Rulings since the 1992 Cable Act

Relatively few program-access cases have come before the FCC. As of September 1994, there had been twelve, and eleven of those had been decided.[8] By late 1996, eleven additional rulings had been made.[9]

Two of the 1994 rulings established models for the commission's subsequent interpretations of the program-access regulations on exclusive contracting. In one of those cases, the commission denied Time Warner Cable the right to withhold its vertically affiliated network, Court TV, from

---

Buy, MULTICHANNEL NEWS, April 4, 1994, at 1. Other news reports, however, have suggested that Viacom was pursuing a sale of its cable systems before the merger. Laura Landro & Jonnie L. Roberts, *Viacom Is Set to Grow into a Media Colossus—or a Burdened Giant*, WALL ST. J., Feb. 16, 1994, at 1.

7. The Primestar settlements, particularly those at the state level, appear to overlap significantly with the FCC's program-access requirements. Those settlements, however, apply only to the seven vertically integrated MSO defendants, and, at least in the federal case, they affect only program suppliers that are controlled by means of a 50 percent or greater equity share held by one MSO or in common by more than one MSO. The state decrees require programming to be made available to other MVPDs on "reasonable" terms, while the Primestar agreement essentially controls collusion only among the MSOs or their controlled entities—one or more party is involved. United States *v.* Primestar Partners, L.P., Proposed Final Judgment and Competitive Impact Statement, 58 Fed. Reg. 33,944 (1993). The Primestar rules would not, therefore, compensate for the shortcomings of the FCC program-access rules that we have identified.

8. 1994 FCC Cable Report, *supra* note 2, ¶¶ 174–75, app. F.

9. Implementation of the Cable Consumer Protection and Competition Act of 1992; Annual Assessment of the Status of Competition in the Market for the Delivery of Video Programming, CS Dkt. No. 95-61, FCC 95-491 (December 11, 1995), at 161–66 [hereinafter 1995 FCC Cable Report]; In the Matter of Annual Assessment of the Status of Competition in the Market for the Delivery of Video Programming, Third Annual Report, CS Dkt. No. 96-133, FCC 96-496 (Jan. 2, 1997), app. H.

Liberty Cable Co., an MMDS operator competing with Time Warner cable franchises in the Manhattan area.[10] In the other case, the FCC permitted New England Cable News (NECN), a regional news channel launched in 1992, to maintain exclusivity agreements with several cable operators for the next eighteen months, after which it would have to petition the commission to continue the agreements.[11] NECN is half-owned by an MSO, Continental Cablevision.

In each of the rulings, the FCC intended to balance the benefits of encouraging competition by alternative MVPDs with the benefits that program exclusivity could have by encouraging entry and investment in new cable program services. In the Court TV case, the commission argued that the network was already well established, so that the balance was in favor of encouraging alternative MVPDs. In the NECN case, the FCC argued that the network was not yet established, so that the balance was in favor of encouraging competition in program supply. The commission has followed similar rationales in more recent exclusivity decisions.[12] Thus, the FCC has taken a rather straightforward infant-firm approach to program access by nurturing newer competitors upstream and downstream.

One can take issue with the FCC's wisdom in deciding which cable firms are most in need of nurturing, with respect to either their financial stability or their potential benefits to program diversity. Under the circumstances, however, the rulings seem reasonable. Early in 1994, *Multichannel News* reported that some nascent local cable news channels were threatened by the program-access regulations and that some entry plans had stalled.[13] The article speculated that third-party packagers were likely to take the place of MSO ownership owing to the vertical integration language in the regulations. Affirming the exclusivity provision in the NECN case presumably

---

10. In the Matter of Time Warner Cable Petition for Public Interest Determination Under 47 C.F.R. § 76.1002(c)(4) Relating to Exclusive Distribution of Court TV, CSR-4231-P (June 1, 1994).

11. In the Matter of New England Cable News Petition for Public Interest Determination Under 47 C.F.R. § 76.1002(c)(4) Relating to Exclusive Distribution of New England Cable News, CSR-4190-P (June 1, 1994).

12. *See* Cablevision Industries Corp. and Sci-Fi Channel Petition for Public Interest Determination Under 47 C.F.R. § 76.1002(c)(4) Relating to the Exclusive Distribution of the Sci-Fi Channel, Mem. Op. & Order, 10 F.C.C. Rcd. 9786 (1995), and NewsChannel, a Division of Lenfest Programming Services, Petition for Public Interest Determination Under 47 C.F.R. § 76.1002(c)(4) Relating to Exclusive Distribution of NewsChannel, Mem. Op. & Order, 10 F.C.C. Rcd. 691 (1994).

13. Kim Mitchell, *Cable Act Fine Print Threatens Local News Channels*, MULTICHANNEL NEWS, Jan. 29, 1994, at 14.

reduced pressures toward ownership separation between MSOs and entering program suppliers. In addition, a relatively new program service is unlikely to be a good foreclosure weapon. Conversely, established networks such as Court TV might be effective foreclosure devices.

The commission has issued only one ruling involving nonvertically integrated programming suppliers.[14] American Cable Company, a cable operator that had overbuilt an established system owned by Telecable, Inc., in Columbus, Ohio, complained that separate exclusivity contracts that Telecable had signed with the Sci-Fi Network and ESPN violated the program-access rules. The commission ruled that those contracts did not violate the exclusivity provisions of the rules because both networks were at the time in question vertically unaffiliated with any cable operator. The commission further held that American Cable failed to meet the burden of proof under the more general "unfair" provisions of the access rules that apply to nonvertically integrated suppliers. Whatever the merits of American Cable's complaint, that ruling puts into relief the cable act's illogical distinction between vertically affiliated and unaffiliated programming suppliers with respect to the program-access rules.

The commission has made only one substantive ruling under the non-disrimination provisions of the program access rules, but that case involved a refusal to deal rather than an allegation of price discrimination per se.[15]

It may be that the low volume of FCC cases to date means that either the current program-access rules or natural economic forces have already broken the floodgates of program flow to alternative technologies. Competition with established cable remains nascent, however. As our discussion of vertical integration by LECs and other alternative MVPDs suggests, program access could prove to be an important element in future competitive battles.

---

14. American Cable Company and Jay Copeland *v.* Telecable of Columbus, Inc., Order, CSR-4206, CSR-4198-P (Aug. 29, 1996).

15. Several of the FCC's program-access rulings have involved complaints of discriminatory pricing, but all were privately settled and the complaints dismissed by the FCC with the exception of CellularVision *v.* SportsChannel Associates, Order, CSR-4478-P, DA 95-2134 (Oct. 6, 1995). In *CellularVision*, the commission ruled that SportsChannel New York had unreasonably refused to deal with CellularVision, a microwave distributor of video programming. *See* 1994 FCC Cable Report, *supra* note 2, app. F; and 1995 FCC Cable Report, *supra* note 9, at 163.

VERTICAL DISINTEGRATION

Should there be vertical divestiture of cable networking from cable system operation? Or should there be limits on the extent of integration? Recall that it was the expectation that cable system operators would favor their affiliated programming that motivated Nixon's cabinet committee to propose complete divestiture of cable system operation from program supply. We not only have documented such behavior by cable operators but have argued that it is essentially impossible to control through regulation. And despite the program-access regulations, there is no guarantee that cable operators will not use their vertical ties with program suppliers to restrict entry at the facilities level.

Why not, then, resolve those issues by complete vertical divestiture? Of course, one can judge the effects of integration on cable program menus to be slight, especially if the net result—as our analysis suggests to be the case frequently—is simply the replacement of one network with a similar one. As long as cable systems retain "bottleneck" monopoly control over the access of program suppliers to final consumers, however, vertical divestiture in cable television is essentially desirable from a First Amendment perspective of ensuring equal access by all programming suppliers to cable subscribers.[16] From an economic perspective, mandated vertical divestiture in the cable industry is unwarranted. The historical record makes clear that vertical ownership ties are only one within an arsenal of devices that cable firms might employ to establish and defend their competitive positions. Program suppliers can use pricing, programming investment, and a variety of arms-length contractual arrangements to carry out competitive strategies—whether procompetitively or anticompetitively motivated. MSOs can employ similar devices to defend their market positions at the facilities level. As a result, there is no assurance that disintegration would meaningfully reduce entry barriers to new cable networks or to alternative MVPDs at the facilities level, because vertical integration does not motivate any of the potentially anticompetitive behavior in the industry with which policy should be concerned. While vertical integration probably facilitates anticompetitive behavior in the cable industry, the evidence does not support a compelling economic case against vertical ownership.

One cannot make as strong a positive case for ownership of both content and conduit in cable television as, for example, in the newspaper industry, where the creation of content seems inextricably entwined with the editorial

---

16. For a recent discussion of that issue, *see* BRUCE M. OWEN & STEVEN S. WILDMAN, VIDEO ECONOMICS 236 (Harvard University Press 1992).

function of assembling the newspaper product. Vertical divestiture would, however, mean a sacrifice of the several benefits of such relationships that we have identified—especially the creative and risk-reducing resources that cable operators can provide.

Finally, vertical separation in cable would have consequences far beyond the dislocations incurred by firms currently holding ownership interests both in system operation and networking. As table 3-2 shows, diversified corporations having a variety of different media interests have held much of the equity in cable networks and MSOs. Such diversification is broadly motivated by risk, cash flow, cost, and long-term strategic considerations.[17] A policy of vertical separations in cable would impede realization of those well-recognized benefits if potential merger partners were unwilling to divest of either cable system or networking interests. If vertical separations in cable were to include not just program packaging but all cable program production, those consequences would be great. The overwhelming majority of major corporations in the U.S. video media industries produces and distributes programming that appears on cable at one time or another. Complete vertical separations would therefore effectively foreclose the resources of all those firms from either video program production or cable system ownership. That conclusion with respect to vertical integration leaves us to consider the possibility of limiting horizontal concentration in the cable industry.

MSO SIZE LIMITS

National market concentration at the MSO level poses several possible threats to social welfare. As discussed in chapter 5, an MSO that monopsonistically reduces input prices could restrict the backward flow of resources to the program-supply industry and thus reduce program diversity and the level of program investments to economically inefficient levels. Such monopsony power could also translate into veto power over the entry or survival of individual cable networks, a primary concern of policy makers. Any ability that a cable operator may have to restrict other MVPDs' entry is also likely to be enhanced by the bargaining leverage over programming suppliers it can obtain through its national share of U.S. cable subscribers. And not least, a central claim of this study has been that whatever hazards vertical integration in cable may pose to the social welfare on economic or other

---

17. *See* Michael E. Porter & M. S. Salter, Diversification as a Strategy (Harvard Business School 1982).

grounds largely depend on the presence of monopsony power at the MSO level.

Preferably, any limits on MSO size would be imposed on a case-by-case basis via Justice Department reviews of MSOs' horizontal merger activity. A major problem with FCC jurisdiction is access to the information necessary to determine an appropriate limit. The faulty logic by which the FCC arrived at the 30 percent limit on the number of homes passed that a single MSO can have demonstrates that point. Our analysis suggests that the limit is excessively high and probably prejudices the Justice Department's ability to challenge potentially anticompetitive MSO mergers.

In a 1993 report the FCC stated:

> A 30 percent horizontal ownership limit is generally appropriate to prevent the nation's largest MSOs from gaining enhanced leverage from increased horizontal concentration. Nonetheless, it also ensures that the majority of MSOs continue to expand and benefit from the economies of scale necessary to encourage investment in new video programming services and the deployment of advanced cable technologies.[18]

That statement recognizes the right trade-off in general: Any limit should be set high enough to allow the realization of economies of scale but not so high that significant monopsony power can be exercised.

Consider first the threat of "leverage" over program suppliers. To specify the level at which such leverage is excessive would require input price data demonstrating the extent of monopsony power exerted by larger MSOs. The FCC has not obtained such data. In defending its limit, the commission has said little more than that 30 percent is a nonthreatening market share by usual antitrust standards and that the level of "MSO concentration" is too low to be of serious concern. In particular, the FCC noted in its 1994 report that the Herfindahl-Hirschman index (HHI) of national market concentration of MSOs fell below one thousand, the level ordinarily warranting further Justice Department investigation.[19] In its 1990 report recommending against any size limits on MSOs, the commission cited numerous commenters who had made that argument or had appealed to economic rules of thumb that a single firm having less than a 35 to 40 percent

---

18. Implementation of Sections 11 and 13 of the Cable Television Consumer Protection and Competition Act of 1992: Horizontal and Vertical Ownership Limits, Cross-Ownership Limitations and Anti-Trafficking Provisions, Second Rep. & Order, MM Dkt. No. 92-264, 8 F.C.C. Rcd. 8576–77.

19. 1994 FCC Cable Report, *supra* note 2, ¶¶ 141–47.

market share was unlikely to have sufficient market power to behave anticompetitively.[20]

The FCC is simply wrong to apply the HHI standards or other benchmarks of firm concentration to the MSO case in that way. As the 1992 Horizontal Merger Guidelines make clear, the HHI standards are concerned with the accretion of market power through unilateral or coordinated behavior that would result from a merger within a particular market in which other firms compete for the same customers (or inputs). The rate at which an MSO can accumulate monopsony power has nothing to do with the standard interpretation of the HHI, because virtually none of the cable system buyers competes with another for programs. The relevant determinants are the degree of economies of scale in cable networking, the market power of the particular networks involved, and alternative distribution routes that the affected program producers may have. Under reasonable assumptions, our analysis suggests that an MSO having a national market share well below 30 percent could exert significant monopsony power over many cable networks. Anecdotal evidence cited in chapter 5 is consistent with that hypothesis.

What about the costs to economic efficiency if an MSO limit were set excessively low? We cannot be certain of the size at which MSOs substantially exhaust economies of scale, but it seems unlikely that it could be as much as 30 percent of U.S. cable subscribers.

Consider the need to "encourage investment in new video programming services" cited by the FCC. It is unrealistic to attribute such capabilities to an MSO simply on the basis of the number of subscribers it serves. To the extent that size is relevant, creative and particularly financial resources arise from the size and diversity of the media conglomerates that parent those MSOs. TCI's and Time Warner's respective market values as of May 31, 1995, were $13.9 billion and $15.0 billion.[21] Several other corporations operating cable networks were in the same class, however, including some with no cable system affiliations.[22] Similarly, it is evident from tables 3-2 and 3-3 that while TCI and Time Warner have large numbers of both subscribers and cable network affiliations, Viacom and Cablevision Systems

---

20. Competition, Rate Deregulation and the Commission's Policies Relating to the Provision of Cable Television Service, Report, MM Dkt. No. 89-600, FCC 90-276, 67 Rad. Reg. 2d (P&F) ¶ 75 (1990); *see also* U.S. DEPARTMENT OF JUSTICE & FEDERAL TRADE COMMISSION, HORIZONTAL MERGER GUIDELINES (1992).

21. *The Global 1000*, BUS. WEEK, July 10, 1995, at 64.

22. General Electric (parent of NBC), $98.2 billion market value; Walt Disney Co., $29.1 billion; and Capital Cities/ABC, $14.9 billion.

Development Corporation, two other MSOs with comparable histories of programming innovation and vertical ownership, account for far smaller fractions of all U.S. subscribers.

Consider also economies of scale in the "deployment of high-cost cable technologies" to which the FCC also refers. Undoubtedly, high-tech system upgrades are subject to economies of scale, as are the management efforts required to implement them. Trade press accounts of the recent wave of mergers and joint ventures among MSOs report, in fact, that the smaller MSO partners involved in those activities fear their subscriber bases may be insufficient to realize economies of scale in deployment of the equipment and technical expertise that will be necessary to deliver video-on-demand services or provide telephone or Internet access services, either in competition or cooperation with the local exchange carriers.[23] It seems unlikely, however, that to exhaust economies in technology deployment on the national or regional level, an MSO would need a larger national share of cable subscribers than the approximately 16 percent share of U.S. local telephone subscribers that the largest LEC (GTE) has.[24] Of course, equipment manufacturing or other costs may well reach minimum levels at larger production runs, but those can be advantaged by means of joint buying arrangements, such as the LECs now make.

Much of the recent MSO merger activity has focused on creating clusters of commonly owned cable systems at the regional level. As the 1994 FCC report notes, there are evident economies in clustering—including management, system interconnection, and economies in marketing—to match those that their prospective video competitors, the LECs, already enjoy.[25] Undoubtedly an important reason for that regional clustering by cable systems is their prospect of competing with the LECs in the telephone services market.[26] Clustering may also increase the potential for excessive cable operator control over regional sports or other localized programming suppliers, but considering the evident efficiencies and the relatively minor economic significance of local and regional cable programming, that problem seems of secondary importance.

An MSO having a sufficient national market share to exert anticompetitive control over programming suppliers is also a much more serious First

23. Geraldine Fabrikant, *Time Warner and Newhouse Form a Joint Cable Operation*, N.Y. TIMES, Sept. 13, 1994; John M. Higgins, *Mid-Sized MSO's Dilemma: Buy, Sell or Hold*, MULTICHANNEL NEWS, Dec. 5, 1994, at 96.

24. FCC, STATISTICS OF COMMON CARRIERS, 1995–96, tables 1.1, 2.3

25. 1994 FCC Cable Report, *supra* note 2, ¶¶ 151–153.

26. *Id.*

Amendment access threat than that posed by vertical integration. That threat is illustrated by a recent controversy over carriage of the '90s Channel, a basic, part-time cable network with "left-leaning" political content, on TCI systems. According to press reports,[27] TCI ceased carrying the '90s Channel on several TCI systems when the network's affiliation contract expired in early 1995. The '90s Channel then resorted to leased-access carriage on TCI systems, which accounted in total for 600,000 of the channel's one million national cable subscribers. A few months later, TCI reportedly imposed a large increase in the '90s Channel's leased-access rates. After failing in an appeal to the FCC to disallow that rate increase, the network went out of business, citing TCI's actions as the reason.

The FCC ruled that TCI had not violated proper procedures in raising the '90s Channel's leased-access rates, and TCI vigorously defended its actions as motivated purely by business considerations. Whatever the particular merits of the case, however, it puts into sharp relief the First Amendment significance of horizontal versus vertical market power of cable system operators. Although the '90s Channel's owner claimed that TCI embraced conservatively oriented cable programming such as National Empowerment Television and rejected the '90s Channel for political reasons, TCI had no financial interests in any politically oriented cable programming suppliers. Obviously, then, TCI was not motivated to carry or to reject any politically oriented programming because of its vertical ownership ties. Having a large share of a cable channel's potential market, however, is the basic ingredient of any plausible theory of how noneconomic motivations of a cable operator could restrict the market survival of "undesirable" programming suppliers.

One can always identify potential economic efficiencies realized by very large MSO subscriber bases, including the greater transactions cost savings possible from vertical integration with programming suppliers. To an extent, monopsony might be beneficial if it reduces the bargaining power of program suppliers upstream. But if the FCC's MSO size limit survives its upcoming judicial tests, it should be set at a prudent level. Though necessarily without support of systematic statistical data measuring monopsony power, we can assume that a 20 percent share of U.S. cable homes passed would be a reasonable, if not generous, MSO size limit. Since effective competition to established cable systems would reduce the need for such a

---

27. The following narrative is drawn from *Will TCI Pull the Plug on the '90s?*, VARIETY, Feb. 6, 1995; Richard Katz, *Programming Takes a Right Turn*, MULTICHANNEL NEWS, March 6, 1995, at 3; Joe Estrella, *The '90s Channel Loses Bid to Remain on TCI*, MULTICHANNEL NEWS, Nov. 13, 1995, at 30.

limit, a sunset clause would be appropriate.[28] The limit would, at least, be very easy for the FCC to enforce and would immediately affect only one existing MSO.[29] Whatever regulatory limit may be in place, however, the Justice Department should actively investigate horizontal merger activity among MSOs in light of the unusual cost conditions of the cable programming industry.

A relevant factor in policy affecting the size of MSOs is the potential for collusion by vertically integrated MSOs, an antitrust issue to which we now turn.

VERTICAL INTEGRATION IN CABLE AS AN ANTITRUST ISSUE

The 1985 U.S. Justice Department's Vertical Merger Guidelines describe the main potential antitrust threat arising from vertical integration: the facilitation of horizontal collusion within either the upstream or downstream stage of an industry. As discussed in chapter 7, that theory was a basis for the government case leading to the 1994 Primestar consent decrees. Two of the relatively few major challenges to vertical mergers by the Justice Department in the past two decades, both of them successful, also involved the cable industry and relied on that theory. The first challenge was to the proposed 1980 launch of Premier, a premium cable network to be started as a joint venture by four movie studios having a combined market share of U.S. theatrical film distribution well over 50 percent.[30] The second challenge was to a joint venture proposed in 1983 that involved a merger between Showtime and The Movie Channel, by which three major movie studios would acquire a combined two-thirds share of the venture. The specific government theory in both cases was that the proposed vertical relationships would foster collusion among the upstream firms to withhold their products from competing premium movie networks, thus threatening domination of the pay cable television networking industry.[31]

To what extent might vertical integration anticompetitively facilitate horizontal collusion in the cable industry now or in the future? There are

---

28. An alternative would be to define the limit in terms of an MSO's national market share of total cable plus noncable MVPD subscribers.

29. We recognize the political obstacles to an FCC regulation requiring a structural divestiture.

30. United States *v.* Columbia Pictures Industries, 507 F. Supp. 412 (S.D.N.Y. 1980).

31. Lawrence J. White, *Antitrust and Video Markets: The Merger of Showtime and The Movie Channel as a Case Study*, in VIDEO MEDIA COMPETITION: REGULATION, ECONOMICS, AND TECHNOLOGY (Eli M. Noam ed., Columbia University Press 1985).

several possibilities. One is that despite regulations or antitrust decrees intended to prohibit discrimination, vertical ties could facilitate collusion among networks to foreclose access to programming by other MVPDs at the local or the national level—essentially as alleged in the Primestar case. Or collusion among program suppliers facilitated by integration could convey excessive upstream bargaining power to those program suppliers in their negotiations with smaller cable operators or alternative MVPDs.

With respect to programming supply, another possibility is that MSO equity-sharing in cable networks could facilitate collusion among those MSOs or among rival, commonly held networks to monopolize particular cable programming categories. Of particular interest, perhaps, is the possibility that vertical integration by MSOs could become extensive enough to facilitate anticompetitive control of the entire cable networking industry or of its major segments, such as premium or basic networking. A necessary condition for such behavior to be profitable is that the cumulative effect of new network entry on subscriber demand for the vertically controlled networks be high enough for it to be in the interest of the colluding MSOs to bar any entry into the cable networking industry or industry segment at hand—even from networks that are relatively poor substitutes for vertically controlled networks. If that condition were met, vertically integrated MSOs might profitably collude to deny downstream access to any new cable networks not owned by one of them.

Essentially, that model was the basis for the government case in United States *v.* Paramount Pictures.[32] Five of the eight theatrical movie distributors brought to trial in 1945 were vertically integrated with movie theater chains. Those integrated theater chains were the nation's five largest and accounted for 70 percent of all first-run box office receipts. Theater ownership by those chains was relatively concentrated at the local level as well; in 74 percent of the ninety-two largest U.S. cities, one chain was dominant, controlling between 50 and 100 percent of first-run theater capacity.[33] The government's case, which the Supreme Court basically accepted, was that the integrated distributors operated as a cartel to exchange access to one another's geographically controlled theater markets—to the exclusion of nonvertically integrated distributors.[34]

A similar theory of collusion by MSOs to trade access to one another's vertically affiliated networks—to the exclusion of any nonaffiliated net-

---

32. United States *v.* Paramount Pictures, Inc. 334 U.S. 131 (1948).

33. *Id.* (Loew's Exhibit L-13).

34. MICHAEL CONANT, ANTITRUST IN THE MOTION PICTURE INDUSTRY: AN ECONOMIC AND LEGAL ANALYSIS (University of California Press 1960).

works—may seem remote at a time when cable operators are threatened by entry from several quarters. As we have discussed, however, cable currently has a dominant position in the MVPD market at the retail level, and TCI and Time Warner together control cable markets serving approximately 47 percent of U.S. cable subscribers. In November 1995 those two MSOs had combined ownership interests in networks accounting for 45 percent and 53 percent, respectively, of all basic and premium networking revenues, in addition to their financial interests in networks, together accounting for dominant shares of the PPV, home shopping, and regional sports network markets.[35] If competition from other MVPDs does not develop as hoped, the Justice Department should actively monitor the pace of vertical acquisitions by MSOs with those facts in mind.

VERTICAL INTEGRATION BY ALTERNATIVE MVPDS

Finally, we ask, What are the implications of this study for legal constraints affecting vertical ownership between program suppliers and competitors to established cable television systems? As we noted, the 1992 Cable Act and the 1996 Telecommunications Act leave all MVPDs free to integrate vertically. The FCC has ruled, however, that pursuant to the 1996 act, the program-access regulations extend to programming suppliers or programmers that are vertically integrated with LEC operators of open video systems (OVSs). That is, programming suppliers in which an OVS operator has an attributable interest may not engage in exclusive contracts with that OVS operator.[36]

This book suggests no justification for any restrictions on, or related to, vertical integration by other MVPDs, including the LECs. Since the analysis is somewhat more involved for LECs than for MMDS, DBS, SMATV, HSD, or other prospective MVPDs, we shall first consider the latter group.

Alternative MVPDs Other than LECs

To date, vertical ties between non-LEC MVPDs and programming suppliers are apparently either nonexistent or insignificant. Pressures to integrate are likely to increase, however, if those competitors become better established in the market.

---

35. The Time Warner–TBS merger shifts control to Time Warner but does not change those percentages.

36. In the Matter of Implementation of Section 302 of the Telecommunications Act of 1996, CS Dkt. No. 96-46, Open Video Systems, Third Rep. & Order & Notice of Consideration (Aug. 7, 1996). In that notice the FCC asked for comments on how the rules should be specifically applied.

Consistent with our analysis of integration by cable system operators, programming ownership by alternative MVPDs poses two general concerns: potentially adverse effects on entry and competition at the MVPD level and potentially adverse effects on the supply of programming.

With regard to the first concern, we have argued that vertical disintegration, or program-access regulations that apply only to programming suppliers that have ownership ties to cable systems, are unjustified to promote entry and competition at the MVPD level. It would be illogical, then, for us to advocate that similar vertical restraints should apply to alternative MVPDs. In any case, the problem at hand is facilitating the opportunity for those MVPDs to compete successfully with established cable systems. Vertical restraints on alternative MVPDs would be counterproductive to that objective.

The second concern about vertical integration between alternative MVPDs and programming suppliers is that, as cable systems do now, those MVPDs would favor program suppliers in which they have an ownership interest—to the disadvantage of unaffiliated suppliers. Our analysis of cable system behavior suggests that, at least for efficiency reasons, alternative MVPDs probably would favor their affiliated programming. First, however, the extent to which alternative MVPDs or cable systems may choose to disadvantage or exclude unaffiliated programming will be limited by the competitive environment that alternative MVPDs create. Recall the numerical illustration in chapter 6. An MVPD that integrated with network A would be less inclined to drop a similar network, B, to the extent that network A's subscribers would be induced to switch providers to get B rather than simply turn their business to network A on the same MVPD's system. In any case, such behavior seems of limited social interest because the established cable system already provides an alternative source of programming within the same market area. Another possibility is that newer entrants in the MVPD industry could use ownership ties with programming suppliers to affect the programming market anticompetitively. But monopsony power is required to implement such strategies—an advantage that newer entrants will not have.

As competitors to cable become better established, there may be strategic battles in which alternative MVPDs use vertical ownership ties to various programming suppliers as competitive weapons to differentiate their program menus. Such behavior could be detrimental to consumers if they were forced to buy from two MVPDs to obtain the same full menu of programming they had previously received from an established cable system.[37] First,

---

37. Michael H. Riordan & David J. Salant, Exclusion and Integration in the Market for Video Programming Delivered to the Home (July 7, 1994; rev. Sept. 12, 1994) (paper presented at the AEI Telecommunications Summit). The authors show circumstances in

however, economies of scale in the physical distribution of programming would severely limit such video menu distribution among alternative MVPDs within a given market over the long term. Second, such strategies could be carried out without the benefit of vertical integration, using arms-length exclusive contracts with program suppliers.[38]

Local Exchange Carriers

While the basic issues are conceptually the same, vertical integration into programming by the LECs is more complex. First, the LECs already offer regulated local telephone service, which raises the issue of cross-subsidization. Second, pursuant to the 1996 Telecommunications Act, the LECs may choose to be OVS operators, a model that imposes common-carrier obligations on them. The vertical ownership issue in the OVS case is also more involved because the programming supply function includes not only the actual suppliers such as CNN or HBO but also programmers—the intermediaries that package and supply programs to consumers over LEC facilities. As we noted in chapter 2, the LECs have always been free to own programming suppliers, but until lately, they were unable to have more than a 5 percent equity interest in any programmer using their transmission facilities.

To date no LEC has directly invested in a cable programming network. Since the FCC's first Video Dialtone ruling in 1992, however, several LECs have acquired financial interests in larger companies having cable programming investments or have formed joint ventures with programming suppliers or packagers. In 1993, for example, U S West purchased a 25 percent interest in Time Warner's Entertainment Group, the entity that owns and distributes Warner Brothers' movies, as well as much of Time Warner's cable programming.[39] As noted in chapter 3, NYNEX has acquired a substantial minority interest in Viacom-Paramount, one of the largest cable programming suppliers.[40] Ameritech and BellSouth are coventurers with Walt Disney Co. in a new entity that will create video programming.[41]

---

which exclusive contracting may make consumers worse off than before.

38. During much of the 1980s, the Time Inc. and Viacom premium networks appeared to engage in strategic attempts to gain market share by contracting with various theatrical movie studios for exclusive exhibition rights. At least before Time's merger with Warner Communications, that competition for exclusive rights did not involve significant vertical integration into production. PAUL KAGAN ASSOCIATES, PAY TV NEWSLETTER (various issues).

39. 1994 FCC Cable Report, *supra* note 2.

40. Geraldine Fabrikant, *NYNEX Aid for Viacom in Its Bid*, N.Y. TIMES, October 5, 1993, at C1.

41. Bart Ziegler, *Staid Phone Giants Try Marriage to Hollywood*, WALL ST. J., May 24, 1995, at B1.

How might those or future ownership ties between the LECs and programming entities create policy concerns different from or more objectionable than those for vertical integration by other MVPDs? First, with respect to the objective of encouraging healthy competition at the MVPD level, it is apparent that cross-subsidization of a LEC's video services with local telephone revenues could have socially undesirable effects. For example, if a LEC were able to artificially shift the allocation of its total costs from its video operations to its local telephone service rate base, it might price its video services below their actual cost—to the disadvantage of established cable operators or other MVPDs. Also, of course, as cable operators are fond of pointing out, artificially inflated local telephone rates would subsidize such underpricing.

In practice, however, the threat of cross-subsidization between regulated telephone services and video *programming* operations in which a LEC has an ownership interest seems slight, because there are few, if any, significant costs in common to those business functions. On one hand, if a LEC uses some of the same physical network facilities for both services, there are very likely to be common costs of video and telephone *transmission*. A transmission-based cross-subsidization threat is thus plausible and was in fact the focus of much controversy leading to the FCC's 1992 and 1994 Video Dialtone rulings.[42] Cable television networking—or a programmer's package and sale of cable networks and other video programming—however, is quite distinct from either video or telephone transmission. We have little reason to think that vertical ownership with programming functions would aid a LEC's ability to cross-subsidize by shifting common transmission costs. Such transmission cost shifting could not be hidden any more easily than it could be in the absence of integration.[43]

Of course, apart from cross-subsidy altogether, a LEC or group of LECs could conceivably develop extensive vertical ties to programming suppliers and then attempt to dominate the MVPD market by withholding those programs from established cable operators. Perhaps, the framers of the 1996 Telecommunications Act had that scenario in mind when they mandated that program-access rules be extended to LECs that operate open video systems.

---

42. Telephone Company–Cable Television Cross-Ownership Rules, §§ 63.54–63.58, Mem. Op. & Order on Recons., CC Dkt. No. 87-266, 7 F.C.C. Rcd. 5069 (1992); Telephone Company–Cable Television Cross-Ownership Rules, §§ 63.54–63.58, and Amendments of Parts 32, 36, 61, 64, and 69 of the Commission's Rules to Establish and Implement Regulatory Procedures for Video Dialtone Service, RM-8221, CC Dkt. No. 87-266 (Nov. 7, 1994).

43. LELAND L. JOHNSON, COMMON CARRIER VIDEO DELIVERY BY TELEPHONE COMPANIES ch. 5 (RAND Corporation 1992).

Recall that LECs that choose the cable operator option are automatically covered by the program-access rules under the 1992 Cable Act.

The same analysis of program-access rules that we developed above for cable operators applies to the LECs. If the scenario of the LECs' anticompetitive use of restricted program access is plausible, then experiences of the cable industry suggest that the LECs could behave anticompetitively in the absence of vertical ownership ties. Any program-access regulations should thus apply to contracts made between OVS operators and all program suppliers.

More generally, however, the threat that the LECs will dominate the video industry seems exaggerated. Much has been made of the LECs' abilities to overwhelm cable systems with their "monopoly power" as a justification for prohibiting or restraining LEC entry into video services.[44] But like other entrants in the MVPD industry, the LECs, notwithstanding their abundant financial resources, are basically fledgling entrants in an industry dominated by established cable systems. Under those circumstances, it seems unlikely that vertical ties to program suppliers or programming functions could give the LECs an anticompetitive advantage. In fact, it may be preferable to exempt them from the program-access rules altogether to encourage their entry into video markets.

We turn now to the potential threat to programming that might arise from a LEC's vertical integration into programming supply functions. If an integrated LEC becomes a cable operator in competition with an incumbent cable system, the LEC would obviously realize the same efficiency advantages that now induce established cable operators to favor their vertically affiliated programming—to the evident disadvantage of unaffiliated program suppliers. In the OVS case, further research is needed to determine how vertical ownership is likely to affect any economic incentives that the LECs might have to favor certain programmers or program suppliers or to disadvantage others. One plausible scenario, however, is that the LECs would realize efficiencies in transacting with affiliated firms and that those efficiencies would result in lower retail prices or more aggressive marketing of affiliated programmers or program suppliers. Similarly, an OVS operator might have an anticompetitive incentive to charge inflated access prices or to provide inferior physical connections to unaffiliated firms.

Whether motivated by efficiency or foreclosure intentions, however, such behavior toward unaffiliated programmers or program suppliers seems

---

44. *Communications Act of 1994: Hearings on S. 1822 Before the Comm. on Commerce, Science and Transportation,* U.S. Senate, 103d Cong., 2d Sess. 259–83 (1994) (testimony of Decker Angstrom, National Cable Television Association).

of little concern for the same reasons we discussed with respect to other MVPDs. As market entrants competing with cable systems in local video markets, the LECs are unlikely to have sufficient bargaining power to influence programming supply anticompetitively. And any favoritism the LECs might show to their affiliated programming would seem of limited social importance since those LECs would be providing an alternative programming source, presumably with a menu offering the same core of popular programming available from competing cable TV suppliers.

In sum, if effective competition for established cable systems successfully develops—whether its source be the LECs, DBS, MMDS, or some other multichannel video provider—most of the cable industry problems with which Congress, the FCC, and antitrust enforcement have been concerned will diminish or disappear. Economic efficiency and First Amendment–related objectives of all kinds will be promoted. The provisions of the Telecommunications Act of 1996 that serve to promote entry of the LECs into video markets—largely without vertical restraints—lead us in the right direction. The issue upon which policymakers must continue to focus to achieve the objective of effective competition is not vertical integration by either cable firms or their potential competitors but the sources of horizontal market power at the level of the cable system operator.

9

Postscript: The Time Warner–Turner Broadcasting Merger

IN JULY 1996 the Federal Trade Commission reached settlement on a highly publicized merger that had been proposed in September 1995: the purchase by Time Warner of 100 percent of Turner Broadcasting.[1] As detailed in chapter 3, Time Warner owns cable systems serving close to one-fifth of U.S. cable subscribers and has a number of cable programming interests, including 100 percent ownership of the premium networks, HBO and Cinemax. Turner Broadcasting owns CNN, TBS, TNT, and some other widely distributed basic cable networks. The FTC settlement, confirmed by the full commission on September 12, 1996, allowed the merger but imposed several terms and conditions.[2] The merger was completed on October 10, 1996, although the FTC did not issue its final approval until February 7, 1997.[3]

Basically, the FTC approved the structural reorganization that the companies originally proposed. Since 1987, Time Warner had held approximately 19 percent of Turner Broadcasting's equity, and TCI had held 23 percent.[4] The FTC settlement allowed Time Warner to increase its stake in Turner Broadcasting to 100 percent by acquiring all of TCI's 23 percent

---

1. David Waterman was a consultant to the FTC in its investigation of the Time Warner–Turner Broadcasting merger.

2. In the Matter of Time Warner, Inc., Turner Broadcasting Systems, Inc., Tele-Communications, Inc., and Liberty Media Corporation, United States of America, Before the Federal Trade Commission, Agreement Containing Consent Order, File No. 961-0004 (Sept. 12, 1996).

3. *Time-Turner Merger OK'd,* CHICAGO TRIBUNE, Feb. 7, 1997, at 3.

4. Those and some other statistics in this postscript differ slightly from those cited in

interest, along with other outstanding stock. In exchange, TCI received an approximately 9 percent equity share of Time Warner.

The FTC imposed three principal terms and conditions. First, TCI's 9 percent share in Time Warner, which under terms of the settlement can be increased to 14.99 percent, are to be held by a new, separate subsidiary of TCI and its programming arm, Liberty Media. The new subsidiary's shares in Time Warner are to be nonvoting. Second, sales of the Turner basic networks to cable operators and other MVPDs cannot be bundled with Time Warner's premium networks, HBO and Cinemax, and vice versa. Finally, Time Warner cable systems are required to carry a second general news channel in addition to CNN. That second news channel must reach at least 50 percent of Time Warner basic subscribers over a period of five years.

In reaching any merger settlement, the FTC faces the constraint that if the firms involved decide to fight an FTC ruling, the commission has the formidable burden of proving in court that the proposed merger violates the antitrust laws. The analysis of this book nevertheless implies that the Time Warner–Turner merger, as approved by the FTC, poses significant risks to competitive behavior in the cable industry. The terms and conditions imposed by the FTC will have a minor influence on the incentives created by the structural reorganization.

The approved merger has two basic structural components: the acquisition of 100 percent of the Turner networks by Time Warner and the up to 14.99 percent acquisition of Time Warner equity by TCI's new subsidiary.

In itself, Time Warner's 100 percent acquisition of the Turner networks does not have evident social benefits, although its effects are difficult to predict. First, the resulting change in vertical ties between the Turner networks and cable operators could cause entry barriers into programming categories now served by the Turner networks—notably general news—to either rise or fall. On the one hand, the incentive of Time Warner's cable branch to protect its own programming investments increases with the rise in Time Warner's equity stake in the Turner networks from 19 percent to 100 percent—a change that may raise those entry barriers. On the other hand, barriers may fall because TCI surrenders its 23 percent stake in the Turner networks. That is, the combined national market share of cable subscribers served by MSOs having substantial equity interests in those networks— Time Warner plus TCI—falls from about 47.4 percent to 19.1 percent with Time Warner's buyout of TCI's interest in those networks.[5]

---

the FTC consent order, presumably because of different dates of compilation or data sources. For consistency, the data reported here are taken from this book.

5. MSO market shares include TCI's joint venture and other minority holdings. See chapter 3 for supporting data.

A more predictable effect of the Turner network acquisitions is unrelated to the merger's vertical aspects but follows from the upstream horizontal combination in programming. As our discussions in chapters 5 and 7 imply, there will be an increase in the bargaining, or input price setting, power that the Time Warner–owned networks will have with all unaffiliated cable operators and other MVPDs. The extent of that increase is uncertain, since Time Warner's premium networks and Turner's basic networks are on their own among the most popular cable services. The input prices paid by unaffiliated MSOs and other MVPDs for those networks are nevertheless likely to rise by some amount. Such price rises would tend to increase the flow of funds into programming supply. In itself, that is a potential social benefit, although permitting mergers to create countervailing market power is generally not good public policy. Of perhaps more significance, higher input prices would also tend to increase the difficulty of successful downstream entry by alternative MVPDs.

The FTC restriction against bundling of HBO/Cinemax with the Turner networks is evidently intended to mitigate the latter threat to competition resulting from the merger. The bundling restriction will make it less convenient for Time Warner to use its increased bargaining power, but it is hard to imagine that the stipulation will have much effect. Time Warner's bargaining power in negotiating terms for any one of its networks implicitly depends on the threat it wields to withhold the supply of all its networks.

Although the above analysis identifies important competitive concerns about the upstream combination in programming supply, one should still give any benefit of the doubt to Time Warner's ability to improve management of the Turner networks or to realize other efficiencies or benign strategic objectives. It is difficult, however, to imagine such value flowing from the second structural aspect of the approved merger, TCI's acquisition of Time Warner equity. By creating an ownership link between MSOs serving well over two-fifths of U.S. cable subscribers, that horizontal tie invites higher entry barriers in cable programming but without any foreseeable social benefit.

The FTC's separate subsidiary–nonvoting requirements on TCI's equity holdings in Time Warner are appropriate because they limit Time Warner's incentive to collude with TCI. More problematical because of TCI's larger national share of cable subscribers, however, are TCI's incentives to collude with Time Warner and to otherwise avoid actions that would diminish the value of its Time Warner equity. Those incentives are basically unaffected by the separate subsidiary–nonvoting requirements. Entry barriers into cable programming could increase because TCI's equity in Time Warner would suffer if it allowed its 28 percent national share of cable subscribers to be used as a platform for programming suppliers competing with any of the

Time Warner networks. Of more concern are direct consequences of the horizontal link at the cable system level. TCI and Time Warner's national market shares of cable subscribers, if used in concert, would give those cable operators even greater influence over unaffiliated programmers and a surely overwhelming power over new entrants into programming supply. TCI's equity interest in Time Warner is conducive to coordination or the granting of reciprocity in making programming carriage or launch decisions. Even if antitrust authorities were to bar further programming acquisitions by Time Warner or TCI, such cooperation could help both firms dominate the launch of new cable networks and thus increase market power in programming over the long term. The long-term cable industry antitrust concerns discussed in chapter 8 thus become more realistic with the Time Warner–Turner ownership link.

Consider finally the FTC's requirement that Time Warner carry a second cable news network. Basically, that is a vertical nondiscriminatory access restraint intended to compensate for Time Warner's increased incentive to favor its affiliated programming service, CNN, at the expense of unaffiliated cable news services. Our statistical analysis in chapter 6 suggests that Time Warner will indeed behave in that way—presumably more so, given its larger equity stake. Our arguments in chapters 5 and 8 that nondiscriminatory access constraints in cable are ineffective or counterproductive, however, suggest dim prospects for the FTC's unusually proactive attempt in the present case.

First, neither the programming content nor the quality of a competing general cable news network is reasonably definable. Beyond the descriptive words "an Independent Advertiser-Supported News and Information Video Programming Service,"[6] the FTC ruling makes no attempt to do so. The marketing behavior of Time Warner's cable operations is also nearly impossible to regulate.

To the extent that the requirement that Time Warner carry a second news channel is effective, that MSO will probably be induced to exclude other programming more desirable to subscribers. As we discussed in chapter 6, there are substantial opportunity costs to the carriage of any network, and those costs will persist into the future for basic economic reasons, even as channel capacities expand.

Amid much publicity, MSNBC and the Fox News channel were launched in the summer of 1996 and brought on a new episode of the cable news wars. In this book we have chronicled CNN's successful dominance of cable news networking since 1979 in both the presence and the absence

---

6. Agreement Containing Consent Order, *supra* note 2, § IX.

of vertical ties to cable operators. We have done similarly for the dominance of single networks in music and some other categories of basic cable programming. In the future as in the past, the main determinants of market structure in cable news networking will be the fundamental forces of economies of scale in cable networking, advertisers' incentives to reach a high percentage of a target audience at the lowest rates, and cable operators' incentives to offer differentiated program menus. For those reasons, the ability of competing news networks to successfully differentiate their content will be especially important. Mandated carriage on an MSO with nearly one-fifth of all cable subscribers could, of course, help launch viable competition with CNN. The history of the cable industry and its regulation, however, suggests that the FTC's attempt to promote cable news network entry with such a vertical restraint has little chance of affecting the final outcome.

References

Amemiya, Takeshi, *Advanced Econometrics* (Harvard University Press 1985).

Andrews, Edmund L., "After Delay, FTC Allows QVC's Takeover," *New York Times*, February 4, 1995, at 17.

Andrews, Edmund L., "Plan to Create MTV Rival Is under Antitrust Scrutiny," *New York Times*, July 23, 1994.

Arrow, Kenneth J., "Vertical Integration and Communication," 6 *Bell Journal of Economics and Management Science* 173 (1975).

Auletta, Ken, "John Malone: Flying Solo," *New Yorker*, February 7, 1994, at 59.

Baumol, William J., and J. Gregory Sidak, *Toward Competition in Local Telephony* (MIT Press and AEI Press 1994).

Besen, Stanley M., and Robert W. Crandall, "The Deregulation of Cable Television," 44 *Law and Contemporary Problems* 79 (1981).

Besen, Stanley M., and Leland L. Johnson, *An Economic Analysis of Mandatory Leased Channel Access for Cable Television* (RAND Corporation 1982).

Besen, Stanley M., Steven R. Brenner, and John R. Woodbury, *An Economic Analysis of the FCC's Proposed Cable Ownership Restrictions* (Charles River Associates 1993).

Besen, Stanley M., Steven R. Brenner, and John R. Woodbury, *Exclusivity and Differential Pricing for Cable Program Services* (Charles River Associates 1993).

Blair, Roger D., and Jeffrey L. Harrison, *Monopsony* (Princeton University Press 1993).

Blair, Roger D., and David L. Kaserman, *Law and Economics of Vertical Integration and Control* (Academic Press 1983).

Braunstein, Yale, with the assistance of Larry S. Levine and Alisa Jones, "Recent Trends in Cable Television Related to the Prospects for New Television Networks," report submitted to the Federal Communications Commission, August 1979.

Brennan, Timothy J., "Vertical Integration, Monopoly, and the First Amendment," 3 *Journal of Media Economics* 57 (1990).

Brenner, Daniel L., "Cable Television and Freedom of Expression," 1988 *Duke Law Journal* 329.

Brown, L., "Home Shopping Is Forever," *Channels*, April 1987.

Brown, R., and S. McClellan, "Programming DBS: Still a Long Way to Go," *Broadcasting*, February 22, 1993, at 36.

Cabinet Committee on Cable Communications, *Report to the President* (1974).

"Cable Impact: Changes Likely in Systems Management," *Broadcasting*, Mar. 13, 1989, at 31.

Cablevision Systems Development Corp., *1994 Form 10-K* (1995).

Caspedes, F. V., and E. R. Hattemer, *Cox Cable (A) and (B)*, Nos. 9-586-045 and 9-587-054, Harvard Business School, 1986.

Cassady, R., Jr., "Exchange by Private Treaty," Bureau of Business Research, Graduate School of Business, University of Texas, 1974.

Chipty, Tasneem, "Horizontal Integration for Bargaining Power: Evidence from the Cable Television Industry," 4 *Journal of Economics and Management Strategy* 375 (1995).

Coase, Ronald H., "The Nature of the Firm," 4 *Economica* (n.s.) 386 (1937).

Conant, Michael, *Antitrust in the Motion Picture Industry: An Economic and Legal Analysis* (University of California Press 1960).

Crandall, Robert W., "FCC Regulation, Monopsony, and Network Television Program Costs," 3 *Bell Journal of Economics* 483 (1972).

"Dallas Dies," *Economist*, Dec. 14, 1991, at 28.

Denisoff, R. Serge, *Inside MTV* (Transaction Publishers 1988).

Dixit, Avinash K., and Joseph E. Stiglitz, "Monopolistic Competition and Optimal Product Diversity," 67 *American Economic Review* 297 (1977).

Dordick, Herbert S., and David Waterman, *Arts and Cultural Programming on Non-Broadcast Media: Past Experience and Future Prospects* (Corporation for Public Broadcasting 1984).

Economists, Inc., *Cable Network Carriage Analysis Update* (June 28, 1994).

Edgeworth, Francis Y., *Papers Relating to Political Economy* (Macmillan 1925).

Estrella, Joe, "The '90s Channel Loses Bid to Remain on TCI," *Multichannel News*, Nov. 13, 1995, at 30.

Fabrikant, Geraldine, "NYNEX Aid for Viacom in Its Bid," *New York Times*, Oct. 5, 1993, at C1.

Fabrikant, Geraldine, "Time Warner and Newhouse Form a Joint Cable Operation," *New York Times*, Sept. 13, 1994.

Federal Communications Commission, *Statistics of Communications Common Carriers,* 1995–1996.

Federal Communications Commission, Network Inquiry Special Staff, *New Television Networks: Entry, Jurisdiction, Ownership and Regulation* (Government Printing Office 1980).

Frasco, Gregg, *Exclusive Dealing: A Comprehensive Case Study* (University Press of America 1991).

Gandal, Neil, and David J. Salant, "Movie Wars," Department of Economics, Tel Aviv University, February 1993.

Gershon, R. A., "Home Box Office, A 20-Year Perspective," in *Cable Television Handbook* (R. Picard ed., Carpelan Press 1993).

Gershon, R. A., "Pay Cable Television: A Regulatory History," *Communications and the Law* 3 (June 1990).

"Glimmering Hopes," *Broadcasting*, Jan. 13, 1986, at 7.

"The Global 1000," *Business Week*, July 10, 1995, at 64.

Granger, R., "Distributors See Program-Access Rules as a Plus," *Multichannel News*, May 10, 1993, at 6A.

Grant, August E., and Kenton T. Wilkinson, *Communications Technology Update: 1993–1994* (Technology Futures 1993).

Hart, Oliver, and Jean Tirole, "Vertical Integration and Market Foreclosure," *Brookings Papers on Economic Activity: Microeconomics* 205 (1990).

Higgins, John M., "FTC Seeks More Antitrust Data on Shopping Nets," *Multichannel News*, Sept. 13, 1993, at 40.

Higgins, John M., "The Heat Is Rising in Home Shopping Wars," *Multichannel News*, Mar. 28, 1993, at 40.

Higgins, John M., "Mid-Sized MSO's Dilemma: Buy, Sell or Hold," *Multichannel News*, Dec. 5, 1994, at 96.

Higgins, John M., "TCI Buying Control of United Video," *Multichannel News*, June 26, 1995, at 1.

Higgins, John M., "TCI Eyes Viacom Buy," *Multichannel News*, Apr. 4, 1994, at 1.

Hilmes, M., "Pay Television: Breaking the Broadcast Bottleneck," in *Hollywood in the Age of Television* (T. Balio ed., Unwin Hyman 1990).

Ivey, M., "Home Shopping," *Business Week*, Dec. 15, 1986.

Ivey, M., "The King of Cable TV," *Business Week*, Oct. 26, 1987, at 88.

Jaffee, Larry, "Thrills and Shills: Home Shopping Net Hawks to Viewers," *CableAge*, Sept. 16, 1985, at C7.

Jerrold Communications, *Jerrold Cable and Television Factbook* (annual).

Jessell, Harry, "Biondi Sees Net Benefit in Cable Act," *Broadcasting*, Oct. 26, 1992, at 38.

Johnson, Leland L., *Common Carrier Video Delivery by Telephone Companies* (RAND Corporation 1992).

Johnson, Leland L., *Toward Competition in Cable Television* (MIT Press and AEI Press 1994).

Johnson, Leland L., and Deborah R. Castleman, *Direct Broadcast Satellites: A Competitive Alternative to Cable Television?* (RAND Corporation 1991).

Johnson, Walter H., "Structure and Ownership of the Cable TV Industry," in *The Cable/Broadband Communications Book* (M. L. Howell ed., Knowledge Industry Publications 1990).

Katz, Michael L., "Vertical Contractual Relations," in 1 *Handbook of Industrial Organization* 655 (Richard L. Schmalensee ed., Elsevier Science Publishers 1989).

Katz, Richard, "Attention Shoppers," *Cablevision*, Nov. 4, 1991, at 25.

Katz, Richard, "High Time for Showtime," *Cablevision*, Nov. 2, 1992, at 23.

Katz, Richard, "Programming Takes a Right Turn," *Multichannel News*, Mar. 6, 1995, at 3.

Kerver, T., "Hubbard's World," *Cablevision*, May 18, 1991, at 24.

Klein, Benjamin, "The Competitive Consequences of Vertical Integration in the Cable Industry," working paper, UCLA, June 1989.

Klein, Benjamin, R. A. Crawford, and Armen A. Alchian, "Vertical Integration, Appropriate Rents, and the Competitive Contracting Process," 21 *Journal of Law and Economics* 297 (1978).

Krasilovsky, Peter, "Interactive Television Testbeds," Benton Foundation Communications Policy Working Paper No. 7, 1994.

Krattenmaker, Thomas G., and Lucas A. Powe, Jr., *Regulating Broadcast Programming* (MIT Press and AEI Press 1994).

Krattenmaker, Thomas G., and Steven C. Salop, "Anticompetitive Exclusion: Raising Rivals' Costs to Achieve Power over Price," 96 *Yale Law Journal* 206 (1986).

Kreps, David, and Robert Wilson, "Reputation and Imperfect Information," 27 *Journal of Economic Theory* 253 (1982).

Lafferty, W., "Feature Films on Prime-Time Television," in *Hollywood in the Age of Television* (T. Balio ed., Unwin Hyman 1990).

Lampert, Donna A., "Cable Television: Does Leased Access Mean Least Access?" 44 *Federal Communications Law Journal* 245 (1992).

Landes, William M., and Richard A. Posner, "Market Power in Antitrust Cases," 94 *Harvard Law Review* 937 (1981).

Landler, Mark, "The Dishes Are Coming: Satellites Go Suburban," *New York Times*, May 19, 1995, at 19.

Landler, Mark, "U S West Continental Ambitions," *New York Times*, Feb. 28, 1996, at C1.

Landro, Laura, "Tele-Communications Sets Cable-TV Agenda," *Wall Street Journal*, Feb. 11, 1986, at 6.

Landro, Laura, and Jonnie L. Roberts, "Viacom Is Set to Grow into a Media Colossus—or a Burdened Giant," *Wall Street Journal*, Feb. 16, 1994, at 1.

Lippman, J., "Home Shopping Rivals Prepare for Merger," *L.A. Times*, July 13, 1993, at D1.

Machlup, Fritz, and M. Taber, "Bilateral Monopoly, Successive Monopoly, and Vertical Integration," 27 *Economica* 101 (1960).

Marvel, Howard P., Review of *Exclusive Dealing: A Comprehensive Case Study* by Gregg Frasco, 8 *Review of Industrial Organization* 127 (1993).

Mayo, W., and Y. Otsuka, "Demand, Pricing, and Regulation: Evidence from the Cable Television Industry," 22 *RAND Journal of Economics* 396 (1991).

Milgrom, Paul, and John Roberts, "Predation, Reputation and Entry Deterrence," 27 *Journal of Economic Theory* 280 (1982).

Mitchell, Kim, "Cable Act Fine Print Threatens Local News Channels," *Multichannel News*, Jan. 29, 1994, at 14.

Mitchell, Kim, "USA and A&E Sue Two Ops over à la Carte Tiers," *Multichannel News*, Mar. 27, 1993, at 1.

Mitchell, Kim, and R. Granger, "Operators Call New Contracts 'Obscene,'" *Multichannel News*, Mar. 29, 1993, at 1.

National Association of Broadcasters, *TV Financial Report, 1991* (1991).

National Cable Television Association, *Cable TV Developments* (Spring 1995).

National Cable Television Association, *Regional Sports Networks: Media Guide* (Mar. 1993).

National Telecommunications and Information Administration, *Video Program Distribution and Cable Television: Current Policy Issues and Recommendations* (1988).

"NBC Cable News Project in Jeopardy," *Broadcasting*, Jan. 13, 1986, at 182.

"NBC Ponders Plan for Cable News Service," *Broadcasting*, Aug. 26, 1985, at 33.

Newcombe, Peter, "Music Video Wars," *Forbes*, Mar. 4, 1991, at 68.

Noll, Roger G., "The Role of Antitrust in Telecommunications," *Antitrust Bulletin* 40 (Fall 1995).

Ordover, Janusz A., with the assistance of Yale Braunstein, *Does Cable Television Really Face Effective Competition?* (Association of Independent Broadcasters 1988).

Ordover, Janusz A., and Garth Saloner, "Predation, Monopolization, and Antitrust," in 2 *Handbook of Industrial Organization* 537 (Richard L. Schmalensee and Robert D. Willig eds., Elsevier Science Publishers 1989).

Ordover, Janusz A., Garth Saloner, and Steven C. Salop, "Equilibrium Vertical Foreclosure," 80 *American Economic Review* 127 (1990).

Ordover, Janusz A., Alan O. Sykes, and Robert D. Willig, "Noncompetitive Behavior by Dominant Firms toward the Producers of Complementary Products," in *Antitrust and Regulation: Essays in Memory of John J. McGowan* (Franklin Fisher ed., MIT Press 1985).

Owen, Bruce M., *Economics and Freedom of Expression* (Ballinger Publishing Co. 1975).

Owen, Bruce M., and Steven S. Wildman, *Video Economics* (Harvard University Press 1992).

Owen, Bruce M., Jack H. Beebe, and Willard G. Manning, Jr., *Television Economics* (Lexington Books 1974).

Park, Rolla Edward, "New Television Networks," 6 *Bell Journal of Economics* 607 (1975).

Paul Kagan Associates, *Cable TV Advertising* (various issues).

Paul Kagan Associates, *Cable TV Financial Databook* (various issues).

Paul Kagan Associates, *Cable TV Investor* (various issues).

Paul Kagan Associates, *Cable TV Programming* (various issues).

Paul Kagan Associates, *Kagan Cable TV Census* (various issues).

Paul Kagan Associates, *Kagan Media Index* (various issues).

Paul Kagan Associates, *Media Sports Business* (various issues).

Paul Kagan Associates, *Pay TV Newsletter* (various issues).

Perry, Martin K., "Vertical Integration: Determinants and Effects," in 1 *Handbook of Industrial Organization* 655 (Richard L. Schmalensee ed., Elsevier Science Publishers 1989).

Porter, Michael E., and M. S. Salter, "Diversification as a Strategy," Harvard Business School, 1982.

Quelch, John A., "Cable News Network," Harvard Business School, 1985.

Riordan, Michael H., and David J. Salant, "Exclusion and Integration in the Market for Video Programming Delivered to the Home," paper presented at the AEI Telecommunications Summit, July 7, 1994; rev. September 12, 1994.

Roberts, J., "How Giant TCI Uses Self-Dealing, Hardball to Dominate Market," *Wall Street Journal*, Jan. 27, 1992, at 1.

Robichaux, Mark, "Cable TV Consolidates Rapidly in the Hands of a Few," *Wall Street Journal*, Feb. 8, 1995, at B4.

Rosenblatt, Robert A., "Meese Approves Rescue Plan for Detroit Papers," *Los Angeles Times*, Aug. 9, 1988, at IV1.

Rosewater, V., *History of Cooperative News-Gathering in the United States* (D. Appleton & Co. 1930).

Rosse, James N., "Daily Newspapers, Monopolistic Competition, and Economies of Scale," 57 *American Economic Review Papers and Proceedings* 522 (1967).

Rosse, James N., "The Evolution of One-Newspaper Cities," in *Proceedings of the Symposium on Media Concentration* (Federal Trade Commission 1978).

Rosse, James N., James N. Dertouzous, Michael D. Robinson, and Steven S. Wildman, *Economic Issues in Mass Communication Industries* (Federal Trade Commission December 1978).

Salinger, Michael A., "A Test of Successive Monopoly and Foreclosure Effects: Vertical Integration between Cable Systems and Pay Services," Columbia University Graduate School of Business, 1988.

Salinger, Michael A., "Vertical Mergers and Market Foreclosure," 103 *Quarterly Journal of Economics* 345 (1987).

Salinger, Michael A., "Vertical Mergers in Multiproduct Industries and Edgeworth's Paradox of Taxation," 5 *Journal of Industrial Economics* 545 (1991).

Salop, Steven C., and David T. Scheffman, "Raising Rivals' Costs," 73 *American Economic Review Papers and Proceedings* 267 (1983).

Samuelson, Paul A., "The Pure Theory of Public Expenditure," 36 *Review of Economics and Statistics* 387 (1954).

Scherer, F. M., and D. Ross, *Industrial Market Structure and Economic Performance,* (3d ed., Houghton Mifflin Co. 1990).

Schmalensee, Richard L., "Entry Deterrence in the Ready-to-Eat Breakfast Cereal Industry," 9 *Bell Journal of Economics* 305 (1978).

Shavell, Steven, "Risk Sharing and Incentives in the Principal and Agent Relationship," 10 *Bell Journal of Economics* 55 (1979).

Sidak, J. Gregory, "Telecommunications in Jericho," 81 *California Law Review* 1209 (1994).

Spence, A. Michael, "Product Selection, Fixed Costs, and Monopolistic Competition," 43 *Review of Economic Studies* 217 (1976).

Spence, A. Michael, and Bruce M. Owen, "Television Programming, Monopolistic Competition, and Welfare," 91 *Quarterly Journal of Economics* (1977).

Spengler, Joseph J., "Vertical Integration and Antitrust Policy," 58 *Journal of Political Economy* 347 (1950).

Steiner, Peter O., "Program Patterns and Preferences, and the Workability of Competition in Radio Broadcasting," 66 *Quarterly Journal of Economics* 194 (1952).

Tele-Communications, Inc. *1995 Form 10-K* (1996).

"Teleshopping: TV's Hottest Ticket," *Broadcasting*, Sept. 1, 1986, at 89.

"Time-Turner Merger OK'd," *Chicago Tribune,* Feb. 7, 1997, at 3.

U.S. Department of Justice and Federal Trade Commission, *Horizontal Merger Guidelines* (Government Printing Office 1992).

Walley, W., "Time Warner, Viacom Settle," *Electronic Media*, Aug. 24, 1992, at 2.

Waterman, David, "Local Monopsony and Free Riding," 8 *Information Economics and Policy* 4 (1996).

Waterman, David, "Vertical Integration and Program Access in the Cable Television Industry," 47 *Federal Communications Law Journal* (1995).

Waterman, David, "World Television Trade: The Economic Effects of Privatization and New Technology," 12 *Telecommunications Policy* 141 (June 1988).

Waterman, David, and Andrew A. Weiss, "The Effects of Vertical Integration between Cable Television Systems and Pay Cable Networks," 72 *Journal of Econometrics* 357 (1996).

Waterman, David, Andrew A. Weiss, and T. Valente, "Vertical Integration of Cable Television Systems with Pay Cable Networks: An Empirical Analysis," paper presented at Telecommunications Policy Research Conference, Airlie, Virginia, Oct. 1–3, 1989.

White, Halbert L., "A Heteroskedasticity-Consistent Covariance Matrix and a Direct Test for Heteroskedasticity," 48 *Econometrica* 817 (1980).

White, Lawrence J., "Antitrust and Video Markets: The Merger of Showtime and The Movie Channel as a Case Study," in *Video Media Competition: Regulation, Economics, and Technology* (Eli M. Noam ed., Columbia University Press 1985).

Wildman, Steven S., and Steven E. Siwek, *International Trade in Films and Television Programs* (Ballinger Publishing Co. 1988).

"Will TCI Pull the Plug on the '90s?" *Variety*, Feb. 6, 1995.

Williamson, Oliver E., *The Economic Institutions of Capitalism* (Free Press 1985).

Williamson, Oliver E., *Markets and Hierarchies: Analysis and Antitrust Implications* (Free Press 1975).

Williamson, Oliver E., "Transaction Cost Economics: The Governance of Contractual Relations," 22 *Journal of Law and Economics* 233 (1979).

Williamson, Oliver E., "The Vertical Integration of Production: Market Failure Considerations," 61 *American Economic Review* 112 (1971).

Zahradnik, Rich, "You Better Shop Around," *Marketing and Media Decisions*, Aug. 1986, at 6.

Ziegler, Bart, "Staid Phone Giants Try Marriage to Hollywood," *Wall Street Journal*, May 24, 1995, at B1.

Zinn, L. "Home Shoppers Keep Tuning In—But Investors Are Turned Off," *Business Week*, Oct. 22, 1990.

Case and Regulatory Proceeding Index

Name Index

Alchian, Armen A., 45n1
Amemiya, Takeshi, 119n29, 120n30
Andrews, Edmund L., 70n43, 71n46, 72n49, 73n52
Auletta, Ken, 65n26

Baumol, William J., 17n19, 144n1
Beebe, Jack H., 63n17
Besen, Stanley M., xii, 13n5, 38–39n18
Blair, Roger D., 45n1, 86n62
Braunstein, Yale, xi, xii, 38–39n18, 43
Brennan, Timothy J., 18n22
Brenner, Daniel L., xii, 18n22
Brown, L., 71n46
Brown, R., 104n20

Cassady, R., Jr., 49n10
Castleman, Deborah, 104n20
Chipty, Tasneem, 66n30, 106n23
Coase, Ronald H., 45n1
Conant, Michael, 133n15, 158n34
Crandall, Robert W., 38–39n18, 66n27
Crawford, R. A., 45n1

Denisoff, Serge, 69n41
Dixit, Avinash K., 18n20
Dordick, Herbert, 104n19

Edgeworth, Francis Y., 103n17
Estrella, Joe, 156n27

Fabrikant, Geraldine, 155n23, 161n40
Frasco, Gregg, 132–33n11

Gershon, R. A., 38–39n18, 133n14
Granger, R., 48n8, 147n5
Grant, August E., 106–7n25

Harrison, Jeffrey L., 86n62
Hart, Oliver, 57–58n7
Higgins, John M., 34n11, 71n46, 147n6, 155n23
Hilmes, M., 133n13

Ivey, M., 71n46

Jaffee, Larry, 71n46
Jessell, Harry, 147n5
Johnson, Leland L., 5n15, 13n5, 104n20, 130n4, 162n43

Kaserman, David L., 45–46n1
Katz, Michael L., 45–46n1, 132n11
Katz, Richard, 46n2, 47nn3–4, 156n27
Kerver, T., 104n20

187

Subject Index

William M. Landes
Clifton R. Musser Professor of
   Economics
University of Chicago Law School

Sam Peltzman
Sears Roebuck Professor of Economics
   and Financial Services
University of Chicago
   Graduate School of Business

Nelson W. Polsby
Professor of Political Science
University of California at Berkeley

George L. Priest
John M. Olin Professor of Law and
   Economics
Yale Law School

Murray L. Weidenbaum
Mallinckrodt Distinguished
   University Professor
Washington University

Research Staff

Leon Aron
Resident Scholar

Claude E. Barfield
Resident Scholar; Director, Science
   and Technology Policy Studies

Cynthia A. Beltz
Research Fellow

Walter Berns
Resident Scholar

Douglas J. Besharov
Resident Scholar

Robert H. Bork
John M. Olin Scholar in Legal Studies

Karlyn Bowman
Resident Fellow

Kenneth Brown
Visiting Fellow

John E. Calfee
Resident Scholar

Lynne V. Cheney
W. H. Brady, Jr., Distinguished Fellow

Stephen R. Conafay
Executive Fellow

Chuck Downs
Assistant Director, Asian Studies

Dinesh D'Souza
John M. Olin Research Fellow

Nicholas N. Eberstadt
Visiting Scholar

Mark Falcoff
Resident Scholar

John D. Fonte
Visiting Scholar

Gerald R. Ford
Distinguished Fellow

Murray F. Foss
Visiting Scholar

Diana Furchtgott-Roth
Assistant to the President and Resident
   Fellow

Suzanne Garment
Resident Scholar

Jeffrey Gedmin
Research Fellow

James K. Glassman
DeWitt Wallace–Reader's Digest
   Fellow

Robert A. Goldwin
Resident Scholar

Robert W. Hahn
Resident Scholar

Robert B. Helms
Resident Scholar; Director, Health
   Policy Studies

Glenn Hubbard
Visiting Scholar

Douglas Irwin
Henry Wendt Scholar in Political
   Economy

James D. Johnston
Resident Fellow

Jeane J. Kirkpatrick
Senior Fellow; Director, Foreign and
   Defense Policy Studies

Marvin H. Kosters
Resident Scholar; Director,
   Economic Policy Studies

Irving Kristol
John M. Olin Distinguished Fellow

Dana Lane
Director of Publications

Michael A. Ledeen
Resident Scholar

James Lilley
Resident Fellow; Director, Asian
   Studies Program

John H. Makin
Resident Scholar; Director, Fiscal
   Policy Studies

Allan H. Meltzer
Visiting Scholar

Joshua Muravchik
Resident Scholar

Charles Murray
Bradley Fellow

Michael Novak
George F. Jewett Scholar in Religion,
   Philosophy, and Public Policy;
   Director, Social and
   Political Studies

Norman J. Ornstein
Resident Scholar

Richard N. Perle
Resident Fellow

William Schneider
Resident Scholar

William Shew
Visiting Scholar

J. Gregory Sidak
F. K. Weyerhaeuser Fellow

Herbert Stein
Senior Fellow

Irwin M. Stelzer
Resident Scholar; Director, Regulatory
   Policy Studies

Daniel Troy
Associate Scholar

W. Allen Wallis
Resident Scholar

Ben J. Wattenberg
Senior Fellow

Carolyn L. Weaver
Resident Scholar; Director, Social
   Security and Pension Studies

Karl Zinsmeister
Resident Fellow; Editor, *The American
   Enterprise*